Consuming Traditions

Modernist Literature & Culture

Kevin J. H. Dettmar & Mark Wollaeger, Series Editors

Consuming Traditions
Elizabeth Outka

Machine-Age Comedy
Michael North

Forthcoming Titles:

The Hypothetical Mandarin
Eric Hayot

The Art of Scandal
Sean Latham

Consuming Traditions

Modernity, Modernism, and the Commodified Authentic

Elizabeth Outka

OXFORD
UNIVERSITY PRESS
2009

OXFORD
UNIVERSITY PRESS

Oxford University Press, Inc., publishes works that further
Oxford University's objective of excellence
in research, scholarship, and education.

Oxford New York
Auckland Cape Town Dar es Salaam Hong Kong Karachi
Kuala Lumpur Madrid Melbourne Mexico City Nairobi
New Delhi Shanghai Taipei Toronto

With offices in
Argentina Austria Brazil Chile Czech Republic France Greece
Guatemala Hungary Italy Japan Poland Portugal Singapore
South Korea Switzerland Thailand Turkey Ukraine Vietnam

Published by Oxford University Press, Inc.
198 Madison Avenue, New York, New York 10016

www.oup.com

Library of Congress Cataloging-in-Publication Data
Outka, Elizabeth.
Consuming traditions: modernity, modernism, and the commodified authentic / by Elizabeth Outka.
p. cm.
Includes bibliographical references and index.
ISBN 978-0-19-537269-4
1. English literature—20th century—History and criticism. 2. Modernism (Literature)—Great Britain. 3. Material culture in literature. 4. Nostalgia in literature. 5. Authenticity (Philosophy) in literature. 6. Consumption (Economics)—Psychological aspects. 7. Commercial products—Psychological aspects. 8. Commerce in literature. 9. Marketing—Great Britain—History—20th century. I. Title.
PR478.M6O87 2008
820.9'112—dc22 2008011262

9 8 7 6 5 4 3 2 1

Printed in the United States of America
on acid-free paper

To Trip, Kate, and Tom
for real and true

Foreword

Every once in a great while, one reads the first few pages of a book and feels instinctively, overwhelmingly, the "rightness" of its argument: the delighted, rather than dismissive, feeling of "But of course!" Elizabeth Outka's *Consuming Traditions: Modernity, Modernism, and the Commodified Authentic* is just such a book. Elegant, eloquent, and wise, it forges a genuinely new argument about the complex relationship between modernist writing and commercial culture with such clarity and force that it immediately opens up new vistas for modernist studies.

Outka's argument builds skillfully on previous work on modernism and commodity culture, while at the same time showing how and why our paradigms need to be stretched. The image of the modernist author as mandarin aesthete, fiddling with words, words, words while society busies itself with the trivial anarchy of contemporary history—an image exalted in the '40s and '50s and pilloried in the '70s and '80s—has for some time now been challenged and complicated by studies showing how modernism was always and already entangled in the web of the social, whether in the form of market conditions informing the production, distribution, and consumption of the books or through the impress, coded with various degrees of obliquity, of other forms of historical modernization on their work. Declared dead in the '60s, the modernist author has come back to life, and she has bills to pay, and friends who died in the war.

Of course, restoring the worldliness of texts in a critically productive way requires more than reminders that aesthetic autonomy was always a fantasy, not a social fact, and *Consuming Traditions* takes us deeply into the conjunction of modernist aesthetics and consumer culture. Thus, rather than simply pointing out a paradox between a desire for authenticity untainted by the forces of the modern marketplace, on the one side, and the self-conscious commodification and marketing of that authenticity, on the other, Outka shows how the two sides of this coin mutually constitute one another. Indeed, the promise of commodified authenticity for early twentieth-century England, Outka argues, was that the very contradiction between authenticity and commodification could be sustained. The paradox, in other words, *was* the appeal.

Outka's chapter on the "model towns and commercial utopias" of the Cadbury Brothers' Bourneville and Lever's Port Sunlight represents a richly material working-out of the large claims made in the introduction. Situated in the transitional and too often overlooked period between late Victorianism and high modernism, Outka's extensive archival work results in a richly detailed discussion. What is most exciting about this analysis, however, is not the relatively unfamiliar material pertaining to these two planned living experiments, or the Garden Cities spawned by Ebenezer Howard's work; instead, what is most impressive is the way that Outka systematically brings this new information to bear on already familiar literary texts and manages to elucidate difficulties that have heretofore been glossed over or insufficiently grasped in their full complexity. In this connection, Shaw's *John Bull's Other Island* and *Major Barbara* come in for significant revisionist readings of key moments. The discussion of *Major Barbara* is particularly striking for its recasting of the long-standing conundrum of its peculiar ending, in which the heroine is suddenly infantilized, a transformation of which Outka is able to make sense in relation to Shaw's critique of the paternalism of planned communities.

The chapter on Forster's *Howards End*, which gives us a way to talk about some of the novel's otherwise unintelligible or unassimilable features—the furniture of Howards End, for instance, or the vexed status of real estate more generally—is likewise powerfully revisionary. The reading here of Miss Avery as a kind of estate agent, trying to "dress" Howards End "to sell," is a savvy interpretive move, as is Outka's account of the "temporal density" of the resulting arrangement. As in her treatment of Shaw, Outka also manages to render newly interesting one of the most notoriously problematic endings in early modernist fiction: Forster's willfully idyllic pastoral retreat, threatened by the creep of London, dismissive of Leonard Bast, yet presented as somehow still sufficient, even visionary. Throughout the book, Outka is able to use what she has learned in the archive—in this instance about the domestic revival energizing planned communities—to breathe new life into texts whose aesthetic status has come under fire in recent decades.

In chapter 4, Outka's characterization of Selfridges as a "mass-market [campaign] to sell a disdain for the mass market" nicely names both what is put in place in Selfridges' marketing strategies, but perhaps more saliently the uncomfortable accommodation to mass markets that remains a kind of schizophrenic blind spot in contemporary culture to this day. Chapter 5, on window shopping, is a tour de force. Building on the work of Rachel Bowlby, Outka makes the consumer gaze through plate glass into her own trope for modernist consumption, while bringing a keen critical intelligence to bear on what is perhaps Virginia Woolf's least studied novel, *Night and Day.* Yet Outka's contextually informed close reading yields more than fresh insight into this one novel. Much of what she argues about *Night and Day*, especially in her excellent pages on its straddling of Victorian and modernist modes, illuminates Woolf's first novel, *The Voyage Out,* as well as issues of form in early modernist fiction more generally. Moreover, Outka's conclusion to *Consuming Traditions* shows how Lily Briscoe reinhabits the window-shopping posture with a significant difference in *To the Lighthouse.*

Outka writes in that conclusion, in which she also makes brief but suggestive forays into the work of D. H. Lawrence and Joyce, "It is not simply that modernists have contradictory impulses toward tradition and originality, toward the past and entirely new futures, toward commerce and the dream of a cultural space outside the marketplace; it is that modernism itself is about the vacillations among these various contradictions, its definition arising as much from this movement as from the extremes themselves." The skill and delicacy with which Outka teases out these constitutive contradictions—never disdainfully, never condescendingly, and with an obvious and infectious enthusiasm—makes *Consuming Traditions* an ideal book with which to kick off the new Modernist Literature & Culture (MLC) series. MLC was established to explore the cultural bearings of literary modernism across multiple fields, geographies, symbolic forms, and media, publishing books that synthesize close attention to literary texts with interdisciplinary cultural approaches: innovative and energetic books that explore the breadth and depth of modernist studies. We could not have hoped to find a better harbinger of the work to be published in MLC in the years to come.

Kevin J. H. Dettmar and Mark Wollaeger

Acknowledgments

I am grateful to many people and institutions. I received helpful support at numerous archives in England. Sue Filmer, Chloe Veale, Margaret Rose, June Searby, and the late Michael Cudlipp, at the History of Advertising Trust Archive in Norwich, offered invaluable guidance on the Selfridges material and window displays. For help with the Cadbury and Bournville materials, I am likewise indebted to Alan Shrimpton, at the Bournville Village Trust; Angela Quinby, Rachel MacGregor, and the rest of the staff at the Birmingham City Archives at the Birmingham Central Library; and Chloe Haynes at Cadbury Schweppes. Margaret Williams and Julie Hayes assisted me at the Port Sunlight Heritage Centre, as did Lesley Owen-Edwards, Robert Pickering, and Claire Tunstall at the Unilever Archives at Port Sunlight. Josh Tidy could not have been more helpful at the Garden City Heritage Museum at Letchworth. Katie Lee and Alan Pinnock, of the Associated Newspaper Print Library, kindly let me examine the early materials on the *Daily Mail* Ideal Home Exhibition. Claire Hill and Margaret Richardson, of the Lutyens Trust, offered helpful guidance on the Lutyens material, as did the staff at the Royal Institute of British Architects in London. Alison Straw, of Selfridges, provided me with additional information about the store and showed me some of the building's original features. In the United States, I received aid from the helpful staff at several libraries: DuPont Library at Sewanee (the University of the South), particularly from Cari Shepherd; Boatwright Memorial Library at the University of Richmond; Alderman Library at the University of Virginia; and Sterling Memorial Library at Yale University. Tammy Elliott was patient and helpful with images, and Josh Harris, Katie Payne, and Katie Volz offered essential research assistance at critical junctures.

A number of fellowships and grants also supported this project, including a John B. Stephenson Fellowship from the Appalachian College Association and an Academic Initiative Grant from Sewanee. Two Faculty Research and Travel Grants from Sewanee helped me to complete the archival work for the project. The James D. Kennedy III Endowed Faculty Fellowship provided crucial funds for supporting the book's images. My former colleagues at Sewanee offered support at every step of the process, and my colleagues at the University of Richmond have continued this support.

The ideas in the book were shaped by several conferences and articles. I am grateful to the seminar group on "Modernism and Authenticity" I co-led with Jesse Matz at the Modernist Studies Association annual conference. Additional feedback on this material was provided at panels at the MLA conference and the Modernist Studies Association conference. Some of the material from chapter 4 appeared in "Crossing the Great Divides: Selfridges, Modernity, and the Commodified Authentic," *Modernism/modernity* 12, no. 2 (2005): 311–328, © The Johns Hopkins University Press; excerpts from chapter 3 in "Buying Time: *Howards End* and Commodified Nostalgia," *Novel: A Forum on Fiction* 36, no. 3 (2003): 330–350; Copyright NOVEL Corp. © 2003; and very brief sections of chapter 5 in "The Shop Windows Were Full of Sparkling Chains: Consumer Desire and Woolf's *Night and Day*," in *Virginia Woolf Out of Bounds: Selected Papers from the Tenth Annual Conference on Virginia Woolf*, edited by Jessica Berman and Jane Goldman (New York: Pace University Press, 2001), 229–235. I am grateful both to the journals and to Mark Hussey at Pace University Press for permission to reprint this material.

I also acknowledge the kind permission to reproduce material and images from the following museums and archives: Letchworth material from the First Garden City Heritage Museum, Letchworth; Cadbury and Bournville material from the Bournville Village Trust, Bournville; Birmingham City Archives, Birmingham; and Cadbury Limited. Port Sunlight material, including quotations from *Progress*, from Unilever, PLC. For a letter by Ebenezer Howard, the Hertfordshire Archives and Local Studies; for a short quotation from Clive Bell's "Play Reading Book" from the King's College, Cambridge, the Society of Authors as the Literary Representative of the Estate of Clive Bell; for an image from the Ideal Home Exhibition, Solo Syndication; for help with research and with window display images, the staff at the New York Public Library Picture Collection and their express research services.

I am deeply indebted to Jennifer Wicke and Alison Booth for their continued support of this project. Rita Felski, Marty Hipsky, Jesse Matz, Marie Hawthorne, John Grammer, Pamela Macfie (a full knowing reader), Virginia Craighill, Kelly Malone, Jennifer Michael, Amanda French, June Griffin, Lisa Spiro, Virginia

Zimmerman, and my father, Gene Outka, gave astute critical readings of the book at various stages. The wonderful Ruby Walker provided time in which to write. My mother, Carole DeVore, braved dusty archives to track down critical information and images. For good cheer and conversation, I thank Sherri Bergman, Nancy Berner, David Coe, Elizabeth Grammer, Kim Heitzenrater, Jacqueline Outka, Jim Peterman, Elizabeth and Oliver Pollard, Laura Willis, and Elizabeth Wilson. My children, Kate and Tom, gave me the joy I needed to finish the book.

I cannot imagine more insightful or more generous editors for Oxford's Modernist Literature & Culture series than Kevin J. H. Dettmar and Mark Wollaeger, who, along with an anonymous reader from Oxford, offered detailed suggestions on every part of the book. My editor at Oxford, Shannon McLachlan, her assistants, Christina Gibson and Brendan O'Neill, and my production editor, Liz Smith, have likewise been terrific. My excellent copy editor, Susan Ecklund, saved me from numerous errors.

Finally, I owe a particular debt to three people: Virginia Cope brought her intelligence, her critical eye, and her wit to this project at every stage; Paul Outka, in addition to being the best brother I could imagine, gave generously of his time and his insight, improving the manuscript in all ways; my husband, Trip Pollard, has provided love, support, and intellectual energy from the beginning, and without him, there would be no book.

Contents

Abbreviations

BCA-BVT	Records of the Bournville Village Trust, Birmingham City Archives, Birmingham Central Library, Birmingham, England. MS 1536.
BCA-CF	Papers of the Cadbury Family of Birmingham, Birmingham City Archives, Birmingham Central Library, Birmingham, England. MS 466.
CL	Bernard Shaw. *Collected Letters.* 4 vols. Edited by Dan H. Laurence. New York: Viking Penguin, 1985. Volume numbers noted in text.
CP	Bernard Shaw. *The Bodley Head Bernard Shaw: Collected Plays with the Prefaces.* 7 vols. Edited by Dan H. Laurence. London: The Bodley Head, 1970–1974. Volume numbers noted in the text.
D	*The Diary of Virginia Woolf.* 5 vols. Edited by Anne Olivier Bell and assisted by Andrew McNeillie. New York: Harvest-Harcourt Brace, 1977–1984. Volume numbers noted in the text.
FGCHM	First Garden City Heritage Museum, Letchworth, England.
HAT-BB	Original press clippings about the opening of Selfridges department store, collected in a large binder covering 1909–1911. Located in the Selfridges Archive at the History of Advertising Trust Archive, Norwich, England.
HAT-Early	Small black notebook on the early advertisements of 1909. Located in the Selfridges Archive at the History of Advertising Trust Archive, Norwich, England, SEL 793.

HAT-GS	Gordon Selfridge's collection of materials gathered as he contemplated his store's design. Located in the Selfridges Archive at the History of Advertising Trust Archive, Norwich, England.
HAT-PIC	From the Selfridges picture collection at the History of Advertising Trust Archive, Norwich, England.
L	*The Letters of Virginia Woolf*. 6 vols. Edited by Nigel Nicolson and Joanne Trautmann. New York: Harvest-Harcourt Brace, 1975–1980. Volume numbers noted in the text.
LGC-Gen P	Letchworth Garden City General Pamphlets. Box of promotional material at the archives of the First Garden City Heritage Museum, Letchworth, England.
Uni-Ar	Unilever Archives, Port Sunlight, Wirral, England.

Consuming Traditions

1. Introduction

Selling Authenticity

"Illusion," said Oscar Wilde, "is the first of all pleasures."[1] Wilde himself was a dexterous purveyor of such illusive pleasures, celebrating stance over character, pose over pedigree. In this he epitomized the late nineteenth-century fascination with new ways to construct illusions, and with the corresponding possibilities for reinventing the self. Over the course of the next century, dramatic changes in advertising, marketing, and shopping would encourage consumers not simply to live a life but to select among lifestyles; not to stay within the given circumstances and time of their birth but to live within multiple pasts; not to remain fixed in one identity but to perform within many. Such popular and enticing new avenues for artifice and performance predictably produced a backlash, fueling anxious efforts to recapture something "real," something authentic and genuine to set against such flux.

The two camps of artifice and authenticity are usually considered in opposition, roughly mapping onto, on the one hand, a cutting-edge modernity, and, on the other, a more conservative impulse to preservation and stability. The obvious contradiction between these camps has, however, obscured their fundamental interrelationship within a seemingly paradoxical phenomenon that was emerging amid the very changes. At the turn of the century, particularly in Britain, what began to arise was the half-hidden but pervasive desire to unite Wildean ideas of artifice and performance and continual self-fashioning with the contrary but appealing ideas of authenticity, stability, and continuity. New marketing strategies—in advertising, in store design, in emerging ideas of community planning, in novel trends in architecture—rapidly created a particular kind of commercial hybrid that fused (or promised to fuse) artifice and authenticity. Innovative possibilities of construction and reinvention were carefully linked to ideas that would, at least at first, seem antithetical to interchangeable identities and lifestyles. New objects and places were packaged and sold as mini-representations of supposedly noncommercial values: nostalgic evocations of an English rural past; appeals to an original, genuine article; and images of a purified aesthetic free from any taint of the mass market.[2] It was not simply that marketers were appropriating areas that had traditionally been seen as noncommercial. What made these efforts so distinctive, and what contemporary critics have largely failed to recognize, is how the commercial origins were intrinsic to the allure of these objects and places. Their noncommercial aura made them appealing; their underlying commercial availability promised to make the simulation better than the original, for these new hybrids were accessible, controllable, and—in their ability to unite seemingly antithetical desires—tantalizingly modern. This noncommercial commerce was certainly a paradox, but the powerful underlying promise was that the intrinsic contradictions could be sustained rather than resolved; indeed, the paradox *was* the appeal.

We remain surrounded by the repercussions of this phenomenon. Marketers still love to sell us nostalgic forms of authentic goods. The United States offers Disneyworld's pristine Main Street U.S.A.; Cracker Barrel's general store, replete with its old-fashioned candy jars and moon pies amid a faux-rusticated interior; Pottery Barn's new distressed furniture, machine made to look old and weathered. Likewise, Britain is awash in the selling of a venerable old England, from the vine-covered cottage, to the proliferation of the heritage industry, to the opening of Dickens World in Kent, to the immensely popular Hovis Bread ads, which featured a young boy delivering loaves of fresh bread down a cobblestone street. In a different variation of the phenomenon, marketers present a refined aesthetic, one miraculously and allegedly free of the vulgar taint of commerce; here we find the soft-focus Ralph Lauren ad; the fireside scene of the L. L. Bean Christmas catalog, with its golden retriever puppies reclining on soft flannel; and the solid sophistication (with lovely wood accents) of the venerable London store Liberty. In every case, the viewer is assured that the real is "real"—and readily available for a reasonable price.

I use the term "commodified authentic" as a helpful shorthand for this enormously complex and important phenomenon. The term does not imply a search for authenticity per se but rather a search for a sustained contradiction that might allow consumers to be at once connected to a range of values roughly aligned with authenticity and yet also to be fully modern. The strategy had many expressions that I detail later, including appeals to nostalgic nationalism, aesthetic refinement, and the genuine original article, but they all promised to deliver a vision of stability and permanence at the same time that they promised equally to be endlessly exchangeable. Instead of choosing between the past and the present, between an alluring sense of endurance and the chance to reinvent and possess, consumers might unite all these desires in one attractive package.

Most of us are suspicious about attempts to commodify seemingly noncommercial values. Indeed, the proliferation of such marketing is matched by the proliferation of critics who decry the phenomenon—or satirize it, as Julian Barnes does so brilliantly in his novel *England, England.* We usually perceive the selling of authenticity as fraud, as the inauthentic masquerading as the authentic. Accordingly, we are adept at (and often smug about) unmasking the commerce behind the facade: the distressed furniture is not really old, the soft-lit reproduction of the villager's house hides the economic hardships that were found there, and at the very least, that new soft sweater is unlikely to deliver the sophisticated atmosphere from the catalogue. Such exposure is important and ongoing critical work, but the rush to condemn (or at least ironically smirk) has limited a critical investigation of either the history of such marketing or its powerful allures. In moving so quickly to unmask, we have missed the opportunity to understand.

Consuming Traditions brings the commodified authentic center stage, arguing that this half-hidden but critically significant phenomenon is a key trope for understanding not only commodity culture but the development of both modernity and literary modernism. I trace the paradox of the commodified authentic in key areas of British culture at the moment it emerges in the late nineteenth and the early twentieth century.[3] The urge to construct, buy, reproduce, package, and sell a range of images and ideas clustered around authenticity began to appear not simply in stores but in new efforts to plan model communities, to build model homes, and in new literary works that recognized, critiqued, and exploited the phenomenon for innovative literary ends. The very idea of the commodified authentic—that one might unite desires for permanence, or commercial purity, or for the absolutely original, with the promise that despite appearances such things might be endlessly remade, constructed, reproduced, and exchanged—was an astonishingly powerful paradox; efforts to align modernism or modernity with only one side of the equation (with, say, the desire to "make it new") miss how the paradox itself, with its heady promise to sustain the contradiction, functioned as a critical tool within the culture. Understanding how this tool performed is, in turn, essential for understanding the intertwined development of commodity culture, modernity, and literary modernism.

The commodified authentic by its very nature crossed boundaries, so our critical approach to it should do likewise. I thus draw on literary, commercial, and architectural examples, considering two significant clusters of activity in differing locations. The first cluster centers on the countryside, investigating how both rural villages and houses, well-established repositories of nostalgic forms of authenticity, became new sites for intense commercialization that were explicitly produced through modern industry and factory work. These developments in town planning and in architecture radically shifted the way communities were structured and the way houses were built, and the power of these transitions in turn spilled into literature, as novelists and playwrights depicted and savagely critiqued the move to construct apparently old towns and seemingly old homes. Yet surprisingly, the appetite for old-new hybrids was also shared by writers, architects, and consumers alike, who all recognized that the emerging power of commerce to produce nostalgic environments was a critical way to negotiate the difficult transition into modernity. With the second cluster, we move to the city to explore how various forms of authenticity often considered antithetical to the modern urban setting were rapidly translated into malleable images for the urban market. This second section investigates the emergence of the British department store, early twentieth-century revolutions in advertising, and the concomitant spilling of commercial possibilities from the store to the store window and out into the urban street scene, as the culture moved from having a life to creating a lifestyle. Such shifts became central to the work of early modernist writers, who quickly recognized the power of constructing objects and spaces seemingly purified of commercial taint, and of sustaining the contradiction between authenticity and its construction. The paradox of the commodified authentic lay at the heart of all these shifts, and it profoundly changed the way we shop and how we read.

The commodified authentic's rapid development in turn-of-the-century Britain was due in large part to its enticing promise to address a series of pervasive, often overlapping tensions at the moment that such tensions threatened to overwhelm public discourse. First, various forms of the commodified authentic addressed the contradiction between the desire to access the past and the heady urge to "make it new." This tension was especially acute for many people living through the anxious transition from the Victorian age to the modern one. Between the 1880s and the high-water mark of British modernism in 1922, Britain revolutionized its art, architecture, and marketing. For those coming of age in the early 1900s—the children of Victorian parents—such shifts were both exhilarating and alarming. As Virginia Woolf noted, "There should have been a generation between [my father and me] to cushion the contact," a buffer to ease the sudden transitions.[4]

In this rapidly changing environment, the commodified authentic emerged as an appealing and dexterous tool, one uniquely designed to satisfy both a longing for tradition and the urgent need to move into the modern era. Stranded between an outmoded past and a rapidly modernizing future, consumers were drawn to the commodified authentic's ability to weave temporal fragments together, sustaining the contradiction between modern imperatives and nostalgic longing while at least temporarily satisfying both. As Henry James says of "The Great Good Place," in his story of that title, "you could . . . never have said if it were the last echo of the old or the sharpest note of the modern."[5] Like James's Place, the commodified authentic combined the old and the new into a single gratifying experience, promising to bring, say, a comforting image of nineteenth-century-tinged tranquillity (updated and shorn of any drawbacks) to the modern moment. Purchase the right object, build the right building, preserve the right relic, and one might possess an appealing aura of the past, maintain a sense of authentic tradition, and, by one's very participation in the novel production of such spaces and things, simultaneously be new, up-to-date, fashionable.

The commodified authentic also worked to soothe the friction between an often elitist desire to escape the marketplace and a contradictory but powerful appetite for its spectacular bounty. It paradoxically promised to democratize the production of commercial purity and to make exclusivity universally available. In effect, the commodified authentic not only participated in the modernist dream of an autonomous aesthetic separate from mass culture and the mass market but also anticipated recent critiques of this separation. The creation of a noncommercial commerce fundamentally challenged the organizing binary that divided the authentic from the mass market, or a pure art from a sullied materialism, declaring without embarrassment that its antimarket aesthetic was exclusive and yet easily accessible. Such a union proved a potent—and lucrative—combination in early twentieth-century British culture. It also provides us with a unique lens through which to view this period, one built on the imbrication of modernity, authenticity, and commerce.

Selling Authenticity

This book explores three central manifestations of the commodified authentic that, taken together, all heralded the profound marketing shift from commodity fetishism to lifestyle design and the possibilities of performance that that move generated. Starting in early twentieth-century Britain, marketers began to focus less on a particular object for sale at a particular price, and more on aura and setting, promising consumers not single products but new identities and new ways to live.[6] Consumers were drawn to the transformative possibilities, and also to the sense of permanence and refinement individual examples might offer. This shift was not simply a transition from formerly fixed identities or lives to the mobile flux brought by modernity, but a simultaneous embrace of modernity's promise of exchange and the equally alluring promise of authenticity. The three versions I explore here—commercialized versions of nostalgic nationalism, of originary authenticity, and of aesthetic purity—all suggested the possibility of stability and beauty, evoking a climate of pleasure and ease; the appeal lay as much in the vision of permanence as it did in the promise of access and interchange.

Timeless . . .

The late nineteenth century saw the rapid emergence of what would become one of the most popular versions of the commodified authentic: an appeal to a nostalgic, often nationalistic authenticity. Such marketing evoked an ideal English rural past, usually one that predated industrial production and modern technology, and often one that was situated in the country. This "Ye Olde England" aesthetic evoked misty images of happy craftspeople at their looms and benches, the gentle pastoral scene, the cozy domestic interior. While nostalgia for a pastoral tradition had long been a staple of British culture, the turn of the century witnessed an especially intense revival of such nostalgia, as well as its aggressive commercialization. Critic Alun Howkins describes the pervasive rise of "Englishness" in this era, a rural myth based loosely on an idealized vision of the late Elizabethan period and on ideas of southern England that involved quaint villages, cultivated land, and a sense of classlessness—or at least class harmony.[7] We can follow strains of such nostalgia in the Arts and Crafts Movement of John Ruskin and William Morris, who were forever extolling the virtues of carefully crafted handmade goods. Traditionally, this type of nostalgic authenticity had been defined in part by its separation from the mass market and the factory system; at the turn of the century, however, there was an explosion of efforts to mass-produce and market this nostalgic vision. Such marketing was reflected both in the rapid rise of town planning efforts such as the Garden City Movement and in new designs of individual domestic homes. Nostalgic authenticity with a nationalist flavor quickly became a staple of advertising and influenced such ventures as the launch of *Country Life* magazine in 1897 and the start of the *Daily Mail*'s Ideal Home Exhibition in 1908. While manifestations of this nostalgia differed in form, what united all these efforts was the central appeal of the paradox: a constructed, marketed aesthetic of things that might be easily obtained and exchanged, infused with the contrary images of stability, permanence, and the noncommercial. Consumers might have it all: the advantages of the country image without the rigid feudal hierarchy, the pastoral without the toil, the old-looking cottage without the primitive plumbing. Late Victorian and Edwardian writers such as Bernard Shaw and E. M. Forster presented scathing critiques of such efforts of nostalgic authenticity, but they also understood how powerful and appealing such images might be, and how essential they were to a changing nation.

Nostalgic authenticity allowed an enticing manipulation of time—fracturing it, disrupting it, expanding it, condensing it. A sense of time's passage might be inscribed onto objects or architectural details, suggesting a range of past moments simultaneously available in the present for a given consumer or reader. The actual or imagined body moving through these settings inverted this, bringing a mobile representation of the modern moment to an older, "timeless," setting. This modern body toured the sites of nostalgic authenticity, bringing the present into contact with the past in a single space and time. The selling of such efforts promised to liberate time from its chronological progression and to heal the disjunction Woolf describes, assuring participants that everything and nothing had changed. Such time-play not only anticipated the modernist novel and the modern cinema—both poised at the start of the century to disrupt time, to stretch out days, and to rearrange years—but turned time into a salable item, one that might be altered, purchased, and owned.

The Genuine Article . . .

Emerging alongside commodified nostalgia was the selling of an alternative version of authenticity, one defined by innovation. This form, what I term the "originary authentic," equated authenticity with the original or the one-of-a-kind, something that was not a copy and that was not derived from previous traditions. The mystique of the originary object had long been felt, but the turn of the century saw its rapid emergence as a powerful advertising strategy. As with the nostalgic form, the originary authentic was in part defined by and valued for its alleged separation from the mass market, and it was likewise aggressively marketed in what are now familiar strategies: appeals to the coterie, to high fashion, to the limited edition. Part of the originary's allure was its evocation of the prototype. One was not buying the general but the genuine, the first model from which others might be made. The originary authentic at times had a nostalgic tint—the aura of an original artwork, for example, might be valued in part for its evocation of a venerable past.[8] At other times, however, the authenticity that was evoked was one of novelty, of being the first, the cutting edge, the new. As with the nostalgic variety, the power of selling the originary authentic lay in its paradoxical promise: middle-class consumers might (allegedly) have both the genuine article and something that they could easily purchase, both the exclusive and the accessible, the original as the perfect reproduction.

Such appeals quickly became a popular marketing technique, and literary modernists, who were themselves often linked to a supposedly nonmarketed originary authenticity, became adept purveyors of such strategies, as I detail below. Writers and marketers alike recognized the power of boldly declaring that something had no precursors, that it was the first of its kind, beholden to no tradition, and at the same time to understand this very appeal as a deliberately and usefully constructed artifice. Efforts to promote the originary authentic were forcefully represented by the particular attractions of literal and literary versions of the modern shop window, where the glass promised simultaneously a cutting-edge availability and an out-of-reach allure, and where new design strategies introduced in the early twentieth century emphasized the single, genuine commodity.

An Exclusive Offer . . .

Alongside the nostalgic and the originary versions of the commodified authentic, there also emerged a third version, one that commercialized the supposedly pure realms of aesthetic pleasure and refinement. Commerce had long been understood as corrupting, always threatening to intrude on the realm of true art. At the turn of the century, however, both marketers and writers imagined new heights of aesthetic and sensual pleasure that were not only not sullied by their union with commerce but purified by it. New department stores such as Selfridges sought to reclaim commerce from its shadowy role as the perverter of artistic refinement, carefully recasting commerce as the powerful and appealing purveyor of bountiful aesthetic pleasures previously reserved for the upper class. Middle-class customers were suddenly promised environments and objects that evoked a high-class aesthetic refinement, where the commercial exchange was de-emphasized to imply that the spaces and objects were always already purchased and that nothing so crass as an exchange of money would be involved. At the same time, customers were invited to reproduce the refined atmosphere within their own homes by choosing from the many goods that surrounded them. Selfridges promised and largely delivered to its "guests" a hushed atmosphere of soft carpeting and beautiful displays, all within a large department store full of a seemingly endless supply of goods. This powerful strategy should not simply be seen as another grim example of how the market was appropriating ever more realms for its material ends, or duping ever more customers by its commercial tricks. The appeal was the *union* of aesthetic refinement and commercial possibility, and the implicit promise was that the union was better than the constituent parts.

Authors such as Henry James understood the appeal of such marketing and, instead of condemning it, presented such unions as one possible way to make aesthetic pleasure and restful contemplation readily available, governed by money rather than the muse. Literary modernism itself would come to depend on the savvy marketing of a refined, noncommercial, high-art aesthetic, as recent critics have suggested.[9] The very idea of a union between aesthetic pleasure and commerce became important not simply in the marketing of modernism, however, but within modernist writing itself. Authors such as Joyce and Woolf understood the power of sustaining the contradiction between something that was constructed and marketed and yet purified and noncommercial. Such a strategy did not imply duplicity, as has often been assumed, but a dexterous deployment of the appealing contradictions that fueled modernism's growth and that were infusing ever larger parts of British culture.

Crossing the Great Divides

The imbrication of authenticity and commerce was a phenomenon that united the marketplace and the literary world, as efforts to sell authenticity overlapped and became intertwined with the early growth of modernism. In arguing these points, my work speaks to some of the persistent contradictions within modernist studies itself. In the past ten years, critical work on modernism has transformed the field, making a broad effort to revise—and revive—modernism, defending it against charges of elitism, and reconsidering critics who have condemned the modernist movement for nostalgically seeking to recapture a lost wholeness. Central to these revival efforts has been a challenge to the alleged separation between modernism and mass culture and the related division between modernism and commerce. Andreas Huyssen's formulation of "the great divide," which describes how modernism defined itself against mass culture, and Fredric Jameson's assertion that modernist writing relies on a "distinction between high and so-called mass culture"[10] have proven irresistible targets for more recent modernist critics.[11] Far from being above commerce, advertising, or even the mass market, literary modernists must be viewed as participants in all three, and critics have productively linked writers from James to Woolf to Joyce to many different commercial concerns.[12] The newer critics tend, however, to dismantle the great divide from a similar viewpoint. Standing on the shores of modernism, they discover the various ways that modernist writers and artists have used commercial strategies—both for good and for ill. Although important contributions to modernist inquiries, these studies often neglect two critical parts of the equation: how commercial ventures in fact deployed and dismantled the vexed relationship between high and low culture, and how literary modernism developed not through a reliance on the great divide or its dismantling but on the uneasy movement between the two impulses, a movement intimately connected to the paradoxical impulse to construct authenticity. If we study only how modernists appropriate the market both within and for their works, we reify modernism as the central cultural location of these tensions, and we further risk treating "the market" as a monolithic entity, rather than as an immensely complicated set of strategies and commercial exchanges, something in fact at least as variable as modernism itself.

This book seeks to undo the circular debates surrounding modernism's vacillating commitments to high and low culture, and to the marketed and the aesthetically pure. Despite modernism's recent critical rehabilitation, the growth of modernism was, in fact, often marked by nostalgia, by a disdain for mass culture, and by attempts to purify an aesthetic from any taint of commerce. It was also, as the newer critics remind us, marked by novel uses of advertising and marketing strategies and by an embrace and celebration of popular culture. Both the older and newer critics are right—even though they contradict each other. I work to unite these historical tensions in modernist studies, arguing via the commodified authentic that the contradictions were in fact constitutive of modernism's development and of the larger culture. As the twentieth century began, both writers and consumers were not simply deciding between, on the one hand, ideas of self-fashioning, of constructed lifestyles and identities, of the urge to make it new and to discard tradition, and, on the other hand, the longing for tradition, for permanence, and for aesthetic purity. Instead, writers, marketers, architects, and consumers were searching for new ways to sustain these contradictions, to bring different sides together in new combinations that animated the many forms of the commodified authentic. It is finally the movement across the gap—by the authors, the marketers, and the critics themselves—the ability both to perform the great divide and to dismantle it when needed, the actions of this, rather than the vantage points on either side—that offers the most vital critical model for both modernism and modernity.

To investigate the symbiotic connections between modernism's growth and the commodified authentic, I consider literary works from the late nineteenth to the early twentieth century, examining in particular texts that lie on the cusp of modernism. I deliberately select transitional works that are hard to categorize as Victorian, Edwardian, or modernist, for such works represent a critical transitional moment. These hybrid texts, by authors such as Shaw, Wells, James, Forster, Lawrence, and early Woolf, show in stark relief the early development of modernism's vexed relationship with commodity culture. As the authors struggled to shape literature into a new form, they searched for ways to bridge the gap between an outmoded but alluring past and tantalizing modern possibilities. This search in turn led them both to criticize and to embrace efforts to sell authenticity. As they recognized the power and the perils of the emerging marketing strategies, they began to explore and develop the paradoxical desires that were intrinsic to the commodified authentic and that would become intrinsic to modernism: both nostalgia for an authentic commercial-free past, and the desire for an authentically new future, one not derived from outmoded traditions; both a dream of exclusivity and a select audience and at the same time a desire for ready accessibility and a wide market. One of the reasons that modernism itself became so notoriously difficult to define is that, like the commodified authentic, it encompasses all these contradictions. Understanding the commodified authentic both within commercial ventures and within transitional literary works in fact leads to surprising new readings of high modernist texts. In the later works by authors such as Woolf and Joyce that I consider at the end of my study, the ideas that fueled the commodified authentic became critical tools for modernism and its construction, for the very idea of a constructed authenticity, implying as it does both an innovative self-fashioning and an elegiac longing for permanence or an enduring originality, lies at the heart of iconic modernist works such as *To the Lighthouse* and *Ulysses.*

I work in this project not only to advance critical discussion of British modernism and commodity culture but also to help reintroduce the maligned concepts of authenticity and nostalgia. Only recently have literary and cultural critics been willing to discuss these themes in anything but pejorative terms.[13] In particular, relations between authenticity and modernism have increasingly been a subject of interest to scholars, leading to investigations of the authentic—and the inauthentic—in art, music, and literature.[14] Despite this renewed interest, when authenticity cavorts with that favorite bad boy, commerce, views on the relationship tend to sour. Examples of commodified authenticity have usually been considered as unholy alliances, mixing things that must not be mixed. Most critics reserve special wrath for commodified nostalgia or "heritage baiting," often perceived as a marketing ploy that sells what is sacred, makes the authentic inauthentic, and, perhaps most disturbingly, simplifies or even invents the past and erases its painful features.[15] Such exposure is essential, and within this volume, I remain attentive to the darker elements of this type of marketing. The key thrust of my analysis, however, is not to debunk but to understand. The impulse to criticize and dismiss has prevented an investigation either of the development of such marketing within Britain or of the potent attractions—as well as the perils—of constructing notions of the authentic. The commodified authentic emerged as a powerful cultural strategy, and this project uses British literary and commercial ventures as models to shift the critical paradigm of the commodified authentic from a *thing* to be unmasked and dismissed to a *locus* of competing imperatives.

Selling Gender, Class, and Commerce

The commodified authentic had particular resonance for three groups of British shoppers: middle-class women, the middle class in general, and modern consumers who felt threatened or overwhelmed by the sheer explosion of commercial possibilities at the turn of the century. For all these groups, the commodified authentic provided a comforting new vision of commerce, one designed to ameliorate some of the specific anxieties each group might have about shopping. The commodified authentic became, in effect, a marketing plan for commerce, packaging and reselling it in a purer, calmer, and more refined form. Selling authenticity was, ironically, a self-preservation strategy, promising through shopping to soothe any anxieties caused by shopping.

For women, especially those of the middle class, the commodified authentic helped to unsettle rigid divisions between, on the one hand, women's historical associations with an "authentic" domestic sphere unsullied by commerce and, on the other, the image of a predatory public sphere of trade. The strategy promised to bridge this artificial division not by severing associations among women, authenticity, and domesticity but by presenting commerce as continuous with authentic realms, rather than separate from them. In newly sophisticated advertising and store designs, marketers began to construct environments that suggested various noncommercial settings, such as a country home or a small community, where women might allegedly remain untainted by trade while still engaging in public activities such as shopping. As actual material transactions were de-emphasized, through displays and advertisements that sold aura over object, the division between the home and the store began to waver (though the store, of course, was presented as a bigger and more perfect version of the home). The implicit promise was that the commercialized authenticity would be preferable to the previous models, for it implied that various forms of authenticity might be performed (and thus changed and more easily controlled) rather than embodied. While hardly a recipe for liberation, the new strategies did offer women more control over *how* to create and present an "authentic" home and self, and granted a larger sphere in which "authentic" performance might be possible.

The commodified authentic likewise promised to grant new forms of mobility to the middle class, presenting appealing samples from both higher and lower economic levels. Seen through the lens of the commodified authentic, trade no longer referenced and reinforced a middle-class status but promised a way to gain appealing aspects of other classes. Customers browsing through the various departments of Selfridges department store, for example, might sample an upper-class country estate aesthetic constructed around the collection of goods on display, or tour the art section as connoisseurs, two activities formerly considered financially out of reach for the middle class. At the other end of the economic spectrum, nostalgic values associated with the laboring classes in rural England might be sampled; tourists arriving at model industrial towns like Bournville or Port Sunlight, built to look like old country villages, could walk within an idealized version of a rural pastoral community without actually being one of the workers laboring in the fields. The middle class was promised a touch of peasant dignity and the flavor of the venerable old estate, shorn of the complications that often went along with such ingredients, and without having to confront class differences. The implicit suggestion, of course, was that the distilled essences of other classes were new and improved—and easier to buy.

The commodified authentic not only promised a purified vision of commerce for women and the middle class; it also promised to soothe any consumer made anxious by the pace of modern life. Consumers at the turn of the century, awash in a sea of goods and the concomitant opportunities to create new identities, were always in danger of being overwhelmed, unable to decide among competing possibilities, and thus unable to purchase. The commodified authentic helped protect commerce from this potential backlash. Tying transformational possibilities to the opposite appeals of buying the real thing, possessing the genuine article, and being the prototype was not only desirable but necessary. Rather than being a strategy that aimed to mislead consumers, the commodified authentic in fact needed consumers to see the authenticity as something constructed. They might be attracted to the object's nostalgic references or aesthetic refinement, but they also had to see such effects as reproducible or they would not see the object as one that they might eventually possess. Part of the brilliance of the commodified authentic as a marketing strategy—and part of the reason it remains a central strategy today—was that it provided an antidote to the very anxieties it helped create, and then in turn demanded its own critique.

Performing Authenticity

The different expressions of the commodified authentic should be considered not only through individual examples but also as performances, ones that involved both staging and acting, both carefully constructed settings and the opportunity for role-playing. Writers, architects, marketers, and consumers could move through various constructions, reinventing identities and shaping lived environments. Each iteration might suggest authenticity, a fixed identity, a nostalgic stability, or an aesthetic refinement untainted by commerce, and yet encompass multiple times, spaces, and identities and be forever open to being remade. In order to encompass the paradox that was involved in these essentially different impulses, participants had to be able to perform in different modes, to flow within images of authenticity and aesthetic refinement while maintaining the ability to acknowledge such images as constructions. The contradiction implicit in *performing* authenticity is the very contradiction that had to be upheld. Only in performance were the possibilities of the commodified authentic released, and only in action were its paradoxes sustained.

Yet part of the consumer appeal of the commodified authentic was the underlying suggestion that it delivered the real *rather* than the performance, that despite its constructed nature it could still give the temporary illusion of the actually authentic. While consumers had, on one level, to remain aware of the artificial quality of the experience in order to see it as available and exchangeable, they could nevertheless look with another lens and also see the experience as real.

What was perhaps even more enticing was the possibility that—through the right combination of clothes or furniture or architecture details—participants themselves could in turn express the originary or the nostalgic or the aesthetic; they could become, in effect, models from which copies or imitative performances might be made. Like a moving picture that freezes momentarily on an image before starting its motion again, consumers could take up the mantle of authenticity, present a particular identity or style, and then exchange it for another if they so desired.

Theorists working within the field of performance studies have traditionally focused on the subversive qualities of performances and performativity, seeing them as challenges or disruptions of existing norms. As Jon McKenzie has noted, performance studies scholars have "long articulated" "theories of transgressive performance," often ignoring the pervasively normative dimensions of many performances.[16] Likewise, critics have traditionally studied performances as resisting the impersonal forces of commercial exchange; Richard Schechner recently observed that few theorists in performance studies "will concede that [the global forces of capital] know very well—perhaps even better than we—how to perform, in all meanings of that word."[17] The various manifestations of the commodified authentic provide potent models for investigating the interchange of commerce and performance, allowing us to explore hybrid performances where subversive possibilities were in fact inextricably linked to normative ones, and where the "global forces of capital" were certainly in play. These strategies were in some sense transgressive in that one might, for example, perform class positions different from one's own material status, playing an art connoisseur or the owner of a country estate. The performative quality of the experience not only hinted that one's own class position might be changeable but also hinted that class position itself might be at least as much about performance as it was about family history or connections. These new commercial strategies could also play normative roles, reifying a cultural and economic hierarchy that made things like country cottages and an original artwork venerable and desirable. In other words, they drew their transgressive power from their performativity, making what had been exclusive and class bound into an opportunity more widely available, and they drew their normative power from their promise to deliver, in effect, quintessentially normative expressions of authenticity, stability, and permanence.

. . .

I organize the book spatially because the commodified authentic was a cultural and material stage on which various models of authenticity were constructed and performed. Part I, "Commodified Nostalgia and the Country Aesthetic," focuses on the marketing of the countryside, examining both literal and literary efforts to create model communities and individual domestic homes that suggested a nostalgic return to a preindustrial age—but a return that explicitly relied on commercial production. What emerged were new ways to imagine a mix between the country and the city, and new ways to bring the past—modernized—into the present. Images of commerce and industry were transformed, as both marketers and writers realized the growing commercial possibilities of a nostalgic version of rural "precommercial" England, and the inextricable link between such nostalgic visions and the commercial ventures that might create and sustain them. Part II, "Urban Authenticities," shifts to urban-based versions of the commodified authentic, and the strategy's promise to ease distinctions not simply between the past and the present, and the city and the country, but between commerce and any sense of the noncommercial. Consumers and readers were invited to shape images of authenticity into a range of new forms and identities, and to see how commerce might deliver a luxurious aesthetic refinement, not only for elites but for everyone. The new commercial hybrids in turn became central to new literary experiments in modernism.

The first chapter in Part I, "The Past Is a Present Country: Model Towns and Commercial Utopias," explores the revolutions in town planning and community design that were inspired by the creation of model factory towns at the turn of the century, as well as by the rapid development of the Garden City Movement. While novel in many respects, model towns such as Bournville and Port Sunlight, and Garden Cities such as Letchworth, presented the illusion of an older economic and cultural time, showing a commitment to past designs that were meant to correct some of the excesses of the industrial age. These literal spaces in part made manifest ideas from a diverse set of literary utopias such as Edward Bellamy's *Looking Backward* (1888) and William Morris's *News from Nowhere* (1890), and they also drew on the Arts and Crafts Movement. What set these places apart from these earlier efforts, however, was their deliberate reliance on the modern factory system to support the nostalgic country vision, and the emerging ways this vision was marketed to sell products from chocolate to soap. Such efforts received enormous publicity and captured the imagination of many, including Bernard Shaw. Through his plays, Shaw became the most incisive critic of the new town planning schemes but also, in ways my analysis makes clear, their surprising champion. Through both the literary and the literal model towns, long static visions of the country and the city were united into appealing new hybrids, and industry itself, rather than being the villain, was recast as the provider of new pleasures. These early efforts to imagine and create whole communities around visions of nostalgic rural lifestyles were the start of what would soon become a massive new industry in community development. Shaw's ambivalent reaction remains an incisive critique of both the dangers and the possibilities of such commercial ventures.

The next chapter, "Buying Time: E. M. Forster and the Neo-nostalgic Home," turns from the model community to the individual country dwelling, analyzing a cluster of efforts to unite modern commercial ventures to the production of the "authentic" home. The chapter examines Forster's subtle exploration of the symbiotic connections between modern industry and country life. I consider Forster's literary critique alongside both the launch of the *Daily Mail*'s Ideal Home Exhibition and new trends in British home building, most notably in the homes designed by the architect Edwin Lutyens, who used a blend of architectural styles to create a patina of age in his work. All these efforts—though in different arenas—imagined new ways that commercial ventures might sustain nostalgic visions within the individual dwelling, and considered together, they reveal how the idea of "home" was suddenly not a given or fixed quality but something that could be deliberately and carefully constructed. The concept of the home makeover, so central to current conceptions of domestic space, was just emerging, and this chapter traces the importance of these early developments through different aspects of the culture.

Town planners, architects, and writers all saw the value (in every sense of the word) of incarnating the passage of time in architectural features, providing an arena in which individuals might experience a visible connection with the past without abandoning the present or a sense of being thoroughly modern. And so they constructed objects that implied time's flow: buildings that combined different styles from different eras, or communities that united a country vision associated with the past, with a city vision of modern amenities. This temporal play in turn allowed for the literal buying of time, for if time could be "applied," like a coat of paint, to objects or dwellings, it could also then be packaged and sold. Blending architectural styles from different eras was not a new trend; what made the architectural spaces of a Bournville, a Howards End, or a *Daily Mail* ideal home unique was their self-consciously constructed nature. The resulting structures not only bore marks of continuity with the past but crucially made an often frank avowal that the very idyllic, "authentic," and noncommercial aura was in fact sustained by modern commerce. It is this contradictory move—to recognize the value of continuity while foregrounding the constructed and commodified nature of this continuity—that allowed these architectural sites to become stages for performances at once modern and nostalgic. To inscribe temporality on new and marketable objects and spaces, and turn time and nostalgic visions into commodities, can be seen as the hallmark of a society particularly anxious both to preserve traditions and to be fully modern. Instead of an outmoded past or a dirty, industrial present, the commodified authentic promised a better hybrid, one that would bring select parts of the past into an updated setting.

Part II of the book, "Urban Authenticities," shifts to somewhat later versions of the commodified authentic that unfolded within the city and that were marked by efforts to manufacture a modern aesthetic refinement. In contrast to a Bournville or a Howards End, which tended to reinforce a hierarchical model of community relations and to emphasize a nostalgic return to an authentic country aesthetic, these urban versions developed a more flexible and more democratic model presented to a broader market, infusing popular culture with highbrow ideas of noncommercial purity.

The first chapter in this section, "The Vanishing Act of Commercialism: Selfridges, Modernity, and the Purified Marketplace," concerns the radical innovations in British retail initiated by the London opening of Selfridges department store, which offered an unprecedented setting for authentic performance and provided its customers a complete education in creating and maintaining different kinds of authentic goods and spaces. In its advertisements, displays, and interior and exterior design, Selfridges worked to redefine shopping by systematically erasing distinctions between commerce and areas most Londoners would have assumed were separate from commercial concerns. On a grand scale, Selfridges perfected the various forms of the commodified authentic, bringing a dash of English country flavoring into the city (and a city sophistication into the country), and providing a hushed atmosphere of aestheticized luxury where customers might escape the press of modern life and commercial frenzy, and where visitors might relax as if they were in an improved version of their own home. At the same time, customers might select among vast numbers of seemingly endless goods. The implications were not simply that customers could have it all, but that these new commercial blends were in fact superior to the previous forms. Selfridges' use of the commodified authentic quickly changed the commercial climate of London, inspiring other stores rapidly to develop a similar approach. The discussion of Selfridges allows new readings of works by Henry James and H. G. Wells, writers who, in their contradictory efforts to revel in and to unmask the commodification of authenticity, captured the powerful and unsettling consequences of commerce's steady advance into ever more areas of the culture.

The next chapter, "'Lustrous behind Glass': Woolf, Window Shopping, and Authentic Display," moves from the store out into the urban street. Focusing on the individual consumer gaze, I analyze literary depictions of window shopping, particularly in the early work of Virginia Woolf, alongside new methods of window display in Britain just before and during World War I. Both the fictional and the actual displays left behind the crowded, though often lavish, arrangements of the Victorian shop window to present less cluttered exhibits with clean lines and single objects—a transformation paralleled in Selfridges' print advertising by a shift in emphasis from price and quantity to a more austere and image-focused modernist aesthetic. A consumer could perform a kind of authenticity and aesthetic refinement that both alluded to and elided its own commercial construction and that, remarkably, even promised after the war to bridge the temporal and cultural gap between pre- and postwar society. Selfridges, Woolf, and the new window displays satisfied in different ways some of the contradictory desires of the modern subject: the longing for the noncommercial, the pleasure in distinguishing between high and low culture, and a modern wish to acknowledge and even celebrate the constructed nature of this satisfaction. These very desires became a critical part of the modernist project, as such strategies promised to transcend distinctions between the "authentic" and the mass-produced, between an aesthetic modernism and a commercial modernity.

As I argue in my final chapter, "Modernist Excursions," tracing the history and development of the commodified authentic is key to understanding later works of high modernism, as well as our own contemporary moment, with its strangely hybridized blend of nostalgia and modernity. This concluding chapter investigates how the commodified authentic became a critical modernist tool, analyzing the way authors such as Lawrence, Woolf, and Joyce deployed the strategy to capture some of the contradictions at the heart of modernism itself. The commodified authentic remains a powerful marketing technique and cultural strategy. Indeed, it derives its continuing strength and relevance from its promise to capture and resolve many current tensions: The desire for a simple, commercial-free space away from the malls and the sprawl overlaps with the wish to be cutting-edge and immersed in the latest thing; the appeal of the coterie, with its exclusivity and select audience, flows into the attraction of celebrity, with its ready reproducibility and mass-market appeal. From Merchant-Ivory films to new heritage villages to Restoration Hardware, the commodified authentic continues to promise a temporary antidote to these conflicts, always leaving, of course, the desire for another dose.

Part I

Commodified Nostalgia and the Country Aesthetic

2. The Past Is a Present Country

Model Towns and Commercial Utopias

> What our rural image does is present us with a "real England." Here men and women still live naturally. The air is clean, personal relationships matter (especially between employer and employee), there is no crime (except "quaint" crime like poaching) and no violence.... It is an organic society, a "real" one, as opposed to the unnatural or "unreal" society of the town.
>
> —Alun Howkins, "The Discovery of Rural England"

> Town and country *must be married*, and out of this joyous union will spring a new hope, a new life, a new civilization.
>
> —Ebenezer Howard, *To-morrow: A Peaceful Path to Real Reform*

In 1898, Ebenezer Howard, a shy stenographer from London, published a short book that revolutionized town planning. His work, *To-morrow: A Peaceful Path to Real Reform*, quickly became an unexpected success and made Howard one of the most influential town planners of the twentieth century. Published in a second edition in 1902 under its better known title, *Garden Cities of Tomorrow*, Howard's compact book introduced the modern idea of a planned development, a community designed specifically to correct the haphazard and destructive expansion of urban industrial centers. *Garden Cities* provided a blueprint for limiting growth and for concentrating housing; more important, it envisioned an unexpected but tantalizing combination of a deliberately constructed "authentic" English country life with a vibrant industrial city.[1] While seemingly as idiosyncratic as the towns his vision spawned, Howard's conceptualization was an organic embodiment of commodified authenticity, creating a product that could be both lived and sold, and inspiring a revolution in the way communities were planned and built.

Howard's Garden City concept, and the first Garden City at Letchworth, were in part the culmination of two earlier efforts. The factory towns of Bournville and Port Sunlight, started by wealthy industrialists to provide better housing for workers, offered models for uniting the power of commerce with a vision of an "authentic" English lifestyle, loosely clustered around ideas of simple but picturesque housing, green spaces, and a sense of getting back to an older—yet modern—way of life. Both the factory towns and the new garden cities refused the impulse to privilege either town or country but instead imagined a new form of community in which industry created the conditions for rural pleasures. Such towns not only anticipated modern commerce's recognition of lifestyle itself as a meaningful product but actually provided the material conditions to create and sustain that lifestyle. What they sold was real, and new, and marketable.

The commercialized utopias of Bournville, Port Sunlight, and Letchworth further represent an important moment in the passage into modernity, one that suggests a highly determined reaction against imminent loss coupled with a desire to sustain the excitement of imminent change. In the move to embrace simultaneously authenticity and its deliberate construction, these model communities pushed toward a modern (and even postmodern) aesthetic. What is remarkable is how pervasive this version of the commodified authentic became. The impulse to unite commerce and a sense of authenticity in community design—both by using industrial profits to support a seemingly authentic English lifestyle, and by in turn marketing this lifestyle to sell particular products—began to permeate British culture in the early twentieth century, and the results remain central to suburban planning today. The towns themselves manifested a cultural imperative that flowed between the material and the immaterial, one that was invoked and critiqued in architecture, in business schemes, and in literature. This chapter follows this flow by analyzing actual versions of commercialized utopias as well as literary ones, considering the towns of Bournville, Port Sunlight, and Letchworth, as well as Bernard Shaw's sustained analysis of model towns and their power to commodify different kinds of lifestyles. His plays not only suggest the interdisciplinary attention the towns received; they also provide a critical lens through which to consider the hidden dynamics inherent in attempts to construct and to market an "authentic" community.

The Housing Crisis and Utopian Solutions

Howard encapsulated the innovative union promised by the new model towns in his "Three Magnets" drawing, a schematic representation of the dangers and advantages of town and country living and a depiction of his new conception of the Garden City (figure 2.1). The first two magnets at the top represent, respectively, the attractions—or "magnets"—of the town and the country and also outline their drawbacks. The town might grant "Social Opportunity" and "Places of Amusement," but these advantages were compromised by the high cost of living, dirty air, and lack of natural beauty. Conversely, the country benefits of clean air and beautiful surroundings were outweighed by the lack of opportunity and small society. Howard's third magnet, however, presented an alternative that merged town and country, forming a city that might bring the "Beauty of Nature" directly alongside "Social Opportunity," one that might combine a low cost of living with a picturesque setting and high wages, offering "Bright Homes & Gardens, No Smoke, No Slums."

Howard's third magnet strove not simply to reform the industrial city but to reimagine and remake it. Industry, so frequently seen as the spoiler of a more

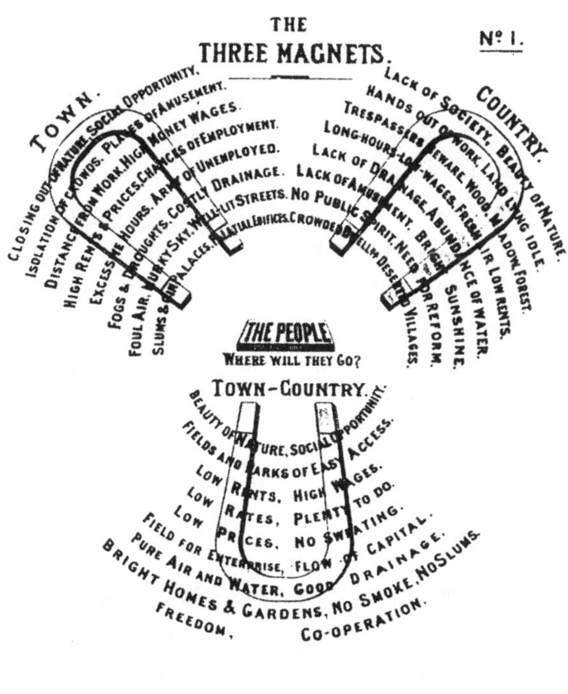

Fig. 2.1
Ebenezer Howard, "Three Magnets" drawing. Originally printed in Howard's *To-morrow: A Peaceful Path to Real Reform*, 1898. Image from *FGCHM*, Howard, Ebenezer: "Three Magnets," Garden City: Diagram No. 1, Howard.1. Reprinted with kind permission from the First Garden City Heritage Museum.

authentic rural England, was recast as a central player in authenticity's production. The newly imagined city would grant an intriguing spatial and temporal conflation. Not only would an idyllic country model be united with a bustling urban one, but this very union would unite a nostalgic, preindustrial past—when the air was clean and life lived closer to nature—with an exciting new future, one that promised to correct the excesses of the industrial era even as it harnessed its potential.[2]

Howard's Town-Country blend was part of a larger response to a growing sense of crisis at the turn of the century, a backlash against city life united with a nostalgic vision of rural ease. As a range of commentators lamented, rampant industrial development was making urban life artificial while simultaneously destroying what was seen as a more organic rural alternative. Cities were plagued by overcrowding, unemployment, poverty, and crime, and increasingly, urban living was considered unnatural, a turn away from the purer life of the country. As one observer noted,

> As we desert the lanes of Nature for the cities of artificiality, we desert quietude, happiness, and integrity for bustle, unrest, and insincerity. . . . Contrast the smiling countryside, the bright sheaths of golden sunrays lazily suffusing across emerald meadow and bronzed upland . . . with the unrest, the clatter and roar of our frowning, grimed, noisy, noisome, never restful, repellent towns.[3]

While such idyllic, natural country visions were repeatedly contrasted with the artificial urban, other commentators decried the increasing poverty and desertion of the countryside. As C. F. G. Masterman complained in his popular book *The Condition of England* (1909), rural communities were being emptied out to provide workers for the new city factories, threatening ancient skills and traditions: "No one stays [in the countryside] who can possibly find employment elsewhere. . . . The villages are left to old men and to children, to the inert, unenterprising, and intellectually feeble. Whole ancient skilled occupations—hedging and ditching, the traditional treatment of beasts and growing things—are becoming lost arts in rural England."[4] For Masterman and many others, the "cities of artificiality" not only served as contrasts to a more natural rural ideal; the cities' growth resulted in the simultaneous destruction of the rural alternative.

Howard recognized, however, the potential of creative fusion. In his plan, he sidestepped the entrenched binary of an idyllic but threatened countryside versus the rapacious and unnatural city. Unnostalgic for country life, he saw the virtues of its cleaner and more beautiful landscape while acknowledging that its faults—such as the isolation, the unemployment, and the low wages—were often intrinsic to rural life rather than a result of the city's vices. In Howard's imagined Garden City, the contradiction between town and country living was not so much resolved or dissolved but sustained in an appealing new package. The virtues of each might continue to define each other, but in new pairings; low rents, for example, might be linked, rather than opposed, to high wages. The new Garden City denizen could experience only the benefits of each way of life, united in one appealing location. Such a union suggested one of the emerging promises of the commodified authentic: the resident could possess previously contradictory elements without strain, joining the country and the city, the commercial and the authentic.

Howard's utopian scheme recognized that at the heart of both the nostalgic longing and the industrial despair was an issue common to both urban and rural areas: housing. Industry and rapid development had produced an acute housing problem, and from the mid-nineteenth century this issue dominated discussions of social reform. Conservative and liberal commentators alike agreed that poor living conditions for both city and country laborers, and even for the growing middle class, led to all manner of social evils, from rampant immorality to drunkenness to disease.[5] Attempts at reform were legion, though largely ineffectual. Model housing for workers became a popular topic; George Eliot's Dorothea in *Middlemarch*, for example, occupies much of her time with designing model cottages and planning a cooperative community—activities, Eliot hints, that, while admirable, were superficial solutions to a deeper problem. Designs for small-scale model towns or villages also began to emerge, especially in the second half of the nineteenth century. A few wealthy industrialists, such as Sir Titus Salt and Colonel Edward Akroyd, attempted to build new towns around an industrial center, with varying degrees of success. William Morris and John Ruskin imagined a beautiful return to older models of architecture and older models of industry, ones that emphasized craftsmanship and handmade quality.[6]

At the turn of the century, however, reformers began to envision more sweeping changes. As the piecemeal and small-scale reforms of the past had proven largely ineffectual, the interest in building both model towns and model cities expanded rapidly. In part, these reforms took literary form, inspiring a rush of utopian novels in both America and Britain. Three of the best-known and most influential—Edward Bellamy's *Looking Backward* (1888), William Morris's *News from Nowhere* (1890), and H. G. Wells's *A Modern Utopia* (1905)—proposed a centralized, marginalized, or even nonexistent role for commerce and industry in the new city. Bellamy, in his wildly successful book, described a city run entirely on the credit system, a place without advertising or the proliferation of stores, and where a centralized state controlled all aspects of production. In contrast, Morris imagined a world without money, one where modern industrial mass production was unknown and workers took careful pride in making expertly crafted goods. Wells proposed an alternative universe where only limited capitalism was allowed and all property was owned by the state. These literary utopian experiments, while differing in many respects, imagined a fundamentally changed role for commerce and industry, abolishing it altogether, taming it to a preindustrial size, or centralizing it into one organization.[7] What none of these books imagined, however, was how commerce and advertising would be harnessed to support, to promote, and to produce a utopian vision.

While novelists envisioned utopias, developers of model towns attempted to realize their own version in full working reality. The factory towns of Bournville and Port Sunlight, and the construction of the first Garden City at Letchworth, offered literal examples of the spatial and temporal union that Howard would outline in his "Three Magnets" drawing. Bournville and Port Sunlight were started in the late nineteenth century by industrialists who sought to blend old-looking villages with modern industrial production, bringing a utopian vision together with an unapologetically capitalist one. Built largely before Howard published his work, and in fact articulating a set of interests different than the ideal Howard had in mind, such towns shared with his vision the innovative union of industry and country living. The more nostalgic models of Bournville and Port Sunlight were transformed and adapted in the construction of the first official Garden City at Letchworth, begun in 1903. While in some respects a continuation of earlier efforts, these new models, with their blend of town and country, past and present, promised to change the automatic association of industrialization with the crowded, urban squalor of a Manchester or a London. Industry would not just be tamed, as Morris and others imagined, but employed as a powerful tool to create and sustain new model communities.

The model towns relied (in different combinations and degrees) on both the nostalgic and the originary forms of authenticity, presenting idyllic visions of the past and a simultaneous insistence on the revolutionary nature of their endeavors. The founders and the commentators of the time repeatedly used words such as "natural," "homey," "picturesque," "pure," "simple," and "clean" to describe these communities, descriptions that presented a picture of nostalgic domesticity and modern efficiency. This combination promised to sustain an English rural authenticity that so many feared was passing away, at the same time that it offered an exciting sense of new possibility.

Bournville, Port Sunlight, and Letchworth were not isolated examples of utopian schemes but in fact represented the modern emergence of lifestyle design in Britain. These communities did not so much produce single objects or especially interesting examples of architecture; they were instead conceived as environments, attempts to construct a new and complete atmosphere that might support specifically imaged lifestyles. Certainly small model towns had been planned before, and many of the popular exhibitions in the late nineteenth century had included reproduced model villages.[8] What Bournville, Port Sunlight, and Letchworth offered, however, was the deliberate commercial production of larger scale communities, ones that included a range of classes and were designed to create a climate of rural ease supported by the latest technology. Today, such lifestyle communities—both actual and in advertising—are so pervasive as to have become a climate, one we often fail to recognize. At the end of the nineteenth century, though, such constructed environments were being produced rapidly and for the first time. Critically, future citizens (and quickly, consumers) were invited to partake in these new communities. They were given a new stage, an entire town within which they might perform a new role. They would not merely be spectators browsing through an exhibition but denizens of a new way of life. These new residents would shape these new towns—and in turn would be shaped by them into modern consumers of lifestyle marketing.

The new utopian communities also possessed another critical element: they were to be created and sustained by the overt, central role of industry. Industry was not to be a silent partner, whose profits were channeled far from the dirty site of production to maintain elsewhere a purified life, free from industrial taint. The factory works were central to all three communities, providing the visible means of support for the lifestyles offered. This link to industry quickly led to a second commercialization, as each community packaged and sold both its lifestyles and its accompanying "authentic" aura to promote a variety of products, such as Cadbury's Cocoa or Sunlight Soap. The careful commodification of authenticity emerged as a powerful sustainer of the towns and their aura.

While seeming to grant a heady and indeed revolutionary blend of industrial profitability and rural purity, the cycle in which authenticity was both produced and sold contained an implicit peril. The more "authentic" and healthy the environment of the towns became, the more it was subject to attempts to sell this as a lifestyle. The authentic environment in turn demanded not only direct and ongoing commercial support but also the commodification of that authenticity as something to be marketed. Inevitably, significant tensions developed, especially between the architects and those in charge of the commercial viability of Letchworth. Nevertheless, Letchworth, Port Sunlight, and Bournville—though compromised—endured when most model communities failed, in part because the cycle of commodification helped fuel their development. As Bernard Shaw—who both supported and criticized the new movement—suggested, any successful model town had to be sustained by profits made in industry. This was not, for Shaw and others, a dirty secret but an inescapable and at times pleasing truth. The new communities derived at least part of their appeal from the very fact that they were newly created representations, built by industry and capable of being reproduced elsewhere.

The Model Village at Bournville

At the turn of the century, George Cadbury, a successful businessman and devout Quaker, began to construct Bournville Village, a model community that was one of the inspirations for Howard's more comprehensive plan. Cadbury and his brother Richard began with the paradoxical idea that lay at the heart of the new model towns: industry, rather than being the spoiler of authentic rural communities, might become the source and preserver of nostalgic authenticity. In their plans for Bournville, they imagined a new type of company town, setting out to remake the kind of village community that so many felt was rapidly disappearing. By the early 1890s, Cadbury Brothers had outgrown its factory in Birmingham, and the brothers acquired land outside the urban center where they could build a new factory in a country setting. As George Cadbury's wife, Elizabeth, sentimentally recalled, the brothers "had resolved to move their factory from smoky town surroundings, to fresh fields and blue skies, amongst trees where birds sang, and the rooks raised their plaintive friendly voice, and where even trout swam in a near-by little brook."[9] The brothers hoped, in short, to redefine industry and reimagine village life.[10]

Bournville not only suggested a new role for industry; it also illustrates several stages of the commodified authentic. First, the "authentic" village atmosphere, carefully produced through architectural details, town planning, and land management, was created and supported by the profits made from Cadbury Brothers' chocolate. The environment of Bournville was then in turn used to sell the products made there. The atmosphere itself was commodified, allegedly infusing the very chocolate with a country atmosphere that might transfer into the bodies and homes of the urban consumer.

Bournville began in part as an experiment in housing reform, as both Cadbury brothers had grown increasingly concerned with housing conditions for workers. They envisioned Bournville less as a company town controlled by a single industry and more as a community development.[11] Bournville was designed to house not simply Cadbury workers but other residents as well. As the historian for the firm notes, George Cadbury "wished to create a village which would be a model of good planning and good and cheap house-building, and in which all those who wished might be free to live, whether they worked at Cadbury's or not" (Williams, 219). By 1900, Cadbury had built 300 houses of various sizes, developed a village green framed by a group of public buildings, and set aside ample grounds both for extensive parklands and for recreation. The same year, he passed over control of the estate to a committee, forming the Bournville Village Trust, which was to regulate the development of the village.

Critically, however, Bournville Village was not to be a philanthropic development; this was to be a new marriage, where industry might profitably produce a natural, countrified lifestyle.[12] As the deed of trust for the village laid out, Cadbury wished to "alleviat[e] the evils which arise from the insanitary and insufficient accommodation supplied to large numbers of the working classes and of securing to workers in factories some of the advantages of out-door village life with opportunities for the natural and healthful occupation of cultivating the soil."[13] This worthy goal, however, had to be made to pay. George Cadbury wanted the town to be a model that might be replicated elsewhere, and so it was important to him to run the village at at least a modest profit. As one Bournville pamphlet explained, the trust "endeavours to operate on an ordinary commercial basis."[14] Edward Cadbury, George's son, further pointed out that treating workers decently was in fact good for business: "Business efficiency and the welfare of the employees are but different sides of the same problem. Character is an economic asset; and business efficiency depends not merely on the physical condition of the employees, but on their general attitude and feeling towards the employer."[15] Profits improved, Cadbury hinted, when employees were educated, healthy, and grateful to their boss.

In both the town and the factory, the Cadbury brothers worked to shape an entire community along village lines, one that served as a direct response to the pervasive fear that the close-knit village communities of the past were dying out; as C. F. G. Masterman had lamented, "'A village which once fed, clothed, policed, and regulated itself cannot now dig its own wells or build its own barns. Still less can it act its own dramas, build its own church, or organize its own work and play.'"[16] Cadbury Brothers attempted to bring back such a village model, recognizing that "houses, by themselves, do not form a community."[17] The workers at the firm, along with the other residents of the village, organized a vast array of activities, including athletic clubs, concerts, lectures, reading groups, a camera club, musical societies, a folk dancing society, social service leagues, and many other groups. The *Bournville Works Magazine*, started in 1902, was distributed free to employees, and it kept all residents up to date on current activities in the town. Bournville worked to change the assumption that industry was necessarily destructive to village life by creating, in effect, a new "old" community.

Bournville was also designed to express physically a temporal and spatial conflation, joining a nostalgic return to preindustrial life with a kind of utopian modernity that promised to bring the latest technology to both town and works. In the actual layout of the town, Cadbury sought in part to replicate the charm of an old country village. He was intent on avoiding the appearance of the notorious "bye-law" streets caused by the Public Health Act of 1875, an act that in an effort to improve housing conditions among the poor in fact resulted in long, monotonous blocks of buildings. Such streets became synonymous with the evils of urban industrial life. As one Bournville pamphlet lamented,

> There are many . . . who have no choice but to live in dismal monotonous streets, so familiar in all our great towns, where gardens are an impossibility, where acres of brick and mortar intervene before the country can be reached, and where those who work during the day in office, factory, or shop must spend their leisure in the club, the theatre, the reading room, or the public-house, instead of in the pure free air of the country.[18]

In contrast, the new village was carefully constructed to blend into the natural surroundings, presenting the appearance of a settled, tranquil town that had been built over time. For the most part, the layout of Bournville followed the natural contours of the land, and every attempt was made to preserve existing trees and to plant new ones. As one contemporary observer noted, at Bournville, the "'undulating nature of the land, which is dotted with coppices and bosky dells, and through which a pretty winding stream runs, gives the special charm that is always connected with old English village scenery.'"[19]

The village atmosphere was further amplified through architectural details. Cadbury's principal early architect, W. Alexander Harvey, designed buildings that reflected tranquil domestic qualities, ones that echoed the past while also standing as examples, in Harvey's words, "of what the village of the future may be, a village of healthy homes amid pleasant surroundings, where fresh air is abundant and beauty present" (15).[20] The public buildings at Bournville evoked a cleansed (some might say sanitized) antiquity. The shops that faced the village green, for example, reproduced the popular half-timbering style, with its vague associations with the Tudor past (figure 2.2). Complete with casement windows on the upper floors, a feature Harvey praised for its "simplicity and homeliness" (56), the shops preserved a village model of shopping quite unlike the grand urban emporiums considered in the fourth chapter of this book. Turning away from the depressing monotony

Fig. 2.2 Bournville, shops on village green, c. 1905
From *BCA-BVT*, 1420-04: Photograph by Thos. Lewis. First Bournville shops, Mary Vale Road, c. 1905. Built 1897. Copy negative BBT/120/1987/4/4. Reproduced by kind permission of the Bournville Village Trust and courtesy of the Birmingham City Archives.

of style associated with most industrial areas, the architecture was deliberately designed with variety in mind; as Harvey notes, buildings of various sizes echoed "so many well-known old villages" (4).[21] Yet these venerable-looking public spaces were not simply reproductions; Bournville was to be a new and improved moral community as well, which meant, for the devout Cadburys, that one of the central institutions of public village life—the pub—was not allowed.

Cadbury focused most of his building energies on designs for picturesque worker cottages and their attached gardens. Following Harvey's convictions, the external architecture was simple; Harvey noted that he always sought to "obtain that rustic appearance suitable to a cottage" (58). Each house had a long stretch of land in the back that was planted (at the owner's expense) by the Bournville Trust. Gardening, which Cadbury thought was "the most natural and healthful of all recreations" (Harvey, 10), would reconnect the workers to the land, a connection that countless books and articles of the time declared had been lost by the vast migration of workers to the urban centers. For Cadbury, gardening represented a healthy leisure activity, much to be preferred to the pub. This was not quite a back-to-the-land movement; workers still spent their days in the factories. Rather, with his regulations and his landscaping, as well as with the architecture, Cadbury brought back bits and pieces of past lifestyles to create a new living environment for his workers.

Cadbury went to great lengths to blend the old and the new. Alongside the newly constructed "old" dwellings, Cadbury reconstructed actual old houses. Selly Manor, a fourteenth-century manor house originally located about a mile from Bournville, was moved near the village green, reconditioned with modern materials, and "restored as far as possible in accordance with its original design" (figure 2.3).[22] Likewise, Minworth Greaves house, dating from roughly the same era, was moved from an area east of Birmingham and reconstructed next to Selly Manor.[23] The interior of Selly Manor was set up, as the historian of the firm notes, to "act as a kind of museum of old English furniture and household objects" (Williams, 225). These reconstructed old homes, alongside the new but old-looking buildings, suggested an amalgamation of times, a carefully constructed new creation that was

Fig. 2.3 Bournville, Minworth Greaves (left) and Selly Manor
From *BCA-BVT*, 1485-24. Reproduced by kind permission of the Bournville Village Trust and courtesy of the Birmingham City Archives.

designed to reference—though not quite reproduce—an older village model as a more attractive setting for modern industry.

Cadbury and his designers were eager to separate Bournville's constructed aura of authenticity and nostalgia from other "artificial" versions. Harvey, for example, carefully distinguished his designs from what he viewed as vulgar attempts at extra ornamentation, which tended "to deprive the dwelling of its homeliness" (5). Echoing the tenets of the Arts and Crafts Movement, Harvey observed, "The soul of beauty is harmony, which may co-exist with the veriest simplicity; and it is in the harmonious treatment of parts, and not in useless and sometimes costly decoration, that a dwelling gains that homely appearance which should be our aim to realize" (5). While the estate as a whole might cast a nostalgic look back, Harvey was cautious about introducing anything that might smack of falsity, complaining, for example, that the inglenook, "like many old-time features which have been revived during the last few years . . . has perhaps been a little overdone" (53). Implicit in these assertions is the claim that Bournville derived its authenticity from its more careful reconstruction. What is interesting is that such a claim was not based on time—the older, "authentic" version versus the newer copy—but on distinguishing among more and less authentic *re*productions. Such distinctions suggested the growing commercial culture, where the contrast between the commercial and the noncommercial gave way to comparisons among various modes of commercial production.

Even within the factory itself, the Cadbury brothers attempted to unite an older, more "natural" economic model with modern industry. As the firm grew rapidly in the years following the move to Bournville, the brothers tried in numerous ways to keep the personal approach of a small company. As historian Standish Meacham observes, many early employees of the firm recalled the sense of connectedness that infused the company: "In these recollections, as in all the accounts of the life of the firm, one senses a cultivated perception of Cadbury Brothers not just as a family firm but as a family."[24] While obviously not a cottage industry, Cadbury Brothers nevertheless attempted to evoke this older model, in which goods were made in the home by family members and various assistants. Along these lines, it also reintroduced the concept of apprenticeship. While Edward Cadbury admitted that "the system of apprenticeship that used to obtain is not adapted to modern developments" (44), Cadbury Brothers developed a modern form of apprenticeship, one that gave boys a broad introduction to the firm's various branches, followed by rigorous training in one particular field. Boys chosen to be apprentices had to "sign[] an indenture to attend classes and to work for the Firm until [they were] 21" (E. Cadbury, 47). While following an older training framework, the boys were nevertheless trained in new methods of production and distribution.

This older model logically extended to some of the more innovative benefits that were provided at the firm. The company started pension funds for most employees and also organized sick leave and vacation pay (supported in part by workers, in part by the firm). It employed two full-time doctors, and medical services were available free of charge. A midday meal was served each day, provided to the employees at cost. While these benefits did not look back to previous industrial models, they did embrace an imagined past, a time when workers in the home might have been cared for in the home by their family. Rather than reproducing a replica, the firm attempted to produce a kind of nostalgic spirit, a theoretical return to a cottage industry model that promised to be both new and improved.

Bournville had its problems, of course, and perhaps the most striking is the paternalistic flavor that inevitably governed the community. Such paternalism reveals how the conscious construction of nostalgic authenticity often implies a wistful longing for hierarchy, for both producer and consumer. The Cadbury family repeatedly resisted the charge, but accounts from the early days of Bournville reveal that the genuine desire to help employees often veered into authoritarian oversight, though this line was often blurred. As one employee recalled, "George Cadbury would go round, on rainy days, to inquire of the forewomen whether all the girls under their charge had changed their wet shoes" (Williams, 59)—a partly kind, partly intrusive gesture. Employees were subject to physical exams, education classes were mandatory for the younger workers, house gardens were planted with a preordained list of plants at the owner's expense, and very stringent guidelines were enforced regarding employee cleanliness. Physical exercise was required for the younger employees, though this was usually done on company time, and married women were never allowed to work in the factory. Infusing this paternalism was a sense of religious morality, as the Cadburys' often admirable Quaker commitments could cross over into assumptions that the company knew what was good for both their workers and the residents of Bournville. In part, all this oversight negatively echoed a past rural system where large landowners governed most aspects of their tenants' lives. As George Cadbury Jr. tellingly observed, "Town Planning is . . . estate management on a large scale."[25]

The Cadbury paternalism should be seen, however, as in part taking on roles that the state would later sustain. The firm did insist on continued schooling for its younger employees, but as it pointed out, "the Firm has assumed a responsibility, which, up to the present, the community has itself refused to undertake" (E. Cadbury, 268).[26] It granted free health care before nationalized care was available and supported education beyond the age of fourteen. More critically, there was substance underlying Bournville's idyllic atmosphere, as the town in fact offered tangible benefits for its inhabitants that arose in part from its attempts to manufacture an authentic style. Such benefits may be distinguished from later attempts to commodify this environment, as Cadbury quickly turned from building the model village to packaging and selling its authenticity.

Mass Marketing the Garden Factory

Cadbury Brothers not only produced a deliberately constructed authentic flavor in its town; it also developed an early model of commodified authenticity in its advertisements, selling products by selling the whole Bournville lifestyle. Indeed, the Bournville experiment had been "a splendid advertisement for the firm," as W. J. Ashley, a former professor of commerce at the University of Birmingham, pointed out in 1912.[27] Consider, for example, two Cadbury ads from the *Daily Mail* of 1911 (figure 2.4). Without mentioning a specific product or prices, the copy insists that purity "is inseparable from every product made in Cadbury's factory in a garden at Bournville." This approach is distinctly different than the typical advertisements in the paper at the time, which generally depicted the specific product for sale and its price (figure 2.5).[28] By contrast, the Cadbury ads subtly mimic the pure environment they market; natural imagery forms a border around the ads, the trademark tree is included, and the font style is simple and clean, two virtues constantly enforced at Bournville. The style of the two Cadbury advertisements in fact echoes the graphic style of the Arts and Crafts Movement, and also the less ornate style employed by the Yeats sisters at the Cuala Press (an institution strongly supported by the Cadburys); such similarities suggested the growing overlap at the time between art and advertising.[29] The authenticity of the model village is (allegedly) made material, and the implication is that such authenticity is intrinsic to the chocolates produced there.

Cadbury Brothers even exported the image of the authentic domestic home that it hoped to provide for its workers. In a related series of advertisements that appeared over several weeks in the *Daily Mail*, for example, a young family is depicted in a warm domestic interior at various stages of the day (figure 2.6). Cadbury's Cocoa—implicitly taking on the role of Cadbury Brothers in Bournville—seems not only to produce this interior but also to protect and sustain it. The cocoa is simultaneously a new and innovative product and the producer of the "authentic" domestic scene. The first ad depicts a mother, surrounded by her three children, calmly pouring out cocoa before the school day begins. Cocoa "is a food as

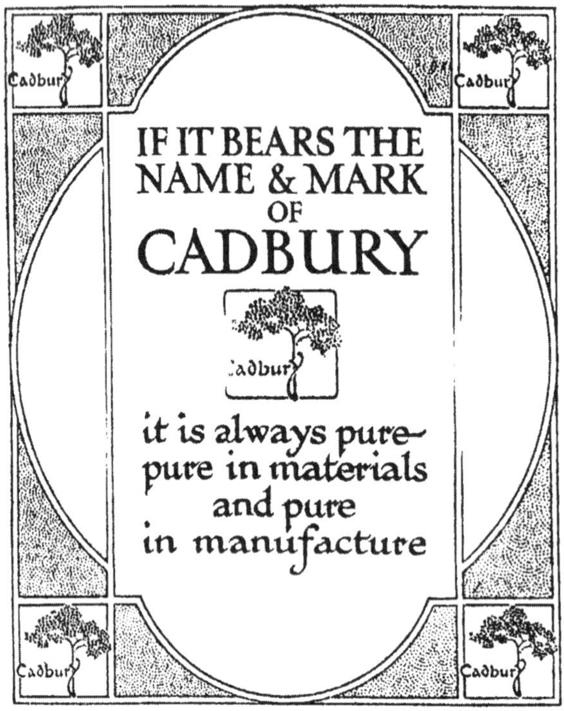

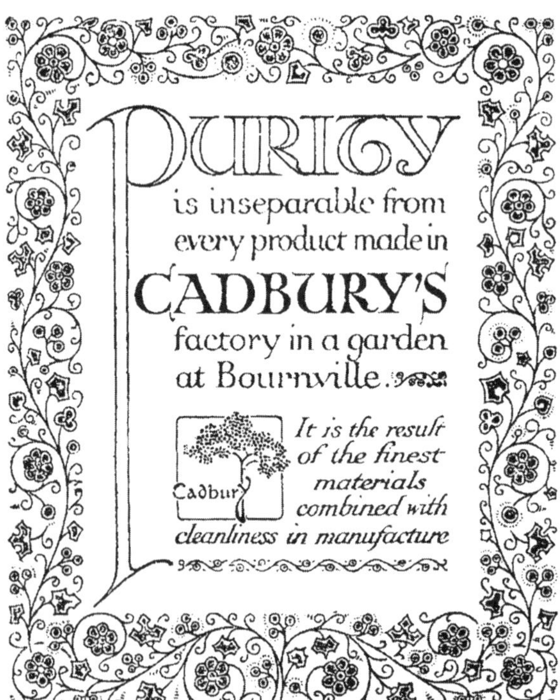

Fig. 2.4
Early Cadbury advertisements from the *Daily Mail*, 1911
A. From *Daily Mail*, 16 January 1911, 4. *B*. From *Daily Mail*, 23 January 1911, 4. Reproduced by kind permission of Cadbury Limited.

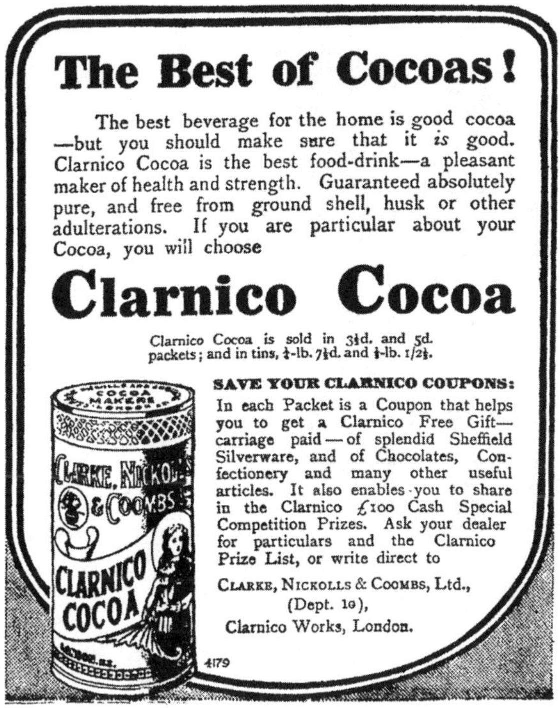

Fig. 2.5
Typical advertisement from the *Daily Mail*, 1911
From *Daily Mail*, 25 January 1911, 9.

well as a drink," one that will "strengthen their little bodies" and help them with their schoolwork. As the children prepare to exit the domestic scene, the cocoa will give energy and protection. Product creates a lifestyle. The second ad depicts the children returning home from school, when cocoa is the perfect drink for "fine healthy appetites" and "a splendid pick-me-up" for Mother as well, "after her busy morning in the house." Here again we see the neat home, with warm steam coming from the cocoa, and clean linens on the table. A week later, the third ad appears, showing the same family, with a father now added. The cocoa will sustain the father "before he starts for the City," bringing the garden factory purity even into the urban setting. As we have seen, modern industrial urban life was believed to weaken the body; Cadbury's Cocoa would infuse the more natural spirit of the village directly into the bodies of its city customers. The final advertisement presents the late evening scene. The children from the earlier ads are sent off to bed, and the parents can indulge not with a visit to a pub but with "the best and safest 'night-cap'": Cadbury's Cocoa.

Cadbury Brothers commodified the virtues it saw as intrinsic to the factory and town—purity, cleanliness, healthiness, and domestic tranquillity—and promised

Fig. 2.6
Series of Cadbury advertisements from the *Daily Mail* in 1911
A. From *Daily Mail*, 6 February 1911, 4. *B*. From *Daily Mail*, 13 February 1911, 4. *C*. From *Daily Mail*, 20 February 1911, 4. *D*. From *Daily Mail*, 6 March 1911, 4. Reproduced by kind permission of Cadbury Limited.

that the products themselves might transmit the purity of the environment in which they were produced. The chocolate products were in fact made in a clean factory, but the advertisements imply a transitive quality for the product, one that has become commonplace in modern marketing and its critiques. While at Bournville the Cadbury brothers could ameliorate housing problems and the effects of industry, the advertisements subtly shift this approach, appealing when selling cocoa to the very anxieties that housing problems produced in the urban body. Like Bournville, the domestic interiors in this narrative set of advertisements implied a space that was neither purely rural nor urban, and that united vaguely

Fig. 2.6B

nostalgic and sentimental images with a modern but authentic product. The narrative approach to these advertisements further implied that the benefits would circulate not only within the body but also within time, throughout the day, hinting that an entire environment was provided, which consumers were invited to reproduce and then perform within in their own homes. The cocoa, like Bournville, would correct urban dangers, strengthen the body, and provide a place of protection.

We often view this progression—from an actual environment to the selling of that environment—as a progression from the authentic to the inauthentic, from the actual and substantive to the empty and chimeric.[30] The shift from Bournville's actual community to the promise that Bournville's community aura might adhere to its cocoa, seems (and is) a move into deceit. Likewise, the model town itself,

Fig. 2.6C

as a suggested re-creation of a previous, more authentic town, further implies the inauthentic. The critic Baudrillard might take this to the logical extreme, finding all models in danger of descending into mere "simulacra," the authentic term in danger of shifting out altogether.[31] Our postmodern sensibilities in fact make us reluctant to locate or define anything as authentic. At the same time, however, the strong critical reaction against commodified authenticity at least partially presupposes an underlying "true" authenticity that the market is manipulating. Without locating or defining precisely what an "authentic" object or atmosphere might be, it is still possible to distinguish among more or less substantive versions of the commodified authentic, as Bournville's move from an actual model town to the commodification of this town demonstrates.

Fig. 2.6D

The Bournville example demands that the commodified authentic be seen on a continuum, from examples that provide significant advantages to those that represent empty promises. At one end, we find the model town itself. Bournville displayed a consciously constructed authentic aura, but it nevertheless gave substantive benefits to support such an aura. Wages *were* higher, benefits *were* greater, the housing *was* better built. The authenticity was constructed and sustained by commerce, but the resulting community possessed many of the attributes that it advertised. At the other end of the continuum, we find the repackaging and selling of this environment. Cadbury's Cocoa had a far more tangential relationship to the benefits of Bournville than the town itself, though many of the advertisements implied otherwise. Ironically, however, this less substantive form could in turn produce surprising new forms of authenticity and nostalgia, as we will explore in the development of Port Sunlight.

Port Sunlight's Utopian Village

In 1887, William Lever, a successful soap manufacturer, began to construct a model town on a rural site near Liverpool, a town where the very name—Port Sunlight—encapsulated the emerging hybrid of commerce and authenticity: a "port," the hub of commercial shipping and exchange, receives not mundane commodities but sunlight. "Sunlight" itself conjures a range of generically positive associations, from the sunny countryside, to a pure and natural image, to enlightenment, to clarity. Put together, Port Sunlight promised the commercial delivery of authenticity, and indeed, Lever's success was intimately connected to his ability to develop and exploit various forms of the commodified authentic.

Lever himself was a frequent speaker and writer on housing issues and industry standards, but unlike George Cadbury, Lever designed Port Sunlight strictly as a business venture, built only to house Lever's workers. Cadbury's devout Quaker lifestyle gave Bournville a sense of philanthropic mission; while religious, Lever was more of a practical businessman, running the town as he did his firm, intent equally on profits and efficiency. As the town's historian, W. L. George, remarked, Bournville was "philanthropic in origin," the Garden City (to which I will turn next) stood "midway between altruism and egoism," but Port Sunlight was intent on "purely business-like transactions informed by good-will."[32] The Port Sunlight community was seen largely as another successful product of Lever soap.

Lever sought not so much to remake the industrial town but to recast the relationship between capital and labor, a relationship that at the time threatened to dissolve into outright warfare. He predicted disaster for both sides if they could not learn to work together, and Port Sunlight was in large part an experiment in creating this new partnership. As at Bournville, part of the solution for Lever lay in returning to a preindustrial model. The key was to "get back again [in] the office, factory, and workshop to that close family brotherhood that existed in the good old days of hand labour."[33] Lever dreamed of a past relationship, one suffused with a paternalistic flavor where "man and master worked side by side. . . . The master knew his Jack and Tom and Joe, and Maggie and Jane and Mary—in fact, every employee in his place. And they all knew him; they all came to him in their troubles. He knew their domestic worries and anxieties, and he helped and encouraged them."[34] Lever's remarks suggest a wistful and largely conservative impulse to return to a (mythical) hierarchy where every employee knew "his place." While Lever admitted that business could not go back to this model, he claimed that "the only thing that can restore to any degree that condition of two centuries ago is Co-Partnership."[35] For Lever, "Co-Partnership" did not mean profit sharing (to which he was violently opposed) but an unofficial agreement between capital and labor that they were working for a common goal. Profits would not be shared directly, but their benefits would be realized in the workers' increased prosperity.

Lever insisted that Port Sunlight be run *on* commercial profits and *as* a profit-making venture. For Lever, "Philanthropy is only another name for charity, and charity can only mean pauperism."[36] No self-respecting worker, Lever thought, would accept any kind of handout. The village life offered at Port Sunlight was made possible by commerce, and both Lever and others repeatedly promoted the commercial nature of Port Sunlight as "its chief value" (George, 204). As a contemporary observer noted, the scheme "pays—and pays well," and "it is the very essence of the village of Port Sunlight that it is claimed to be a sound business enterprise" (Davison, vii–viii, 5). Lever did admit that many of the buildings and houses at Port Sunlight were not, in fact, profitable, and regretted that in most places, "a village such as Port Sunlight is not commercially possible at the present time."[37] Nevertheless, the aim for Lever was to find or create ways to allow industry to use profits to sustain an authentic, modern lifestyle.

As the Cadburys did at Bournville, Lever carefully combined architectural styles, town planning, and land management to manufacture the "authentic" climate of his new rural village. Seeking to return his workers to the land, Lever believed that "a child that knows nothing of God's earth, of green fields or sparkling brooks, of breezy hill and springy heather, and whose mind is stored with none of the beauties of nature" could only be reached by returning to more natural (in both senses of the word) surroundings.[38] While Lever did not provide individual gardens for each house as at Bournville, he set aside large areas for allotment gardens, parks, and recreational fields. An early visitor to Port Sunlight remarked on the peaceful, rural aura surrounding the town:

> The *impression* of country is strongest when one walks through the Village. . . . one is immediately struck by something unusual, for the footpaths are not entirely paved as one might expect in a town of 3500 souls, but are *made* of beaten earth like those that are found along some of our high roads, while the middle of the path is paved with flagstones. This trifling circumstance, together with the many trees, both old and newly planted,

> which often intrude upon the footway, *produces* a singularly vivid *impression* of rusticity. Apart, however, from the roads themselves, nothing seems to have been neglected which may *produce* in the town-dweller *the illusion that he has indeed gone back to the land.* (George, 61–62, emphasis added)

The italicized language here indicates that the viewer knows the natural image is a manufactured effect, and that part of the pleasure lies in knowing that such effects can be produced. The visitor implies, in fact, that this new hybrid might be better than actual rusticity, uniting the pleasing effects of the country while maintaining the benefits of a town. It might have been something of a relief to the viewer to see that a village that echoed a disappearing rural way of life might be newly constructed, a safeguard, as it were, against the total disappearance of a country model.

Even more than at Bournville, Port Sunlight manufactured a sense of age in many of the buildings. The "English cottage" style was used in numerous places (George, 47), and Lever credited two of his principal architects, the brothers William and Segar Owen, with endowing the early buildings with a "distinctive English village character."[39] One deliberately old-looking block had a small shop that later became the post office (figure 2.7). The half-timbering here is solid oak, and in the construction the builders attempted "as nearly as the Modern Building Act will allow" to follow techniques that "would have been employed had the shop been erected 300 years ago."[40] As one observer remarked, many of the structures "may some day very well pass for ancient buildings" (Davison, 34). Designs on the whole were kept simple and picturesque, and as at Bournville, commentators were careful to distinguish the buildings at Port Sunlight from those that had added "freaks or features created simply for picturesque effect" (Davison, 25–26). The "old" style appearance, however, was united with modern advances; a London journalist reported in 1900 that Port Sunlight "has all the picturesqueness of mediaeval England. It has all the conveniences of the nineteenth century. Sanitary science of the Victorian era has married the picturesque of the days of Bluff King Hal, and the offspring is a village of health and loveliness."[41]

Alongside his efforts to build a neo-nostalgic village, Lever also renovated an entire old village, Thornton Hough, which was adjacent to Port Sunlight. On the one hand, like Howard, he was alert to the significant problems with country living and was far less apt to wax sentimental about rural life than was George Cadbury. Lever worked to expose a misplaced sentimental affection for older villages, pointing out that while "the exteriors of some of the old cottages in the Village were very picturesque when seen in fine weather . . . unfortunately, the more picturesque

Fig. 2.7 Port Sunlight: post office, c. 1913
From *Uni-Ar*, Post Office, 1913, LBL-PS-7J-6. Reproduced with kind permission of Unilever PLC from an original in Unilever Archives.

the exterior appearance, the more dirty, dark, damp, unhealthy, and at variance with all ideas of common decency was the interior."[42] On the other hand, however, Lever worked toward preservation. While he tore down the worst cottages, any that allowed for "the slightest possibility of reformation were altered, repaired, and adapted to modern requirements," and he tried wherever possible to build the cottages in their original places "so as to preserve the general outline of the Village."[43] By reconstructing Thornton Hough, Lever increasingly blurred the line between his new old village and the old new village.[44]

Lever used the authentic aura of Port Sunlight to sell his soap, though he drew on the purity of the town less than Cadbury Brothers did within its marketing of Bournville. Small, idyllic photographs of picturesque scenes from Port Sunlight were scattered throughout the company's magazine, *Progress*, and the authenticity of the village was occasionally evoked in advertisements. Consider, for example, an advertisement from a 1903 edition of the *Graphic* (figure 2.8). The copy proclaims that "Port Sunlight is a fairy village rather than a Soap Works," where "an Efficient

Fig. 2.8
Advertisement for Sunlight Soap, 1903
From *The Graphic*, 7 March 1903, *Uni-Ar*, LBL 1998-110. Reproduced with kind permission of Unilever PLC from an original in Unilever Archives.

staff of Chemists test each boiling to ensure that it shall be sweet and clean as the Morning Dew." Modern industry (the efficient staff of chemists) unites with the pastoral to manufacture the purity of Sunlight Soap. Central to the advertisement is a large drawing of the public school at Port Sunlight, a modern building specifically designed to look older than it was, both evoking a misty sense of tradition and serving as an exemplar of modern education. Lever wrapped modern efficiency in a traditional or pastoral environment, promising that this unique blend adhered to the soap's very nature.

While the advertisement for Sunlight Soap certainly offered less tangible benefits than Port Sunlight itself, familiar advertisements and brand names could in turn inspire a sense of authenticity and nostalgia. In a letter published in *Progress*, a soldier in the Boer War writes

> I was on patrol the other day in the direction of Colesburg, riding by myself. I was thinking about dear old England, and the old folks at home.

> Suddenly I came across the remains of a Boer Laager, and being a Lancashire lad hailing from the birth place of SUNLIGHT SOAP I was astonished at seeing an empty SUNLIGHT box. I cannot describe the feeling that came over me: It brought with it recollections of old times and of the old home.[45]

The publication in which this letter is found is certainly a mouthpiece for the company, but the sentiments expressed in the letter are in fact some of the very sentiments that make the commodified authentic such a powerful marketing strategy. Familiar products with familiar brands and images become themselves objects of nostalgia and the sites of authenticity. As transportation grew ever more efficient and individuals went farther from accustomed surroundings, the power of familiar brands to remind travelers of home grew rapidly. Lever was an early master of such techniques, recognizing in Port Sunlight how products might produce and imply not simply a bar of soap but an entire environment.

Building old-looking new buildings or renovating old ones was certainly nothing new in Britain at the time. What made Port Sunlight and Bournville unique was their role as early examples of how an authentic atmosphere might be commodified. The towns helped redefine industrial life in England by crossing a rural ideal with modern business practices and using these new hybrids to construct a new kind of industrial community. In part, these towns are troubling examples of the now ubiquitous selling of "ye olde England," with its vague references to a mythic, generalized past. As many commentators have pointed out, too often historical specificity is left out of such ventures in favor of a sanitized, ahistorical illusion. While both towns did attempt to form a new community, the rigid corporate structure in each place critically distinguished the towns from actual old villages that were less centralized and that had developed over time. Furthermore, the implicit suggestion that industry could always re-create village life—even if it was destroying it in other places—was not finally a solution to housing problems or the damaging effects of industrialization.

Yet there remains an important difference between these fantasy towns and later attempts to market such authenticity, often read as Disney-fied efforts to create a false past. The problems inherent in Bournville and Port Sunlight can be read alongside the advantages granted by these towns, including education, health care, safer work, and better housing; the health statistics and death rates in both communities were significantly better than in other industrial areas.[46] Both Cadbury and Lever worked to export these benefits; Cadbury was instrumental in implementing housing reform in Birmingham itself, and Lever was a popular speaker and a prolific writer on planning issues and labor questions, advocating, among other things, higher wages and the six-hour day.

My aim here is not to make a definitive judgment on the mixed results of Bournville and Port Sunlight but to see these attempts at factory utopias both as practical responses to an important social crisis and as early instances of a community-based version of the commodified authentic. Bournville and Port Sunlight presented a tantalizing blend of the nostalgic and the originary forms of authenticity, allowing residents to feel both part of a tradition (however sanitized) and part of a modern endeavor, a heady combination in the unsteady transition into modernity. Residents could, in effect, have one foot in the past and one in the present, occupying a transitional space in which to accommodate change. The commercialized nature of these spaces, and the reproducibility this implied, suggest an incipient model for later efforts to construct communities around a particular environment or lifestyle, as Howard attempted to do in the first Garden City.

Building the Garden City

Bournville and Port Sunlight served, at least in part, as an inspiration to Ebenezer Howard as he formulated his plan for the Garden City.[47] In Howard's more socialist vision, however, no one industry would be in charge. Howard's efforts marked a dramatic expansion of the factory town ideal, one that was less governed by the individual whims of an industrialist designing a particular community. Howard offered a far more comprehensive model that might serve as a blueprint for numerous towns. He presented the intriguing idea that an entire new city might be built not piecemeal or haphazardly, or based on its proximity to certain geographic features, but around a particular idea or theme, designed to provide a particular lifestyle. Unlike Bournville and Port Sunlight, which marketed their atmospheres to sell particular products, the board of the Garden City at Letchworth marketed Letchworth itself, seeking new residents and new businesses in a targeted campaign. Letchworth reflects an important step in the growth of the commodified authentic, when the community itself became a commodity.

With astonishing speed, a year after Howard published *To-morrow*, the first Garden City Association was formed; the association held its inaugural conference at Bournville in 1901, and the next a year later at Port Sunlight. By 1903, plans were fully under way to build the first Garden City at Letchworth. Few utopian planners could have seen their ideas take practical shape so quickly. As Howard proposed in the "Three Magnets" drawing, the Garden City promised both a spatial and a temporal compression. The small communities of the past would be united with the modern city; a kind of rural authenticity would exist alongside an urban vibrancy. These unions might be made available not simply to those who worked in or near a particular industry but to everyone from the skilled worker to the wealthy industrialist. As with most ideal plans, however, Howard's concept of the Garden City, so carefully laid out in his work, was quickly altered, and it is in these very changes—the way the project shifted to suit the competing interests of different factions—that the commodified authentic begins to shape, and to take further shape in, the Garden City. On the "authentic" side, Howard and the principal architects of Letchworth, Barry Parker and Raymond Unwin, developed a dual set of models that united a utopian originality with a nostalgic return. On the "commercial" side, the investors and governing board at Letchworth worked to make the community economically viable, which involved franchising the Garden City concept and marketing the community ideal to various buyers.

As several commentators have pointed out, Howard was an inventor rather than a city planner.[48] While he embraced a return to nature and the country life, Howard saw the Garden City as a new invention, and his vision remained largely unnostalgic. He begins *To-morrow* with a quotation from the poet J. R. Lowell, declaring that we must not "attempt the Future's Portal / With the Past's blood-rusted key,"[49] eschewing any sense of a nostalgic return for his new creation. Howard imagined a modern city that would solve the crisis in urban living, presenting an intricately detailed layout that he claimed would allow industry and citizens to coexist peacefully. In Howard's plan, a central garden of five acres would be surrounded by various public buildings, including a "town hall, principal concert and lecture hall, theatre, library, museum, picture-gallery, and hospital" (Howard, 14). From this center would extend six wide boulevards. Around the central area would be 145 acres, surrounded by the "Crystal Palace," an enclosed glass corridor that would function both as a Winter Garden for strolling and as a place where "manufactured goods are exposed for sale, and [where] most of that class of shopping which requires the joy of deliberation and selection is done" (Howard, 14). Around this ring would be a circle of houses in various architectural styles, all on tree-lined streets. Circling these would be Grand Avenue, a park of 115 acres where the schools, playgrounds, recreation grounds, gardens, and churches would be located. Surrounding the whole would be an outer ring of "factories, warehouses, dairies, markets, coal yards, timber yards" and railroads, as well as an agricultural "green belt" for farming and dairy production (Howard, 16). Howard explored in great detail the way this scheme would support itself: land would be held by the municipality, which would, once the investors had been repaid, reinvest profits in the community. Central to every part of Howard's original plan was the image of futuristic tranquillity, a new form of living that might correct the terrible conditions of the past.

Alongside Howard's utopian vision, the architects Parker and Unwin imagined a different, though finally compatible, model. Heavily influenced by William Morris, John Ruskin, and the Arts and Crafts Movement, Parker and Unwin brought a distinctly nostalgic turn to the Garden City.[50] Attracted to the utopian handicraft colonies of Ruskin and Edward Carpenter, and to William Morris's many ideas for bringing a sense of craftsmanship and pride back to working conditions, the two architects created individual dwellings and a larger community that would reflect the simplicity and purity found in these previous models. Having built a model village on a smaller scale at New Earswick—for another Quaker chocolate baron, Joseph Rowntree—Parker and Unwin sought to give Letchworth the aura of a picturesque country village, where buildings blended naturally into their surroundings and where all levels of society might work as a harmonious whole. Their offices at Letchworth, for example, were in a small cottage of their own design, complete with a thatched roof.[51] In their writings, the architects wax nostalgic about past design, musing that "wherever one finds a street or part of a street dating from before what may be called the modern period, one is almost sure to see something pleasing and beautiful in its effect."[52] Parker and Unwin returned repeatedly to ideas of hominess and simplicity, set against the speed and artificiality of the modern city:

> In these old towns and streets we read as in an open book the story of a life governed by impulses very different from our own; we read of gradual growth, of the free play of imaginative thought, devoted without stint to each individual building; while the simplicity of treatment, the absence of decoration or ornament in the majority of the cases, and the general use and skilled handling of the materials most readily accessible, tell of the usual avoidance of what could be called extravagance.[53]

The architects knew they could not simply reproduce such an effect at Letchworth, but at every point they aimed to create a modern version, one that would draw on these principles to create a new kind of authentic life.

Alongside Howard's utopian authenticity and Parker and Unwin's nostalgic model, the commercial energies at Letchworth also shaped the final form of the city. As Aneurin Williams, who helped run Letchworth, wrote, "'We must remember that "no manufacturers, no Letchworth's" is absolutely a true statement of the case.'"[54] Financial concerns existed on several levels. First, enough initial investors had to be convinced to set down money for the original land purchase, a task that proved difficult. Second, companies had to be convinced that moving to Letchworth granted substantial benefits in terms of rents and healthy, well-educated workers; third, potential residents needed to be lured with the promise of a better life. These demands often resulted in dramatic changes in Howard's vision and compromises with Parker and Unwin's designs. No benevolent manufacturer could step in to provide extra benefits, as at Bournville or Port Sunlight, and as the stern general manager of the company, W. H. Gaunt, pointed out, Letchworth had "'to be organised on an economic basis rather than as a rich firm's toy or luxury.'"[55]

The economic concerns at Letchworth led to a massive sales effort. To survive, both the Garden City ideal in general and Letchworth in particular had to be packaged and promoted. Thomas Adams, the secretary of the Garden City Association and the man in charge of publicity for Letchworth, prepared pamphlets and picture books, arranged tours and conferences, and worked to sell the idea of Letchworth to investors, industrialists, and possible future residents.[56] Adams and his successors presented Letchworth as a careful blend of country and city life. The agricultural belt would secure "for all time the proximity of the country to the town with the fresh air and freedom that the country gives."[57] Books and small pamphlets of pictures were published with idyllic scenes of town life.[58] Future residents were assured, as one pamphlet stated, that Letchworth was "the first completely new town in England, built so that fresh, clean air and sunshine reach every part of it. Planned to provide every comfort of civilization, yet losing nothing of that freedom, health and beauty which Englishmen need and love." As Howard had promised, residents might enjoy shops, theaters, and railways and would "sacrifice nothing of material convenience or comfort," all "amid beautiful surroundings."[59] Like Cadbury's Cocoa, Letchworth would produce strong bodies, for it was "a gloriously healthy place" where children grew "robust and sturdy, and work-tired men and women [found] new vigour."[60] As one promotional poster promised, Letchworth would combine the "Health of the Country" and the "Comforts of the Town." Wrested loose from its original concept, the vision of the Garden City morphed into a variety of new forms, becoming a convenient label for many new housing schemes, whether or not they bore any resemblance to Howard's ideas.

Taken together, the competing concerns at Letchworth, as well as at Bournville and Port Sunlight, offer a microcosm of the tensions implicit in the commodified authentic. We might see in all three towns both a nexus of desire and a hedge against loss and change. While the authenticity of each place was a carefully produced effect, one that was (and is) often troubling in its manipulative or paternalistic feel, it was also an attempt to remake the industrial city in a better form. We can certainly draw a line from these efforts to later examples of the commodified authentic, from re-creations of old villages, to the selling of heritage cited by recent critics, to the absurd extreme of plastic sheets of prefabricated thatching.[61] All attempts at the commodified authentic should not be lumped together, however, as simply bad-faith efforts to seduce or control the unwitting consumer. Bernard Shaw, a wary contributor to Letchworth, provides a nuanced literary response to the very real workings of these utopian models. As I analyze in the final section of this chapter, Shaw's critical engagement with the model towns offers a probing assessment of their troubling failures and their very real benefits, and further reflects the larger cultural debates they inspired.

Shaw's Utopian Challenge

In a letter to his friend Edward Rose, Shaw painted an unflattering portrait of Howard and his Garden City schemes: "On Monday Ebenezer the Garden City Geyser lectured in Hindhead Hall, with a magic lantern giving views of that flourishing settlement in the manner of Mr Scadder in Martin Chuzzlewit."[62] Shaw recounted the less than enthusiastic audience response to Howard's speech and the much warmer response to his own more pragmatic talk that followed. Shaw was applauded, while Howard was treated as "a mere spring of benevolent mud" (*CL* 2, 119). On the one hand, Shaw was too much of a realist fully to believe Howard's utopian schemes would work, and he expressed deep skepticism that cooperative landownership would ever be supported by capitalist ventures. On the other hand, Shaw was too much of an activist to dismiss the schemes altogether, and he eventually contributed to the Letchworth effort and admitted that Howard was "one of those heroic simpletons who do big things whilst our prominent worldings are explaining why they are Utopian and impossible."[63]

Shaw translated his ambivalent reaction into two plays, *John Bull's Other Island* (1904) and *Major Barbara* (1905), offering a peculiar critique of company towns such as Bournville and Port Sunlight, as well as of the Garden City Movement in general.[64] In these plays, Shaw presents two possible readings of town planning efforts that are striking and instructive in their quite different conclusions. In *John Bull's Other Island*, Shaw unmasks a Garden City scheme as utopian window dressing hiding the rapacious commercial venture that lurks beneath. In this play, any attempt to commodify authenticity is met with derision. In *Major Barbara*, however, Shaw introduces a more startling utopian vision, presenting a company town along the lines of Bournville and Port Sunlight, constructed on the village model with a central "estate" company to manage it. This company, far from making the rather benign products of chocolate or soap, manufactures armaments, representing, in Shaw's own words, "the most sensationally anti-moral department of commerce."[65] Surprisingly, however, Shaw does not go on to cast the company as a corrupting force, but to argue that the idealized authenticity of the town is in fact inextricably linked to the commercial venture, and that this surprising but powerful union of forces might blast outmoded conventions to create a new political and aesthetic ideal. Read together, these plays present an insightful guide to the critical role the commodified authentic may play in constructing entire communities, exposing both its rapacious underside and its surprising power.[66]

John Bull's Garden City

In Britain, the nostalgic version of the commodified authentic perhaps most often appropriated the ideal of a rural, largely southern England; as Shaw understood, however, efforts to market authenticity in general, and the Garden City schemes in particular, were also easily adapted to exploit an allegedly "primitive" culture for colonial ends. In *John Bull's Other Island*, Shaw specifically exposes how easily Irish culture and traditions were turned into commercial spectacle and performance, revealing how a false authenticity is ascribed to Irish towns and the Irish body. He supposedly wrote the play for W. B. Yeats's Abbey Theatre.[67] Launched in 1904, the Abbey was to breathe new life into Irish and Celtic art and drama. Shaw and Yeats admired each other, and in a series of letters, Yeats asked Shaw if he would write a new play on Irish themes, and Shaw tentatively agreed.[68] The resulting play, however, was far from what Yeats imagined. Rather than a celebration of Irish culture, *John Bull's Other Island* was a scathing critique; as Shaw noted, the play was " 'uncongenial to the whole spirit of the neo-Gaelic movement, which is bent on creating a new Ireland after its own ideal, whereas my play is a very uncompromising presentment of the real old Ireland.' "[69] Shaw wanted to "reduce[] the sham Ireland of romance to a heap of unsightly ruins," exposing the actual conditions in Ireland at the same time that he exposed the easy exploitation of a false Irish authenticity.[70] The play concerns two business partners, the English Thomas Broadbent and the Irish Laurence Doyle. Broadbent plans to develop a new community in Ireland, one that he claims would be based on the Garden City model. By exposing Broadbent's motives and gullibility throughout the play, Shaw in turn exposes both the flaws in the Garden City ideal and any attempts to market an "authentic" culture.[71]

At the start of the play, Broadbent describes his plans to build a Garden City in the small Irish village of Rosscullen. He discusses his plans with Tim Haffigan, a lower-class Irishman whom Broadbent hopes to hire to help him win the trust and affection of the Irish residents:

> [Broadbent]: "Have you ever heard of Garden City?"
> [Tim]: [*doubtfully*] "D'ye mane Heavn?"
> [Broadbent]: "Heaven! No: it's near Hitchin. If you can spare half an hour I'll go into it with you."
> [Tim]: "I tell you hwat. Gimme a prospectus. Lemmy take it home and reflect on it."
> [Broadbent]: "Youre quite right: I will. [*He gives him a copy of Ebenezer Howard's book, and several pamphlets*]. You understand that the map of the city—the circular construction—is only a suggestion."
> [Tim]: "I'll make a careful note o that" [*looking dazedly at the map*].
> [Broadbent]: "What I say is, why not start a Garden City in Ireland?"
> (*CP* 2, 508)

As Shaw wryly hints, Broadbent's Garden City will be much less like heaven than Hitchin; Howard's construction designs, used to give the scheme legitimacy, will not necessarily be followed. Later in the play, Broadbent enlarges on his grand schemes for improvements to Rosscullen: "'I shall bring money here: I shall raise wages: I shall found public institutions: a library, a Polytechnic (undenominational, of course), a gymnasium, a cricket club, perhaps an art school. I shall make a Garden city of Rosscullen: the round tower shall be thoroughly repaired and restored'" (*CP* 2, 606). Broadbent sketches out a sweeping vision, describing some of the commonly imaged features of the Garden City, features that would in fact have been familiar to residents of Letchworth, as well as to those in Bournville and Port Sunlight.

Through Broadbent's schemes, Shaw offers a double critique, first of the Garden City ideal itself, and also of the way the ideal might be changed and exploited for monetary gain. Shaw was extremely skeptical of Howard's claim that citizens might be convinced to act cooperatively, and he was especially suspicious of the claim that land could be held in common, as Howard proposed, or that businesses would ever agree to such a scheme. Shaw brings these reservations into the play, revealing the residents of Rosscullen as unable to agree upon any group plan, and showing that cooperative landownership was never part of Broadbent's vision. Shaw's revelations can also be read, however, not simply as a critique of Howard's ideal but as an exposure of the ideal's easy exploitation. Shaw suggests in the play that despite all his talk, Broadbent has no intention of pursuing the Garden City ideal, and that in fact Broadbent represents a corruption of Howard's plans, using the ideal as a cover for his more questionable exploitation of Rosscullen. As critic Bernard Dukore has explored, in the original manuscript of the play, Shaw presents a much more explicit exposure of Broadbent's schemes: "[Broadbent] calls the Garden City plan a dodge, refutes the notion that the idea has turned him into a socialist, and says that his method will require no outlay of capital since the enthusiastic voluntarism of warmhearted Irishmen, not labor for decent wages, would do the job."[72] Under this reading, Shaw offers less an attack on the Garden City itself and more an illustration of how the name might be manipulated to dubious capitalist ends.

Shaw's critique of Broadbent's Garden City is part of the play's broader critique of the commodification of authenticity and the way Irish culture in particular may be exploited for profit. The allegedly Irish Tim Haffigan, for example, plays on Broadbent's image of an "authentic" Ireland and an "authentic" Irish character—one with a fondness for drink, a romantic spirit, a loquacious manner, and many quaint expressions. Broadbent expects in Haffigan the very stereotype that the average English audience member might have expected, what Shaw and others called "the stage Irishman."[73] Haffigan plays on these expectations, speaking in "*a rollicking stage brogue*" and peppering his speech with clichéd Irish expressions such as "the top o' the morning to you" (*CP* 2, 505) and "More power to your elbow!" (*CP* 2, 508). Figure 2.9, from an advertisement for Peter Walker Beer, displays a standard image of this Irish stereotype, with a jovial, drunken Irishman giving the "Erin Go Bragh!" toast. Haffigan charms Broadbent, and he promptly hires the Irishman to help him with his schemes for Ireland. Doyle, Broadbent's partner, later exposes Haffigan as a swindler, revealing that he was in fact born in Glasgow and has never been to Ireland. Haffigan, Doyle reveals, has learned to sell a fake authenticity to the easily duped English. As he tells Broadbent,

> "Man alive, don't you know that all this top-o-the-morning and broth-of-the-boy and more-power-to-your-elbow business is got up in England to fool you, like the Albert Hall concerts of Irish music? No Irishman ever talks like that in Ireland, or ever did, or ever will. But when a thoroughly worthless Irishman comes to England, and finds the whole place full of romantic duffers like you, who will let him loaf and drink and sponge and brag as long as he flatters your sense of moral superiority by playing the fool and degrading himself and his country, he soon learns the antics that take you in. He picks them up at the theatre or the music hall." (*CP* 2, 513)

Fig. 2.9
Stereotyping the Irish.
Advertisement for Peter Walker & Son
From *Daily Mail*, 17 March 1911, 10.

Haffigan exploits the English desire for an authentic Irishmen for his own profit. Broadbent is untroubled by the deceit, for in fact he plans on a much larger scale to exploit the aura of the Irish village, selling it in his turn to English tourists.[74]

In the last act, Shaw brings together his critiques of Broadbent's Garden City schemes and his attacks on selling Irish authenticity. After Broadbent has proclaimed his good intentions to the village and has listed the many institutions and improvements he will bring to Rosscullen, Keegan, a former priest and something of a local prophet, exposes Broadbent's plans:

> "I have no doubt the golf links will be a triumph of your art. . . . You may even build the hotel efficiently if you can find enough efficient masons, carpenters, and plumbers, which I rather doubt. . . . When the hotel becomes insolvent . . . your English business habits will secure the thorough efficiency of the liquidation . . . and when at last this poor desolate countryside becomes a busy mint in which we shall all slave to make money for you, with our Polytechnic to teach us how to do it efficiently, and our library to fuddle the few imaginations your distilleries will spare, and our repaired Round Tower with admission six-pence, and refreshments and penny-in-the-slot mutoscopes to make it interesting, then no doubt your English and American shareholders will spend all the money we make for them very efficiently." (*CP* 2, 607–608)

Shaw here, in the voice of Keegan, exposes the destructive results of Broadbent-like developments and offers a bitter denunciation of the commodified authenticity they represent. Broadbent will package and sell Ireland's culture as a commodity both to England and back to Ireland itself, turning the historic Round Tower into a tourist site, and the citizens into laborers with quaint accents. Broadbent will even turn Keegan into an attraction, declaring after his impassioned outburst, "He's a character: he'll be an attraction here. Really almost equal to Ruskin and Carlyle" (*CP* 2, 611).

John Bull's Other Island reflects a central part of the debate on the commodified authentic in general and on the Garden City in particular. Shaw's underlying aim in the play is to reveal the profit motive of Broadbent's schemes and to expose the schemes as a scam on a gullible public. Keegan's powerful denunciation finds its modern counterpart in any number of current critiques of the heritage industry and the corporate exploitation and even invention of cultural traditions.[75] English and Irish heritage were being marketed as never before at the turn of the century, and Shaw's play encapsulates the unmasking of such activities, an approach that still dominates critical reactions to the commodified authentic. Surprisingly, however, in his next play, *Major Barbara*, Shaw presents an entirely different critique of the Garden City and model factory towns, one not concerned with English-Irish relations or the selling of a particular national heritage. Instead, Shaw exposes the power of industry to remake village life—and then grants his seeming endorsement.

Major Barbara*'s Utopian Paradox*

The opening act of *Major Barbara* is set in the library of the well-appointed home of Lady Britomart Undershaft.[76] Replete with leather armchairs and handsome furniture, the room presents an established, comfortable atmosphere. Shaw quickly reveals, however, that this comfort has been made possible by the enormous profits made by Lady Britomart's husband from the sale of armaments. In part, this unveiling continues themes presented both in *John Bull's Other Island* and in earlier Shaw works such as *Widower's House* (1892) and *Mrs. Warren's Profession* (1894), whose main protagonists learn that the source of their wealth is tainted, in the first case, from slum landlords, and in the second, from prostitution. In *Major Barbara*, however, the capitalist "unveiling" that forms a central part of the action in the earlier plays is condensed in the opening scene; all the characters are aware from the start of the play that the money that supports them comes from the vastly profitable munitions trade. Only the audience needs to be informed. The central action of *Major Barbara* will, ironically, consist of a second, more radical unveiling: the moral cowardice of any attempts to distance oneself from the munitions profits, and, in fact, the surprising embrace of such profits as a possible source of salvation. The ideal model town that Undershaft has built with his money—Perivale St. Andrews—is finally revealed as a modern utopia, a place that exposes the relationship between commercial ventures and the lifestyles they make possible. Perivale St. Andrews presents the risks and also the very real power that commodified authenticity might provide.

Throughout the play, Shaw demands that both Barbara and the audience recognize that there is no purified realm outside of industry. This is not, Shaw reminds us, an ugly secret but a surprising and uncomfortable truth. As Undershaft tells Barbara, her very soul has been saved by his profits:

> "I fed you and clothed you and housed you. I took care that you should have money enough to live handsomely—more than enough; so that you could be wasteful, careless, generous. That saved your soul from the seven deadly sins . . . : Food, clothing, firing, rent, taxes, respectability and children. Nothing can lift those seven millstones from Man's neck but money; and the spirit cannot soar until the millstones are lifted. I lifted them from your spirit." (*CP* 3, 171–172)

Barbara's apparent disregard for money and her ability to give her time to the Salvation Army are in fact made possible by Undershaft's earlier support. Commerce and profits cannot, Shaw contends, be kept in some kind of corrupt compartment where they are carefully separated from lives or spaces seemingly purified of commercial stain. As Shaw writes in his preface, "The notion that you can earmark certain coins as tainted is an unpractical individualist superstition" (*CP* 3, 35). Indeed, he insists that most profits have a sordid origin if they are traced back far enough, and that citizens must recognize the vexed and troubling connections between profits and a good life. Summarizing this stance, Undershaft decries people who attempt to "keep their morals and their business in water-tight compartments" (*CP* 3, 89).[77]

In the final act, Shaw presents a dramatic and unexpected conclusion to these moral dilemmas. London theatergoers, more accustomed to the tidy conclusions of the melodrama, might have expected the performance to end with Barbara finding a way to continue her religious work at the shelter while maintaining her moral and commercial-free appearance, all without contradiction. Audience members more familiar with Shavian drama might have anticipated a conclusion along the lines of *Widower's House*, with Barbara simply accepting the moral quagmire and continuing as before, or of *John Bull's Other Island*, with the commercial concerns set to continue their destructive path. The final act of the play, however, subverts all these expectations—as was surely part of Shaw's design—and offers a much more controversial ending. The central characters finally embrace the munitions factory not as a sign of moral capitulation but seemingly as a sign of moral virtue.

Despite Barbara's assumption that the munitions town would be a kind of Manchester-like hell, "'a sort of a pit where lost creatures with blackened faces stirred up smoky fires and were driven and tormented by [Undershaft]'" (*CP* 3, 154), Perivale St. Andrews turns out to be, in the words of Barbara's fiancé, Cusins, "'horribly, frightfully, immorally, unanswerably perfect'" (*CP* 3, 158). As the setting notes tell us, the town "*lies between two Middlesex hills*" and far from a dark pit is in fact "*an almost smokeless town of white walls, roofs of narrow green slates or red tiles, tall trees, domes, campaniles, and slender chimney shafts, beautifully situated and beautiful in itself*" (*CP* 3, 157). The town is, as one character points out, "a perfect triumph of modern industry" (*CP* 3, 159) and boasts nursing homes, libraries, and schools, provides an insurance fund and a pension fund, and even includes a building society and "various applications of co-operation" (*CP* 3, 159). The town seems an amalgamation of the amenities of a Port Sunlight or a Bournville, with a central industry supporting and maintaining the town and its citizens; it also hold elements of Garden City schemes, with its long list of community offerings and cooperative groups, though the town is clearly not a cooperative venture or communally owned in the way that Howard might have imagined.

The perfection of the town and the apparent happiness of its citizens produce an additional crisis for Barbara in particular. Undershaft appears diabolical in part, but he is also undeniably, as Shaw writes in his preface, "the hero of *Major Barbara*" (*CP* 3, 27), the savior of the town. Shaw is careful not to present Undershaft as the villain but as the only character who is intellectually honest enough to admit that poverty is the worst of crimes, and to do whatever it takes to abolish such a crime in his town. Undershaft is likewise not quite a Nietzschean superman (despite Shaw's interest in aspects of Nietzsche's ideas), as Undershaft's efforts concentrate not on power over others but on bringing the town's inhabitants out of poverty, though admittedly he does this with no philanthropic fervor. After listening to her father, Barbara realizes she cannot go back to her Salvation Army work, for she sees that she wins souls only by giving away food, but she struggles to accept the town and its moral consequences.

Shaw deliberately cuts off one of Barbara's possible escapes: an artistic life that would shun any taint of mass culture or vulgar profits made from armaments. Barbara mocks this possibility. As she tells Cusins, "'If I were middle-class I should turn my back on my father's business; and we should both live in an artistic drawing room, with you reading the reviews in one corner, and I in the other at the piano, playing Schumann: both very superior persons, and neither of us a bit of use'" (*CP* 3, 183). This sort of aesthetic seclusion is presented not as a moral choice but as a useless one. An artistic authenticity that shuns the market and retreats into exclusivity is portrayed as the worst type of philistine solution. Shaw himself satirizes the related work of William Morris and John Ruskin in his preface to the play, and the kind of aesthetic reform they advocated. "They want handsome cities," he writes, and for the poor to appreciate art and design, but the poor "do not want the simple life, nor the esthetic life," they want more money (*CP* 3, 28–29). Give people enough money to live decently first, Shaw argues, and let them choose art or religion with a free will.

Unlike Bournville and Port Sunlight, which joined a kind of nostalgic authenticity for the past to a commercial venture, Perivale St. Andrews gestures more toward an originary version of authenticity, one where the only solution lies in blowing up—both literally and figuratively—older models or outdated creeds. As Undershaft tells Barbara,

> "You have made for yourself something that you call a morality or a religion or what not. It doesnt fit the facts. Well, scrap it. Scrap it and get one that does fit. That is what is wrong with the world at present. It scraps its obsolete steam engines and dynamos; but it wont scrap its old prejudices and its old moralities and its old religions and its old political constitutions. . . . If your old religion broke down yesterday, get a newer and a better one for tomorrow." (*CP* 3, 170–171)

Undershaft advocates blasting away tradition and creating new creeds or new religions, ones not based on stale beliefs. Doing anything else—or living anywhere else in artistic or moral seclusion—is mere hypocrisy.

Barbara and Cusins decide, ultimately, to stay in the town, with Barbara working for the salvation of the contented, well-fed citizens, and with Cusins being groomed as Undershaft's successor. These choices are portrayed not as the wrong ones, or the morally destitute ones, but as the only morally responsible choices to be made. The last moment of the play, however, offers a second surprising finale. Having made the decision to marry Cusins and to stay and preach in the town, Barbara abruptly retreats into infancy, running off declaring, "I want Mamma," "*clutch[ing] like a baby to her mother's skirt*" and crying, "I want a house in the village to live in with Dolly. [*Dragging at the skirt*] Come and tell me which one to take" (*CP* 3, 184–185). Considering that Barbara is the most independent and strong-willed character of the play—next to Undershaft—this regression comes as a shock.

Not surprisingly, critics have long been puzzled by the final act, which leaves Undershaft in triumph and Barbara in retreat, seemingly with Shaw's approval. The critical reviews at the time, while occasionally expressing admiration, were dominated by bewilderment and even horror. The *Morning Post* declared the play in "distressingly bad" taste and saw the characters as merely dupes of Undershaft: "The model town created by the objectionable firm so impresses [the characters] by its decorum, its prosperity, and its admirable institutions that one by one they fall easy victims to the long-winded logic of the cynical capitalist."[78] Beatrice Webb called it "a dance of devils" and lamented that it ends "in an intellectual and moral morass," an "anti-climax of evangelising the Garden-City!"[79] A review in the *Clarion* proclaimed the third act "diabolically cynical" and aesthetically marred but doubted that it could represent Shaw's real beliefs.[80]

Modern critics tend to view the final act less cynically and without the moral outrage, but they also tend to read around the play's divided ending, privileging either the final, optimistic union of the three central characters or, alternatively, Barbara's final disturbing retreat into infantile behavior. Critics in the first camp read the union of Cusins, Undershaft, and Barbara as a kind of new trinity of possibility, one that might create an even better town than Undershaft alone could produce, and one that would unite Undershaft's rare power, Cusins's intellectual curiosity, and Barbara's radical altruism. As critic Martin Meisel summarizes,

> The whole play moves to the union of the three: of Undershaft, who makes the power for the world to use as it will or must; of Cusins, the man of intellect and imagination who can envisage alternative realities and channel the energy accordingly; and of Barbara, the woman of spirit and redemptive purpose, who can rescue both energy and intellect from pointlessness. The end of the play—and the residual impression—is pleasant rather than unpleasant.[81]

In the same camp, critic Michiyo Ishii argues that "the ending of *Major Barbara* suggests solidarity to fight for a better future for society," and Nicholas Grene declares it "an almost unironized utopia."[82] For the most part, however, these readings ignore the troubling ending to the play, when Barbara's regression disrupts the utopian possibilities. Critics in the second camp read the final moments in the play as erasing any optimistic union; Harold Bloom, a spokesman for this alternative, reminds us that Barbara's "pathetic dwindling remains a dark tonality at the conclusion."[83]

What both camps miss, however, is the critical importance of the dual ending and the paradox it suggests, a paradox best understood by reading the play alongside the larger Garden City Movement and the phenomenon of the commodified authentic. Shaw captures the real possibilities of places such as Bournville or Letchworth, towns that might help alleviate poverty and that recognized that a decent life could only be possible with enough money for decent housing. Despite the advantages of such communities, however, Shaw remained attentive to the paternalism present in such schemes, paternalism that informs Barbara's final moments. Shaw repeatedly warned against the dangers of model towns, feeling they should "be kept clear of philanthropy & utopian socialism because people (the tenants) will not stand being kept in a nursery."[84] Barbara's final plea for "a house in the village to live in with Dolly" (*CP* 3, 185) suggests that Perivale St. Andrews might eventually reduce people to coddled children, threatening the remedies to social ills that such towns sought to promote. Within the play, Shaw reminds us of the infantilizing tendency that lies just beneath many expressions of nostalgia, and hence within the atmosphere of the model towns. Nostalgic desire often implies a desire to regress, a refusal to live within an adult world of complexity and change. As we have seen, closely related to this desire is a hunger for a paternalistic hierarchy, for an ordered system of clear authority. The appeal of the commodified authentic lies, then, in part in the promise to return consumers to an idealized vision of childhood, one where the atmosphere that surrounds them is ordered, safe, and produced by an outside force. The dual ending must be read as Shaw's ongoing paradox, a critical model for understanding the commodified authentic in town planning, one that remains suspended between a radical ideal and its radical unmasking.[85]

Examining how the commodified authentic functions when it is produced within a community-wide design reveals some of its myriad roles. The aura of the model towns—themselves consciously produced and constructed as "authentic," and actually holding some tangible benefits for residents—in turn is infused (allegedly) into particular products. The product itself becomes a kind of vessel for the essence of the model town, a manifestation of a particular way of life. Once within the consumer's home, the product might then empty its contents, supposedly reproducing the atmosphere of authenticity found in the original model (which was itself a copy). We have today almost eliminated such a progression; no actual model town is now needed to produce the commodified authentic, or it is only needed as the vaguest of references. The progression offered here, however, alerts us to some of the intricate ways the commodified authentic works and morphs to suit its customers. Much of its power, in fact, lies in its dexterous capacity to shift and re-form.

The imbrications of various forms of authenticity with commerce, as depicted in Port Sunlight, Bournville, and Letchworth, and as so clearly and brutally depicted by Shaw, suggest their uneasy relations in early twentieth-century British culture. The next chapter, on Forster and the domestic architecture movement, examines these relations on a concentrated scale, on individual dwellings rather than on whole communities, and explores how the commodified authentic presented an innovative concept of home and a radical new way of controlling time.

3. Buying Time

E. M. Forster and the Neo-nostalgic Home

Efforts to build model towns along nostalgic lines arose in part from earlier attempts in English domestic architecture to create individual dwellings that evoked a countrified past. From the 1800s on, architects working in the "picturesque" tradition designed both cottages and great estates that drew on vernacular styles and sought to recapture the rustic aura of country dwellings. Turning from neoclassical models that offered symmetry and clean lines, architects began to design asymmetrical buildings and to use a variety of materials to create seemingly more natural, authentic homes; such dwellings appeared as if they were constructed, bit by bit, room by room, over time. Hundreds of "cottage books" appeared in the first half of the nineteenth century, showcasing a range of designs for various dwellings. Styles included everything from an Old English look to the Gothic Revival to an Italianate country aesthetic. What the designs shared, however, was nostalgic replication, an evocation of a different time and place that might connect the viewer to the past in the present moment.[1]

The start of the twentieth century saw a continuation of these architectural styles but also an important new development: the explosion of efforts to market the nostalgic image of the individual country house. Idyllic pictures of rural retreats had long been staples of English fantasy, but the marketing of that vision became a powerful force at the century's beginning, when the very idea of an authentic country residence was for sale in ways not previously seen in England. As we have found with the model towns, the desire to protect an idealized notion of English rural life from the contaminating forces of commerce and urban bustle in fact opened this vision to ever-increasing commercialization. An ironic feedback loop resulted, where efforts to keep the countryside "pure" granted more opportunities to market this purity. Advertisements such as the ones in figure 3.1, from the *Times* of 1909, suggested that, with careful buying, a slower time—and a rural home—awaited London readers. Buyers could maintain a house in the city but still take advantage of the readily available "beautiful old country residences" or "picturesque old cottages." Likewise flourishing at the turn of the century was the Domestic Revival in architecture, which featured new houses designed to evoke age, quiet, and rural living at its best. Other ventures actively promoted the rural home, even to those who might not be able to afford a new house in the old style. The magazine *Country Life* began publication in 1897, devoted to selling the idea of a leisured rural lifestyle, with articles showcasing various ways to decorate and maintain the traditional country home. The *Daily Mail* launched the Ideal Home Exhibition in 1908, designed both to promote advertising and to bring a modern version of the countrified residence to the middle-class consumer.[2]

Efforts to commodify the country home have led in part to the ubiquitous images of English rural cottages that now adorn everything from placemats to coffee mugs. At the turn of the century, however, this version of the commodified authentic was just emerging as a mass-market venture, creating what I will call neo-nostalgic homes. That such dwellings proved enormously appealing should come as no surprise, for they implicitly made an extraordinary promise to consumers both wealthy and middle class: neo-nostalgic homes offered a powerful model of controlling time, one that brought different times and their places—as represented by objects and by architecture—into a new moment where they might be viewed or experienced simultaneously. The *Daily Mail* Ideal Home Exhibition, for example, created replicas of small country houses of the past, replicas in which visitors might not only engage in fantasy time travel but also buy some of the weathered objects for sale in the old houses, thus incorporating a past time into their own home.

This manipulation of time is essential to understanding another important moment in the transition to modernity. Caught between an alluring but outdated past and a tantalizing but unknown future, consumers could reconstitute temporal relations, collecting time's fragments into one space to create a harmonious connection to an updated past, a connection that would potentially satisfy both modern needs and nostalgic longing. Such time-play reflects the strategy used by architects, writers, and merchants to market the past: inscribe temporality on material objects and interior space and make time into a commodity, a maneuver that reaches across disciplines and can be seen as the hallmark of a society in

Fig. 3.1
Advertisements for county living
A. "Country Cottages," *Times*, 19 April, 1909, 16. *B*. "Country Houses," *Times*, 22 April, 1909, 3.

transition from the old to the new. Ironically, commodified nostalgia became a peculiarly modern gesture, conflating time and space in ways that allowed the past to live on, revitalized, in the present.

By turning from town planning to focus on examples of individual dwellings and interiors, I turn more to issues of commodification and individual accessibility. Few citizens had the opportunity to live in a Garden City or factory village, and even fewer had the financial resources of a Cadbury or Lever that might have allowed them to support a model town. The commodification of cottage authenticity, however, made at least parts of the ideal accessible to citizens other than old English families or the new industrialists and their workers. Those who could not build the model city might nevertheless build a model home. These individual examples of neo-nostalgic spaces did not, moreover, make references simply to past architectural styles or past historical eras but to a (potentially fictitious) personal history, promising the chance to showcase an authentic and storied personal life.

In this chapter, E. M. Forster's novel *Howards End* (1910) serves as the structuring nexus for a discussion of neo-nostalgic homes. *Howards End*, often read as nostalgic capitulation, in fact reveals a surprisingly nuanced understanding of commodified authenticity and its power to transform domestic space.[3] Forster presents both a scathing critique and a more subtle investigation of its powers; the fact that he finally fails to maintain his critique suggests one of the central temptations of the commodified authentic: the wish to erase the commercial "taint" once the purchase is complete. Forster's literary model of the neo-nostalgic home comments on—and is brought into sharper relief by examining it alongside—actual versions of such spaces, and this chapter explores two such versions: the opening of the Ideal Home Exhibition, and the new surge of interest in vernacular design by the Domestic Revival movement in architecture, most notably in the homes designed by the architect Edwin Lutyens. Forster's experiments with mapping time onto place paralleled both the domestic spaces displayed at the Ideal Home Exhibition and Lutyens's own designs, which used a blend of architectural styles to create, as historian Peter Inskip terms it, "fictitious histor[ies]" in his work.[4] While Lutyens's designs were generally affordable only for the well-to-do, the Ideal Home Exhibition promised the middle-class consumer the chance to tour and possibly buy—or buy into—such a model (a democratization that reached its full potential in the urban examples discussed in the next two chapters). Read together, these three versions of neo-nostalgic homes reveal the rapidly expanding marketing of the authentic residence to the individual consumer, and the transformation of the "home" into something fungible and marketable.

Neo-nostalgic homes also presented opportunities for performance. Their authenticity could be accessed by moving through such spaces in a kind of willing suspension of disbelief. For commodified authenticity to obtain value, viewers had to experience the domestic space as real or "authentic" while still maintaining a sense that such spaces might be changed, re-created, transported, and most important, purchased. Like audience members watching a realist play, the viewers were invited to believe in the illusion while maintaining the awareness of illusion; at the same time, viewers were asked onto a kind of stage that, through a careful arrangement of objects and architectural details, suggested a variety of possible new roles for the viewers.

This chapter explores two central aspects in the creation and performative possibilities of neo-nostalgic homes. The first considers the paradoxical desire both to erase and to acknowledge the role of commerce in supporting these domestic spaces. At the turn of the century, the long-present wish to purify the home of commercial taint and to construct an "authentic" countrified dwelling met a growing realization of the money required to support this nostalgic vision (money earned in the very commercial ventures that the ideal purported to erase), and of the powerful ability of commercial efforts to market this very authenticity. Such a contradiction acknowledged the ironic symbiotic relationship between the desire for purity and the concomitant rise of ventures that sought to sell this purity.[5]

The second, and related, vein in the discussion of neo-nostalgic homes concerns the various constructions of time they made possible, and the way these constructions became commodified, or available for purchase. Forster, the Domestic Revival architects, and the creators of the Ideal Home Exhibition saw the value of showing the passage of time itself, of providing a material connection to past moments. As they knew, nostalgic desire usually seeks a passage back, a way to reach a wished-for past time or a desired past space. Satisfying such a nostalgic hunger would involve a kind of time travel, but even should such a move be possible, it would potentially involve a troubling denial of the present. The commercial solution was to locate or create objects that in themselves imply the passage of time—such as a weathered piece of furniture or a new home that, through a combination of different styles from different periods, offered a sense of time's flow. Such objects or dwellings made multiple pasts and the present moment available at one place and time. Placed onto objects or dwellings, time could in turn be packaged and sold to a wide market. Neo-nostalgic homes became constructed spaces of time's passage, nostalgic memorials, we might say, of things that never existed.

Any venerable building or antique chair, however, might suggest the passage of time, and the ideal of a rural cottage was not new. The innovative quality of *Howards End*, Lutyens's homes, and the Ideal Home Exhibition lay in their deliberately constructed nature that arose from their intimate ties with commerce. Halfway through his novel, Forster carefully reconstructs the countrified estate of Howards End, building it from past models and present history, the new creation openly supported by commercial money.[6] In a similar mode, Lutyens created old-looking homes for his wealthy modern clients, infused with references to architectural styles from different eras. The Ideal Home Exhibition took this commercial support a step farther and began to sell such a model to a wider audience. For Forster, the architects, and the home show, the resulting structures not only bore marks of continuity with the past but crucially made an often frank avowal that the very idyllic, "authentic," and noncommercial aura of the houses was in fact sustained by modern commercial ventures. It was the simultaneous move to affirm authenticity and its construction that turned these architectural sites into neo-nostalgic homes—and that in turn transformed the idea of home into something that might be constructed and remade.

Killing Time: Failed Efforts in Time Management

Critics frequently observe that Forster's *Howards End* dwells, somewhat obsessively, on houses; as Daniel Born notes, "Real estate permeates the novel."[7] While it is true that houses and interiors are exhaustively described, Forster includes another dimension in these descriptions of spaces that speaks to a much broader cultural phenomenon: a sense of changing private time. Using various dwellings, Forster constructs a series of different temporal zones, letting both the interiors and the objects within them convey a varying sense of time's passage, each with its own relation to commercial ventures. Forster presents a series of failed projects, places where time has been critically, and often disastrously, altered. A quick tour of these architectural landmarks in *Howards End* reveals a central tension between two kinds of real estate, both with a distinct relationship to time: the city home that is transitory and representative of an urban commercial economy, and the authentic English country home, rooted in the past and, although tied to an agricultural economy, theoretically far removed from any monetary transaction.[8]

In the first category, the cheap flat of Leonard Bast and his fiancée, Jacky, the novel's lower-middle-class characters, and the sumptuous London home of the wealthy Wilcoxes represent two socioeconomic ends of the same suspect market, a market where time is static and discontinuous. Leonard's home is part of the larger "Block B" of flats, which in turn is part of a seemingly endless set of flats of "extreme cheapness" (Forster, 36) rising over London, built to house, the narrator tells us, the new urban workers who pour into London from the countryside (the same workers who so troubled the Garden City reformers).[9] Likely to "be pulled down" (36) in a few years time, these flats will offer no lasting dwellings. The apartment's interior is no more distinctive, composed from a set of transitory objects, newly made and newly purchased, and closely linked to their mass-produced origins. Forster, with a hint of condescension, presents his description as a catalogue of lower-middle-class consumer taste:

> The sitting-room contained, besides the armchair, two other chairs, a piano, a three-legged table, and a cosy corner. Of the walls, one was occupied by the window, the other by a draped mantelshelf bristling with Cupids. Opposite the window was the door, and beside the door a bookcase, while over the piano there extended one of the masterpieces of Maud Goodman. (37)[10]

The flat presents a sham respectability, a space that Forster implies reflects a bankrupt aesthetic fueled by a desire to attain middle-class respectability. Leonard Bast is not attempting to reconnect to his own past; as the narrator nostalgically and patronizingly observes, he would be far better off in the country: "Had he lived some centuries ago, in the brightly coloured civilizations of the past, he would have had a definite status, his rank and his income would have corresponded" (35). As it was, "One guessed him as the third generation, grandson to the shepherd or ploughboy whom civilization had sucked into the town" (84). For Forster, the objects in the flat are too obvious in their idealizations and, like the room itself, lack any sense of continuity with Leonard's history. Time here is shallow, and this shallowness links to ownership: Leonard rents the flat and almost all the objects within it. As the narrator observes, the flat "struck that hollow, makeshift note that is so often heard in the modern dwelling-place. It had been too easily gained, and could be relinquished too easily" (37).

Mr. Wilcox's London flat at Ducie Street achieves a similar, if more luxurious, shallowness, one that the heroine Margaret Schlegel observes when touring it with Mr. Wilcox:

> The dining-room was big, but over-furnished. . . . Margaret viewed with relief the sumptuous dado, the frieze, the gilded wall-paper, amid whose foliage parrots sang. It would never do with her own furniture, but those heavy chairs, that immense sideboard loaded with presentation plate, stood up against its pressure like men. . . . Even the Bible—the Dutch Bible that Charles had brought back from the Boer War—fell into position. Such room admitted loot. (118–119)

While not as ephemeral as Leonard and Jacky's flat, the interior here is awash in an easy luxury unconnected to the history of the family. The signs of empire are overt: the wallpaper depicts not an English scene but a nonspecific tropical one, with parrots in the foliage. The Bible from the Boer War is not a religious text or a record of family lineage but an ahistorical marker of British imperialism.[11] The room reflects a static time, a series of usable (and exploitable) moments that suggest not continuity but a compendium of markers newly acquired in the present.

Mrs. Wilcox's Howards End stands as Forster's somewhat obvious antidote to the impermanence and commercial ties of these urban dwellings. Stephen Kern, in his work *The Culture of Time and Space: 1880–1918*, outlines a break between public and private time in the early twentieth century, a break that in Forster's work splits between the hurried, unconnected, urban time of London and the slower, continuous, and indeed timeless time of the country.[12] Early in the novel, while the first Mrs. Wilcox is alive, Howards End is bathed in a nostalgic glow, representative of an older England with authentic traditions. It is, as Helen writes at the start, "old and little, and altogether delightful" (5), and "old" seems synonymous with "delightful" in these early pages. Critic Stephen Bernstein equates Howards End with Jameson's conception of romance, involving a place governed by "homogenous time."[13] Time here moves differently, mythically: it is slower, more in tune with the seasons, continuous.

Forster is dismayed that the fast, unconnected urban time is speeding into the country, represented both by the new motor car and by Mr. Wilcox, who is "a little Ten Minutes moving self-contained through its appointed years" (178). Mrs. Wilcox, however, is a protective foil to this speed, becoming almost an extension of the house itself; as the narrator tells us, "She seemed to belong not to the young people and their motor, but to the house, and to the tree that overshadowed it. One knew she worshipped the past, and that the instinctive wisdom the past can alone bestow had descended upon her. . . . Assuredly she cared about her ancestors, and let them help her" (18). The house and Mrs. Wilcox become markers for vague and nostalgic notions of something essentially English. For all its value, however, and as much as Forster seems enamored with this golden vision, this nostalgic sense of time, set apart from the vulgar speed of both London and the other Wilcoxes, is finally declared inadequate. While Howards End offers a sense of continuity missing from the London flats, time here remains fixed, unable to accommodate the modern age and urban time. Mrs. Wilcox, its purest representative, succumbs early, having stayed too long in London. There are continuous foreshadowings that country time will prove no match for urban time, that, like the dust left behind from the speeding automobiles, it will disappear into the past.

The death of Mrs. Wilcox produces in part a crisis of real estate. A central question for the characters—Who will inherit Howards End?—reflects, as Trilling famously observed, the larger question, "Who shall inherit England?"[14] Yet the crisis is also inextricably related to time. None of the dwellings discussed so far—the London flats or Mrs. Wilcox's Howards End—can finally respond adequately to the crisis of time, to a critical need that Forster shared with his contemporaries: to find a way both to salvage what was worthwhile from the past and still to find an adequate home for distinctly modern desires.

A contemporary solution to such a crisis was the nostalgic form of the commodified authentic, a packaging of time reflected in the fetishized selling of country houses and their aura. The scenes set at Oniton Grange present Forster's biting commentary on these trends of commodified authenticity, where country houses and the accompanying traditions are purchased by urban tourists. The old estate Oniton, the narrator informs us, "had been a discovery of Mr. Wilcox's" (149). It had been so remote "that he had concluded it must be something special. A ruined castle stood in the grounds" (149). He discovers, to his dismay, that despite the ruins and the country setting, there was little play to be found there—poor shooting, bad fishing, and not much scenery. He orchestrates his daughter's wedding at Oniton (for Evie "had a fancy for something rural"), but otherwise only thought "to get it off his hands" (149). The wedding party roars into the village, spreading dust and chaos, only to roar out again.

Margaret, however, is "determined to create new sanctities" (159) among the hills near Oniton and to treat the house as a permanent home. Margaret views the new dwelling with a semiaestheticizing, semireligious fervor, seeking sanctity in this sanctuary. Thrilled with the surrounding countryside, Margaret imagines living an idealized country life:

> Margaret was fascinated by Oniton. She had said that she loved it, but it was rather its romantic tension that held her. The rounded Druids of whom she had caught glimpses in her drive, the rivers hurrying down from them to England, the carelessly modelled masses of the lower hills, thrilled her with poetry. The house was insignificant, but the prospect from it would be an eternal joy, and she thought of all the friends she would have to stop in it, and of the conversion of Henry himself to a rural life. (156)

While Margaret appreciates the home and the setting more than the rest of the wedding party, Forster hints that she too quickly seeks an atmosphere of tradition and stability; her nostalgic thrill at the rounded Druids, her sense that the view would be a continual joy, and her naïve expectation of converting Henry to a rural life are premature. The narrator has already informed the reader that "Oniton was to prove one of her innumerable false starts" (150). Margaret assumes she might quickly make of Oniton another home, to enjoy the "prospect," as if she is literally prospecting, attempting to capture, ready-made, a nostalgic and romantic atmosphere. For Forster, Oniton reflects the ugly side of commodified nostalgia, which assumes a buyer might appropriate quickly and easily the benefits of a rural tradition.

Forster also mocks, however, both the artistic and the philanthropic impulse to enshrine authenticity. Like Shaw's Major Barbara, Forster seems to reject the aesthetic retreat summarized in the voice of Mr. Wilcox, who scoffs at the nostalgic longing for the country ideal. As he tells Margaret, "Small holdings, back to the land—ah! philanthropic bunkum" (147). Despite the renovations at Howards End, Mr. Wilcox proclaims that "one could still tell it's been an old farm. And yet it isn't the place that would fetch one of your artistic crew" (148). The narrator concurs, "No, it wasn't; and if he did not quite understand it, the artistic crew would still less: it was English" (148). Forster cues his readers that they should not view Howards End as a representation of an ideal but as the ideal itself—not its re-creation but the genuine article. Mr. Wilcox did not "quite" understand, but to Forster, the artistic crew would be worse, viewing what was "English" and fundamental as merely an especially attractive new style.[15] Despite his vague mysticism surrounding authentic "English" qualities, for Forster, the problems come—surprisingly—in part from the *elision* of commerce. Howards End, Forster insists, is supported by cash. It is the artistic crew's failure to acknowledge the material necessities of a place like Howards End that Forster seems to condemn.

Forster further parodies the "artistic" solutions of a Ruskin or a Morris, recalling but expanding on Shaw's sharp critique of their aesthetic approaches to housing reform discussed in the last chapter. The only time the reader sees Leonard Bast in his flat, he is reading Ruskin and his description of the grand old architecture of Venice. Leonard "was trying to form his style on Ruskin" (38), making notes as he reads. He wants to bring Ruskin into his flat, seeking—as the new domestic architects themselves sought—"to adapt [Ruskin] to the needs of daily life" (38). Forster makes clear, however, that through no fault of Leonard's, such an endeavor is impossible. Leonard imagines a description of his flat in Ruskin's prose: "'Let us consider a little each of these characters in succession, and first (for of the absence of ventilation enough has been said already), what is very peculiar to this flat, its obscurity'" (38). The language Ruskin used to describe Venetian architecture cannot be adapted for the makeshift flat. The rhetoric fails, as will, Forster hints, Leonard's search for culture. Translating Ruskin is fraught with difficulty, and Leonard's appropriation of Ruskin's language to describe his flat both casts doubts on the architects who did attempt to appropriate Ruskin and also suggests that their very turn away from ugly flats to the new domestic architecture still left the Leonard Basts struggling to escape.[16]

Forster makes clear that not only the aesthetic but also the philanthropic position in regard to old buildings and the natural landscape is critically inadequate unless it includes the role of commerce. In one telling scene in the novel, a group of women have assembled to debate how a millionaire on the brink of death should distribute his money. Margaret and Helen introduce the figure of the nearly impoverished Mr. Bast, whom they have recently met, and debate how best to help him. Margaret is supposed to be speaking "in the interests of the Society for the Preservation of Places of Historic Interest or Natural Beauty" (92), in other words, in support of sustaining a vision of the past—an arguably nostalgic position. But she speaks out of turn, insisting (in a way that recalls Shaw's Undershaft) that the best way to spend the millionaire's money would not be to preserve old buildings but to give men like Mr. Bast the money directly. Independent thoughts, she argues, come from independent means, and without money, "she denied that [Mr. Bast] will ever explore the spiritual resources of this world, will ever know the rarer joys of the body, or attain to clear and passionate intercourse with his fellows" (93). Before money is spent to preserve the past, funds should be given to people directly, so that there will be more chance of producing people who care about preservation in the first place. The unadulterated nostalgia of a Mrs. Wilcox, Forster implies through Margaret, would not finally be enough to preserve the very things she found most precious.

Despite Forster's rejection of commodified nostalgia within the real estate market, this kind of commodification—where the passage of time is desired, packaged, and sold by being mapped onto a domestic structure—suggests an important model of time that Forster modifies when constructing a modern version of Howards End, one that finally captures two competing impulses in Forster's novel and in the culture at large. Forster rejects commodified nostalgia as embodied by Oniton, but he also repeatedly acknowledges the vital role of money earned from commercial ventures; such money not only supports the cultured life of the Schlegels but also revitalizes Howards End as a marker of authenticity incorporating different models of time.[17] Margaret insists, for example, on acknowledging the "islands of money" on which her comfortable life depends and declares, "I refuse to draw my income and sneer at those who guarantee it" (127)—to the point, of course, when she actually marries one of these guarantors. Likewise, she knows Howards End itself, and the way of life it represents, depends at least in part on Mr. Wilcox's money. He has, as he informs Margaret, drained the fields, thinned out the brush, rebuilt the kitchen, and generally kept the house from falling down. When Margaret meets Miss Avery at Howards End, Miss Avery admits (though with caveats) that people like the Wilcoxes "keep a place going" (195). Forster makes clear that while these monetary contributions are not sufficient to maintain the house's spirit, they are necessary prerequisites. Margaret may claim, "Discussion keeps a house alive. It cannot stand by bricks and mortar alone," but as Mrs. Wilcox points out, "It cannot stand without them" (58).

For Howards End to survive, then, it must be rebuilt. It must become a place of paradox: separate from commercial urban spaces yet acknowledging the role of commerce in supporting such a "purified" vision, and embodying a modern sense of time that might address the anxiety of loss without creating a static temporality. Forster in fact offers such a space. Midway through the novel, the newly married Margaret Schlegel Wilcox returns to the titular country house to find it the recipient of an unexpected makeover. Closed since the death of the first Mrs. Wilcox and for months used as a warehouse for the Schlegels' possessions, the house has been unpacked and reconstituted by the housekeeper, Miss Avery, who creates a new interior built from moments of Margaret's own history. As Margaret moves through the house in surprise, she takes a virtual tour of her past: her umbrella stand greets her in the entranceway, the infamous sword of her father hangs on the wall, her brother Tibby's books make up the library, her mother's cheffonier stands in the dining room, and everywhere, "many an old god peeped from a new niche" 94). The carefully placed goods even link events from the more distant past with recent ones: Tibby's old bassinet is, significantly, in the room where Helen stayed during her brief liaison with Paul Wilcox. A newly created space, Howards End is nevertheless temporally dense, not showcasing discrete moments, or even the passage of time from past to present, but suggesting rather a more free-flowing exchange among various times, uniting people, objects, and the house in a connective temporal web.

Under this reading, Miss Avery's neo-nostalgic Howards End parallels commodified architectural nostalgia, appealing in part because of its ability to package time, to collapse past moments onto present place. Howards End, of course, is not for sale on the open market, though Miss Avery, as any consummate shop owner might do, has arranged goods to make Howards End as appealing as possible to her primary target—Margaret. It is easy to cringe at this last image, introducing as it does the idea of a mercantile Miss Avery, recognizing that she stands to gain financially in these arrangements. This runs counter to most conceivable readings of Miss Avery's motives, but I have introduced the image to suggest that the scene lies in complicated critical territory, with Forster insisting on the central role played by money raised in commercial ventures in the construction of spaces seemingly purified of such alliances. Howards End becomes contested terrain, one that exposes both the desire to purify a space from commercial interests and Forster's own recognition that such "purified" spaces must necessarily be self-conscious constructions. Such recognition in fact lay at the heart of new attempts to market a nostalgic aura in home design.

Temporal Density: The Domestic Revival

Forster's move to condense different times onto a domestic structure reflected larger developments in British architecture at the turn of the century, developments that provide material examples of Forster's vision of the neo-nostalgic home.[18] The new architectural trends were summarized by Hermann Muthesius, a young architect from Berlin, who wrote the influential book *Das englische Haus.*[19] Around 1900, Muthesius had been posted at the German embassy in London, where he quickly became a devoted convert of English building techniques for domestic dwellings, techniques he carefully catalogued in his three-volume work. He found in Britain a refreshing style, not ostentatiously modern but one that was both "an up-to-date national art" (4) and yet bathed in nostalgic references to the past. In the new dwellings, Muthesius wrote,

> Everything breathes simplicity, homeliness and rural freshness, occasionally, indeed, verging on the vernacular. But a fresh breath of naturalness wafts through the house and a sound down-to-earth quality is combined with a sure feeling of suitability. What we principally find here is a practical, indigenous and preeminently friendly house; and instead of a sham modernity expressing itself extravagantly in whimsical artificiality we find purely functional, unaffected design that many may already regard as more modern than all the fantastic excesses of a so-called modern style. (4)

The established architects who were producing such dwellings, such as Philip Webb, William Eden Nesfield, and Norman Shaw, as well as a range of younger ones like C. F. A. Voysey, Charles Rennie Mackintosh, and Edwin Lutyens, were, according to Muthesius, returning to traditional building techniques and craft traditions to create individual examples of new yet "authentic" British dwellings.

Muthesius's work has become the basis for most subsequent discussions of vernacular architecture, so it is worth tracing both his history and his description of the movement. In the mid–nineteenth century, Muthesius notes, art, literature, and architecture began looking backward to Gothic traditions. The Pre-Raphaelites, most notably William Morris, looked longingly to the Middle Ages, and Carlyle and Scott likewise extolled an idealized feudalism (13–14). The Gothic Revival in architecture was producing new buildings complete with turrets and towers. By the mid-1840s, Ruskin emerged as "the prophet of a new artistic culture" (13), praising Gothic architecture as forever embodying the work of innumerable anonymous craftsmen. He extolled the qualities that were later to become the basis of the Arts and Crafts Movement: "simplicity and naturalness in art, honesty in tectonic design . . . [and] a synthesis of artistic creation and observation of nature" (13). Above all else, however, Ruskin valued "good, decent, solid workmanship like that practiced so splendidly in the hand-made objects of old" (13).

For Muthesius, Ruskin's ideals received their practical realization in the designs of William Morris, and while he oversimplifies the connection between these men, certainly the influence is present. Morris was one representative of a larger movement in design, one that encompassed groups such as the Century Guild and the Art Workers' Guild, which organized the Arts and Crafts exhibits in London from 1888 on. In addition, the journal the *Studio* was launched in 1893, which in its initial years focused on English designers. All these efforts, while they differed in the details, were devoted to making objects and designing houses that emphasized simplicity and careful craftsmanship (Muthesius, 13–14).

Muthesius was pleased to find that by the late nineteenth century architects had started to focus not simply on exterior design but on the details of the interior as well. Plans included furnishings and even art, as architects began to consider all aspects of the house as part of the larger design. The young architect Baillie Scott, for example, argued that a house was "an organic whole to be designed consistently inside and out" (51), a localized place for authentic craftsmanship. These architects were creating, in effect, earlier, more concentrated versions of the community-wide authentic aesthetic we explored in the model towns. This "new" architectural movement was not trying to return to any particular time or any particular style. While trends in architecture are often to some extent returns—to the classical, the Gothic, the Regency, and so forth—the Domestic Revival returned instead to method, to a way of building (Muthesius, 15).[20] As such, the style tried to evoke not a particular period (other than one generically preindustrial) but a particular, nostalgic atmosphere that was located in an undetermined bygone day.

With its emphasis on a nostalgic evocation of a rural past, the movement nevertheless turned on a contradiction similar to that addressed in *Howards End*: it was supported largely by money from new commercial interests. Gavin Stamp and André Goulancourt, in *The English House 1860–1914: The Flowering of English Domestic Architecture*, outline the ironies of this trend:

> The new movement was fundamentally anti-urban, anti-industrial, anti-modern, yet it depended for its life and success upon the wealth and technology of Victorian Britain. [The architect Philip] Webb may have enjoyed occasional aristocratic patronage, but most of [the architect Norman] Shaw's clients were *nouveaux riches*: brewers, solicitors, industrialists—and the money came from *trade*. (27)

The work of Edwin Lutyens, one of the most well-known vernacular architects, serves as an instructive guide to this blend of nostalgia and commerce. Lutyens built a wide range of houses and commercial structures both in England and in India, as well as numerous war memorials after 1918. A contemporary of Frank Lloyd Wright, Lutyens was born in 1869 and began studying architecture by examining the vernacular structures near his home in Surrey with Gertrude Jekyll, the famous British gardener who is credited with infusing new life into the informal English country garden. From his office in Bloomsbury Square, Lutyens planned houses for clients much like Mr. Wilcox: new industrialists or businessmen who wanted a house that looked established.[21]

Commentators at the time frequently noted the sense of naturalness that seemed to permeate Lutyens's early work. A review of articles from *Country Life* magazine—itself an example of early twentieth-century packaging of a country house aesthetic for an upper-class and middle-class audience—reveals a continual emphasis on the quintessentially English qualities of Lutyens's homes. Such Englishness is tied to simplicity and recalls Forster's descriptions of Howards End and many dwellings in Bournville, Port Sunlight, and Letchworth. Gertrude Jekyll, writing for the magazine about a Lutyens-designed house, Orchards, declares that the architect "faithfully follows the country's best traditions."[22] Her description of the interior might have been written by Forster or by the first Mrs. Wilcox:

> All the woodwork is of honest English oak, designed and wrought as this grand stuff deserves. The bedroom doors are of a fine old local pattern of moulded boards, with hinges and latches made to suit. The bedrooms are planned so that no bed need face the light, and give the impression, as does all the house, of the perfection of simple comfort, and that most precious quality of restfulness, as well as delight to mind and eye, that only comes of the right and dignified use of good and simple material. It is a house that has the true home feeling—good to live and die in. (Orchards, 279)

The word choice of this passage, emphasizing the honesty and simplicity of the design, builds a picture of new yet nostalgic authenticity, implying that here is a recently built house that is natural, that, in Jekyll's words, "sits at home upon its ground and could not be other than the right house in the country" (Orchards, 272). The house design appears to evoke in Jekyll aesthetic rapture as well as moral fervor. Orchards is not merely pleasing to the eyes—it is honest and good. Jekyll conjures a tantalizing blend of established old money and back-to-the-land workmanship, suggesting a hybrid of classes and a union of the beautiful and the true. These combinations arise in part from a deftly executed paradox: on the one hand, there is little sense that this house was just built or that it was ever for sale; indeed, it is appealing because within the photographs, the construction and the monetary transaction have dropped out of sight. On the other hand, the house is on display for the readers, its recent construction detailed (but finished), accessible through the sale of its image within *Country Life* magazine.[23]

Country Life thus became itself a synecdoche to the authentic atmosphere of the country estate, distilling in photographs and articles the essence of the essential naturalism of both Lutyens's homes and others. The product for sale—the magazine—*was*, in part, the atmosphere of high-class originary and nostalgic authenticity that emanated from its pages. Many if not most of the readers could not afford to build a Lutyens-style estate, so it was not the houses that were being sold but the magazine's descriptions of neo-nostalgic homes and the "Life" that allegedly adhered to its pages. In some respects, the magazine was a product just like Cadbury's Cocoa, both commodities allegedly holding a connection to an authentic space. The magazine, however, was directly tied to the original atmosphere. It was not produced there, as Cadbury's Cocoa was produced at Bournville; rather, its very content was the country atmosphere of individual domestic homes. What emerges is the versatility and mobility of the commodified authentic as a marketing tool, able to sell products by presenting a transitive link to an authentic atmosphere (as with the cocoa) or by turning the imagined atmosphere into a product, as we see in *Country Life*.

Many of the Lutyens houses themselves reflected a time-play made possible by carefully constructing a weathered appearance. Lutyens inscribed the passage of time on interior design and on architectural features. Furniture was often austere, built from old wood and stripped of polish. At Gertrude Jekyll's house, Munstead Wood, Lutyens sandblasted the oak he used in order to produce the appearance of age; at another house, Little Thakeham, he treated the stones to give them, as Peter Inskip notes, "the appearance of three centuries of wear" (27). More than simply using old material—or material that had been treated to look old—Lutyens created an imagined history within his houses. Details from different styles and different periods were included in the same house to hint that changes had been made over the centuries. In one design, for instance, he set an eighteenth-century-style chimneypiece amid an even older interior style to create the illusion of an earlier attempt at modernization. The passage of time Lutyens sought to convey might work progressively, as with the chimneypiece, giving the sense that the house had been improved slowly over the years, or alternatively, might hint of disintegration (Inskip, 28–29). At Nashdom, for example, Lutyens built a door many feet off the ground to imply the previous existence of a staircase below; such features present a constructed nostalgia, hinting of a storied past that never existed.[24] With these architectural features, Lutyens sold a temporal density to his clients, offering not simply a mix of styles but the visual sense of time's passage in a single contemporary space.

The new vernacular style was on tricky ground, of course. While the new buildings incorporated older models, the architects and owners were careful to distinguish their work from buildings they saw as fake or artificial re-creations of older forms, much as the designers of the model towns were quick to separate their "authentic" reproductions from cheaper imitations. Consider, for example, Gertrude Jekyll's description of her new house, Munstead Wood:

> [It] does not stare with newness; it is not new in any way that is disquieting to the eye; it is neither raw nor callow. On the contrary it almost gives the impression of a comfortable maturity of something like a couple hundred years. And yet there is nothing sham or old about it; it is not trumped up with any specious or fashionable devices of spurious antiquity; there is no pretending to be anything that it is not—no affectation whatever.[25]

Munstead Wood was to occupy an innovative architectural position: at once new, and yet giving the impression of age; hiding its origins, yet not appearing as a sham. For Jekyll, houses should not be marked by a bogus antiquity, or a kind of fake nostalgic atmosphere. The new houses should, as much as possible, erase the signs of their recent production, but not in an obvious way, and look as natural—and as authentic—as if they indeed reflected a "comfortable maturity."[26]

This attempt to hide the newness of the building in turn implies an attempt to hide its commercial origins. Yet, like Forster's Margaret, Lutyens sought to encompass a possible contradiction: his artistic efforts were supported by new commercial money, and his clients wanted an old, established-looking house. As Lutyens noted in a telling phrase, " 'The visible result of time is a large factor in realised aesthetic value.' "[27] Lutyens recognized the aesthetic and financial use of temporal density, of a building or object that reflected the passage of time, and that was in fact supported and produced by new commercial ventures. Janus-faced, Lutyens worked to promote his ties to industrial money at the same time that he sought, gently, to elide them in his work.

Marketing the Neo-nostalgic: The *Daily Mail*'s Ideal Home Exhibition

Lutyens's neo-nostalgic homes remained by and large accessible only to his wealthy customers, and by extension to the largely elite readers of *Country Life*. Lutyens also participated, however, in another, broader enterprise that brought the commodified authentic to a far larger group of consumers: the *Daily Mail* Ideal Home Exhibition, which was started in 1908.[28] The exhibition, the brainchild of the *Daily Mail*'s Special Publicity Department, was originally designed to induce the various industries involved in home building and interior design to market their products directly to consumers, rather than working through builders and architects, as they had been doing. Wareham Smith, the man in charge of advertising for the paper, immediately saw the financial advantage that might be gained—for the *Daily Mail* as well as for the building industry—from convincing companies to reach buyers through newspaper advertisements and by displaying their wares at the Ideal Home Exhibition. Smith launched a series of competitions at the show for the best ideal home design in various price categories, securing the well-respected Lutyens as the most appropriate judge of such a contest.[29]

The Ideal Home Exhibition, held roughly every other year after its initial launch, literally showcased the many goods and products available for furnishing and for building the home, contributing to a surge in efforts to present the "home" as something that might be created through careful shopping. Advertisements for and articles on the exhibition continually emphasized the various ways to construct an "ideal" home, an ideal that focused on the union of the originary and the nostalgic forms of the commodified authentic. In the exhibition's marketing materials, the desire for a home was repeatedly declared to be fundamental, "the deepest and truest of all instincts, an instinct possessed by the whole animal creation."[30] This authentic construction required blending the best of the old with the promise of the new. In part, the exhibition cast a fond look backward, evoking a specifically English domestic tradition. The promotional materials declared the very idea of "home" was fundamentally English and promised "an eager return to the old ideal of the craftsmen who helped more than others to make the word 'home' the most English of all English words."[31] Alongside this nostalgia, however, the exhibition looked relentlessly forward, promising its customers that they would leave behind the tired constraints of the Victorian home to be dazzled by the most modern, most up-to-date, most scientific products ever conceived. This neo-nostalgic blend captured and made available to the middle class the unions of the old and the new, and the authentic and the commercial, suggested by both Forster and Lutyens, and the promoters began to market such blends in a vast campaign (figure 3.2).[32]

The Ideal Home Exhibition promised not only to unite past times and different spaces into one place in the present but also to make these new unions available to everyone who came to see the exhibition. Quaint old customs from centuries past might be viewed right next to the latest modern technologies. The exhibition's temporal and spatial unions played out over both the physical space of the show and within the objects for sale. By moving through the all-indoor exhibition hall,

Fig. 3.2 From an early *Daily Mail* Ideal Home Exhibition
Picture found in the archives of the Associated Newspaper Print Library, London. Reproduced with kind permission from Solo Syndication.

visitors might engage in fantasy time travel, visiting sanitized representations of the past alongside the present. At the 1910 exhibition, for example, a complete reproduction of a Tudor village was created with a village green, old shops occupied by businesses that had existed for at least 100 years, a well, a maypole, a full street of picturesque gabled houses, and even a waterfall. As an article in the *Daily Mail* noted, the visitor could pass "from the twentieth century back to the days of Elizabeth" and then, just as quickly, "step[] back to modern times."[33] The temporal blending adhered to objects as well. At the 1908 show, for instance, the Devon fire grate was promoted as "one of the most modern scientific forms of open grate, and while retaining all the simplicity of the old fireplaces does away with the complaints of smoke dust, draught, and the extravagant consumption of coal."[34] Customers might have both modern science and old simplicity; the grate was not simply a nostalgic reproduction but a better creation that was marketed as a temporally ideal combination.

By 1912, the exhibition's organizers were praising architects for creating new domestic homes with simple designs that offered a harmonious blend of different times. As one article noted, "The modern architect . . . does not keep strictly to a particular style in house design"; instead, he "pays more attention to real home convenience and solid comfort in his planning."[35] The owner and the architect together could pick from a range of periods and styles to create a new dwelling. The praise for simple architecture of "perfectly plain materials" with "no added ornamentation" recalls both the insistence by the model towns' architects on the absolute simplicity of the dwellings and also Forster's Helen Schlegel, who expects Howards End to be "all gables and wiggles" and is surprised to find instead a house of aged simplicity.[36] Here we find a similar sentiment—but within an explicitly commercial setting.

The temporal blendings in fact led to a surprising nostalgia of commerce. Business—so often seen as the evil foil to all that was authentically pure about England—became venerable. In the Tudor Village of 1910, for example, the visitor was promised the "aristocracy of commerce," for the old firms that had re-created stores in the village showed how "from tiny cramped old shops . . . sprang some of the great, world-famous firms of today."[37] Visitors were invited to "admire the old cottages and to admire no less the long and successful trade history of the old firms exhibiting there."[38] Even Cadbury Brothers had a regular booth (though not in the village), and a *Daily Mail* article commented that the term "factory in a garden," inspired by Bournville, had "passed into proverb," and the firm was now "so well known that it is difficult to say anything that does not appear old."[39] Commercial ventures are here carefully repositioned (a move discussed at length in the next chapter on Selfridges), as commerce becomes not the spoiler of an authentic England but its embodiment.

The Ideal Home Exhibition further promised to manufacture and import the best features of the country directly into the heart of the city. Elaborate gardens, for example, were created within the exhibition hall, immune to any kind of weather. The visitor in 1908 might find a fully prepared model English garden, where "sparkling pools and waterfalls delight the eye, and the musical murmur of the water mingles with the hum of bees. . . . Where bountiful nature has not done her duty by a garden, Messrs. Pulham and Son step in and supply what she has left out."[40] Such a garden captured (the text implies) an authentic country aesthetic; the display even improved on nature by commodifying it, allowing bountiful nature to be revised, updated, and sold by Messrs. Pulham and Son.

In addition to such generic packages of pastoral aesthetics, the exhibition presented two more specific versions of the countryside: the aura of the high-class country estate, and idyllic views of rural cottage industries. Visitors of all classes were invited to partake in an upper-class country life and to enjoy the places "where one will be able to stand amid beautiful grounds as on a great country estate."[41] Viewers might, in effect, perform at least temporarily the role of landed gentry or wealthy industrialist. Alternatively, visitors were invited to visit the related but opposite extreme of the humble country dwelling; they might explore, for example, "the first complete small holding under glass," composed of "[a] neat, vine-clad, furnished cottage, with the surrounding gardens and lawns, the latter provided with rustic seats . . . and a miniature orchard in fruit."[42] Visitors were shown how they too might buy such a house, or even, as one exhibit in 1912 offered, how they might move to one of the emerging Garden City estates.[43] In a similar vein, an extensive area of all the early exhibitions was devoted to cottage industries and the arts and crafts. Visitors might see the actual artisans at work, "a Welsh lassie presiding, dressed in proper Welsh costume, and an old peasant woman . . . rush-making."[44] The original goods that these workers created, allegedly endowed with the "authentic" rustic aesthetic, might be purchased at a reasonable cost, allowing (the marketing materials promised) the visitors to bring part of the country atmosphere back to their own homes.[45]

The Ideal Home Exhibition suggests a democratization of authenticity, offering to a larger audience at least a few aspects of the higher class versions of the commodified authentic found in Forster's novel and Lutyens's homes.[46] The goods displayed were presented as readily available and plentiful—although unique and one-of-a-kind—and even visitors who could not afford them could nevertheless tour within the space and perform a different class role. Of course, the exhibition's version of the commodified authentic often had less substance than a Munstead Wood or a Howards End. The organizers might claim that the stall of St. Ivel's, makers of the nourishing bouillon cube, gave off "the atmosphere of the country that one seems to breathe when in the vicinity of their stalls," but Forster reminds us of the depressing reality, with Leonard Bast dissolving "a soup square" in hot water for dinner in his dingy flat.[47] Amid all the hype, however, visitors were shown some marked improvements in home design and in labor-saving technologies. Regardless of which of the show's claims were valid, the popularity of the exhibition reflected the emerging power of marketing the authentic. The organizers successfully played both to fears that a precious past was disappearing and to the hope that modern technology might offer relief from present difficulties. The Ideal Home Exhibition derived much of its appeal from its dexterous blending of various forms of authenticity with products and spaces that were reproducible and accessible to the middle-class buyer.

The new design possibilities further marked a shift in the very idea of "home." To evoke a venerable past, a home no longer needed to have actual ties to a family estate or to be an old country cottage; the home instead could become referential, gesturing to previous models but remaining accessible and controllable by a customer who might not posses (or even want) an actual old dwelling. The value of having personal ties to a particular place was recognized and re-created as a product that might be packaged and sold. The very idea of the home makeover, so popular in the current culture, arises in part from this earlier move to turn the home into something that might be *made*.

Reconstructing Howards End

The final chapters of Forster's *Howards End* give a snapshot of both the power of temporal density in shaping the neo-nostalgic home and the very real temptations intrinsic to these early models of commodified authenticity. The Howards End that Miss Avery has created by unpacking the Schlegels' possessions becomes the solution to the central crisis near the conclusion of the novel. Margaret has lured her sister, Helen, to England from Germany, ostensibly to visit their gravely ill aunt. Worried that her sister's recent erratic behavior indicates a mental imbalance, Margaret meets Helen at Howards End, only to discover that the unmarried Helen is pregnant. This development brings to sudden intensity the spatial and temporal crisis present throughout the novel. Much of the earlier story had revolved around the question "Where to live?" (Born, 142), with displaced families being the order of the day: Mrs. Wilcox was displaced in London, the Schlegels had to move from Wickham Place, Leonard Bast belonged (so the narrator tells us) in the country. Helen's pregnancy, however, adds new urgency to the issue. Helen recognizes that she is no longer simply displaced but an exile; as she tells her sister, "'I cannot live in England'" (209) and more specifically, cannot stay at her sister's house. "'Imagine a visit from me at Ducie Street! It's unthinkable!'" Helen remarks, and "Margaret could not contradict her" (209). Unlike Margaret, however, Helen does not seem unduly troubled by this crisis of place; the temporal crisis, however, proves more difficult. Helen believes she must cut herself off from her past life, represented by her siblings and her old possessions. "'I am glad to have seen you and the things,'" she tells Margaret, and "She looked at the bookcase lovingly, as if she was saying farewell to the past" (210).

Such a spatial and temporal dilemma suggests the larger cultural tensions outlined by Forster, Muthesius, and the Garden City reformers, and addressed (allegedly) by the Ideal Home Exhibition: a sense of mass displacement and disruption from existing homes and ways of life, simultaneously cutting people off from their dwellings and from their own history. Such tensions would in turn contribute to several staples of the modernist diet: alienation, displacement, and a sense of discontinuity with the past. As discussed earlier, the rural solution to this crisis has often been read as an almost embarrassing nostalgic gesture, a return to a naïve and simplistic vision of a slower, happier country life. Yet Miss Avery's version of Howards End is not a nostalgic capitulation but in fact modernity's evolving answer to the need both to retain the past and to move into the present.

Forster offers a new model of time, part of a larger cultural project to find a way, however uneasily, to respect the past without falling into stasis. Miss Avery's Howards End, with its old traditions and the Schlegel furniture, proves to be a potent model; Margaret and Helen resolve at least part of their crisis simply by walking through the new temporal space of Howards End. After they have decided to part ways, they take one last look at their furniture within the house and end up taking an almost cinemagraphic tour of their own history, moving from room to room to find not simply objects representative of their past but the narratives that adhere to those objects as well. On one of the dining room chairs, for example, is a stain, and the sisters debate whether it was from the soup or the coffee that Tibby had spilled years ago. They finally place the stain in history, identifying it as soup since their father had been alive, but the debate triggers a memory trip to their aunt's and a short childhood rhyme that was the inadvertent cause of another spill. This remembrance of things past, generated by layers of objects and their temporal significance, offers the sisters a sustaining continuity. They have no wish to freeze the arrangement; they move furniture, debate other changes, and imagine future alterations. Unlike the "dead house" that Margaret sees at the start of the scene, the house, as Helen proclaims, "seems more alive even than in the old days, when it held the Wilcoxes' own things" (209). The Schlegels' possessions appear almost animate. Even their chairs, feeling the sun for the first time "in thirty years," seem to have come to life; as Helen remarks, "'Their dear little backs are quite warm'" (211). It is a new arrangement of old things, and thus a new arrangement of the past made accessible to the present. This is not merely a return to some quintessential "Englishness"; the Schlegels are German, after all, and the interior reflects not only a temporal melding but a cultural one as well, with its combination of English and Continental objects and styles. These temporal and spatial connections reunite the two central characters. Far from a static hold on the past, the new Howards End grants the characters both a vital continuity and a chance to remake time's passage to accommodate their current needs. It was, as the narrator tells us, "the past sanctifying the present; the present, with wild heart-throb, declaring that there would after all be a future" (212).

It must be acknowledged, however, that this new temporal continuity, delivering that rare satisfaction of nostalgic desire, does represent a denial of the earlier explicit links among commerce, culture, and a nostalgic longing for a country retreat. Margaret may previously have insisted on the connection between her cultured life and the businessmen who guarantee it, and Helen may have attempted to give her money to Leonard Bast as some kind of reparation, but this meeting at Howards End finally excludes both Henry Wilcox and Leonard Bast. The moment of dramatic reconnection for the sisters is also the moment that the nostalgic vision of the country house starts to become "purified" from ties to commerce or its disturbing repercussions. Once the new Howards End—with its tempting offer of temporal continuity—is available, and construction is more or less complete, the underlying connections between Howards End and commerce seem to slide out of sight.

The final scene of the novel presents the logical and deflating conclusion to this move to separate Howards End from market forces. Critics have, in fact, long savaged the ending as a nostalgic capitulation, although there is disagreement over whether this failure belongs to Forster or to the two sisters.[48] The novel's finale presents Mr. Wilcox almost on his deathbed, revealing the final distribution of his estate among his children and daughter-in-law: Howards End will pass to Margaret and her nephew; the Wilcox money will be carefully channeled away from Howards End, going directly to his children. It is Margaret's inheritance that will presumably maintain the house, though much of this (which itself comes from investments in trade) is also being given away. Likewise, the disturbing results of commercial interests, represented in the novel by the terrible plight of Leonard and his fiancée, Jacky, have been ruthlessly and effectively purged. Leonard is dead (Margaret instructs Helen to forget him), and Jacky is never mentioned, seemingly so far beneath notice (or so potentially threatening) as to be written out of the text.

This final ambivalent gesture toward purification in fact confirms the central tension inherent in relations between nostalgia and commerce. On the one hand, we see the desire to reveal the connections, to uncover the ties between commerce and an architecturally based nostalgia, to be explicit—and in most ways unapologetic—about the complications of creating monuments of temporal density. On the other hand, there is always present the wish and the promise that this unmasking might itself result in a purified space, that the final results of these connections would be a space apart from the problems of modernity and the terrible repercussions of a commercial age, a place where past moments might be united with the present rather than alienated from it. The final moments of Forster's novel suggest capitulation, but they also suggest an imaginary space for nostalgic desire itself—not a place of actual idyllic beauty, or a space that is actually separate from the commercial, but a place where the desire that these things might be realized can be maintained and protected. These places sanctifying nostalgic desire were an enormously tempting vision for Forster, for Lutyens, and for the shoppers at the Ideal Home Exhibition. We misread Forster, however, if we isolate this nostalgic vision from the rest of the novel and simply condemn it, declaring that however much Forster may have protested, he capitulates to nostalgic mistiness in the end. Easy critical condemnation of Forster's nostalgia should, in fact, be resisted as strongly as this simplified country vision. While the final nostalgic tableau is, to borrow a commercial term, a sellout, this vision must be read as part of a larger meditation on the perils and appeals of the commodified authentic. Forster gives, in a sense, the whole advertisement. He explores the financial and human costs of producing this country vision, its careful construction, its illusion of purification, and finally the overwhelming desire to purchase this illusion, a desire Forster undeniably shares. A single-minded critical focus on condemning the blindness of Forster's nostalgia not only misses the contradictory treatment of nostalgic space in *Howards End* but in fact partakes of the very blindness such a focus seeks to correct.

A Locus of Neo-nostalgic Desire

The critical importance of neo-nostalgic homes such as Howards End, Munstead Wood, and the models at the Ideal Home Exhibition lies both in their power to manipulate time and in their self-conscious acknowledgment of this manipulation. These newly constructed spaces offer the viewer—or reader—an opportunity to become a time traveler, to experience spatially a temporal continuity that—nostalgically—helped erase modern industrialization and mechanization. Yet such spaces, as all my examples acknowledge, were made possible by a grant from industrialization, and this tension is instructive of the very contradictions and possibilities inherent to selling time. Creating nostalgic spaces in the present requires that they be both constructed and, to various degrees, commodified. These spaces are both literally for sale, in that it is possible to buy a Lutyens house or a copy of *Howards End*—both popular, incidentally, in part because of the nostalgic atmosphere they evoke—and also more figuratively for sale, in one present space for our viewing pleasure. The spaces become shimmering new commodities, the ideal of a modern nostalgic who wishes not quite to go back to the past but to bring the passage of time to the present, to inscribe onto both space and objects a sense of temporal continuity, to continue time by disrupting it. That this move produces both benefits and very troubling failures and exclusions suggests that our analysis of commodified authenticity must be equally nuanced.

Forster, Lutyens, and the Ideal Home Exhibition, then, not only provide vital models of neo-nostalgic spaces but also create spaces that through their very ambivalence and self-consciousness suggest a potent critical approach to the commodified authentic itself. I want to put pressure on the final word in this term—spaces—and argue that this openness demands an equally dexterous critical response. While maintaining our suspicion of trafficking in nostalgic desire, we might also avoid being overly content simply to unmask it and proclaim it a sham, for these neo-nostalgic homes remind us that this is not the end of the story. Rather than approaching sites such as the new Howards End as single places, we can view clusters of the commodified authentic as reflecting a nexus of contradictory impulses, one that requires us to acknowledge both desire and failure, both a powerful new ability to manipulate and to sell time, and a clear sense of the limits and costs of this manipulation.

Coda

Forster has now become an icon for the Edwardian age; his novels—and the movies they have inspired—are powerful sites of commodified nostalgia. Most notable, of course, are the highly popular (and lucrative) Merchant-Ivory adaptations of his works, a quintessential instance of nostalgia as a profitable sales technique.

Even before these films, however, Forster himself had been endowed by observers with a romantic aura, an Edwardian relic still living in his rooms at Cambridge until his death in 1970. Visitors to Forster in his later years and commentators on the film adaptations of his novels return again and again to the sense of place, to the nostalgia evoked by Forster or the films that emanates from the location, from the dwellings and the objects within them.[49]

As P. N. Furbank relates in his well-known biography of the novelist, Forster found himself without a home in 1946, when he was nearly sixty-eight. At the last minute, a friend worked behind the scenes on his behalf, securing him first a residence near Cambridge, and then an actual apartment at King's College.[50] He had frequent visitors in these later years, and almost all of those who recorded their recollections of visiting him comment on his rooms and their contents. Weaving through all the accounts is a sense of thrill, the sense of traveling to the past and of being in the presence of one of the greats, someone, and someplace, authentic. One visitor contrasted the cold and dark outside world with the bright, warm atmosphere in the apartment, an enclave where "the furniture was old, solid, and comfortable."[51] Another visitor, Frank Hauser, to whom Forster was "mythical," wrote that "the beautiful set of rooms that King's had granted him seemed more like a cocoon than ever."[52]

The objects in the rooms are described with similar enthusiasm, seen as reflecting Forster's personal history. Observers frequently commented on the number of items that came from various members of his family, that had been with him in childhood, or that had lengthy personal stories associated with them. As one visitor notes, "The oval table at which we had had lunch, was the nursery table at which he had sat as a child. Everything in the room had been given to him, everything had a personal history. Nothing had been bought or collected."[53] Forster himself, perched amid all his belongings, seemed part of them, almost—to use the term of several visitors—a mystic. "Altogether," noted L. P. Wilkinson, "the furnishings gave the impression of being accretions round him, evidences of his past and personality."[54] In his later years, Forster became a Mrs. Wilcox figure—a representative of the past, a keeper of objects marked by time and personal history, a safeguard of dwellings linked inextricably to their inhabitants.

We can, of course, be wary of these observations, repeated by the commentators with such frequency as to become almost parodic, bestowing on Forster a flavor of caricature and making his apartment a stage set of authenticity.[55] For many critics, the Merchant-Ivory films have compounded this uneasiness, stripping Forster of his complexity and ambiguity and offering in its place the rarefied, glowing, picturesque Edwardian stage set. The Edwardian era (about which Forster himself was decidedly not nostalgic), always a popular site of wistful longing due to its position before the Great War, has become ever more idealized. Anne Billson, in a review of the film *Howards End* for *New Statesman and Society*, laments that the movie seems like an "Edwardian theme park" and recommends that it "be bought up by the National Trust, though it doesn't need to be preserved. It has already been pickled in the formaldehyde of nostalgia."[56]

How suspicious should we be that both the novel and the movies sell well at least in part because of their own nostalgia? Like Mrs. Wilcox, are we to parcel out a space of authenticity (say Howards End, or Forster's novels), and declare that the copies (poor flats, houses from the English Revival, the models at the Ideal Home Exhibition, or the Merchant-Ivory films) are outside the true original, mere and even dangerous imitations? It is tempting—and tempting for all the reasons that give Forster's novel such power in the first place—to find a space that might be purified, sanctified, set apart. We are poised, though, to lurch between two extremes, to put nostalgia and commerce into an oppositional relationship (The books are pure! The movies are moneymaking schemes!) or to join them together as fatally compromised (selling the "formaldehyde of nostalgia"). Here we can return to Forster, however, and find him ahead of the critics. What *Howards End* finally demands is at once to understand and maintain the powerful cultural desire for an authentic domestic space, and at the same time to hold on to the necessarily ambiguous, complicated, and constructed nature of such space. Forster asks us to survive the contradiction between authenticity and its construction without losing sight of either end of the equation.

Part II

Urban Authenticities

4. The Vanishing Act of Commercialism

Selfridges, Modernity, and the Purified Marketplace

> What the public have yet to realize is that business is a science, or at its greatest an art. . . . Sheer commercialism, the desire to make profit and to accumulate money, may determine the organization of a business, but business to-day has passed beyond that mere money-grubbing stage.
>
> —Selfridges' advertisement, "London's Greatest Store," *Times*, 24 February 1909

The commodified authentic achieved its full power in the urban setting, which is the focus of the second part of the book. While it was a critical strategy within the largely rural and suburban models considered in the first section, the commodified authentic in the city became a dexterous and flexible tool to bring various forms of authenticity to a far wider audience. The commodified authentic promised the urban dweller an accessible and fabricated enclave of serenity within the city. Such enclaves might reference rural images, but these images were firmly incorporated within urban space, suggesting a cultural location both outside the metropolitan bustle and within it. The shift to urban examples also marks a shift fully to commodification. The first part of the book analyzed the striking new unions imagined between industrial money and various versions of nostalgic authenticity; industrial profits supported the lifestyle design of model towns like Bournville or Port Sunlight, and in turn the atmosphere of the villages could be packaged and sold to a public hungry for nostalgic images of a rural past. This second part examines the explosion of efforts to bring elaborate fabrications and enticing promises of perfect aesthetic artifice to the urban consumer. Radical changes in urban advertising, store design, and window displays deftly united heady possibilities of self-fashioning, artificial pleasures, and seemingly endless possibilities of reinvention with the equally appealing but contradictory attractions of the original model, of a refined, commercial-free aesthetic, and of rural life and domestic tranquillity. The urban versions let consumers (and readers) shape images of authenticity themselves, allowing them to unite different times and identities—and then to exchange these for new ones if they desired.

The urban form of the commodified authentic also promised to democratize the search for commercial purity. In contrast to the model towns or a Howards End, which tended to reinforce (or reinstate) a hierarchical model of community relations and to emphasize a nostalgic return to an authentic country aesthetic, the urban versions developed a more egalitarian model. Various notions of authenticity were presented to a broad market, infusing highbrow ideas of commercial purity into popular culture. The urban models also allowed for greater access; while few consumers had the opportunity to live in a model village, and even fewer could afford a Lutyens house, the urban models were more widely available, as I started to explore in the example of the neo-nostalgic country homes of the Ideal Home Exhibition in London.

The accessibility promised by urban examples of the commodified authentic corresponded to the greater spatial reach of commodity culture. In turn-of-the-century London, as well as in other British cities, the divisions between commercial and noncommercial enterprises were dissolving. Elaborately designed window displays extended the store to the city street; the proliferation of newspaper advertising, while certainly present in the nineteenth century, expanded with the launch of the *Daily Mail*, and even crept into the venerable *Times*. Exhibitions, popular since the Great Exhibition of 1851, were a weekly occurrence in the city, uniting, as the Ideal Home show did, commerce with museum-like displays. Department stores such as Harrods rapidly expanded, and new stores such as Selfridges provided larger and ever more spectacular places to shop. Commodity culture was everywhere, and the commodified authentic provided crucial assistance in this expansion, promising to hold together various forms of authenticity considered *outside* the marketplace *within* the marketplace itself.

This chapter begins the trip into the city, examining the extraordinary commercial changes set in motion by the launch of Selfridges department store in 1909. Two literary models serve as bookends to the analysis of this commercial venture. First, Henry James's short story "The Great Good Place" (1900) captures with precision the emerging commercial revolution in early twentieth-century British culture; James presents a fantasy of escape, a commercial ticket out of the press of urban modernity. H. G. Wells's novel *Tono-Bungay*, analyzed at the end of the chapter, offers a derisive critique of this same commercial revolution, mocking advertising in general and attempts to commodify authenticity in particular. Taken together, the two authors present a critical model for investigating Selfridges' innovations, and, in their contradictory stances, they articulate the divisions that would come to dominate reactions to the emerging commercial strategies.

The Great Good Place

Henry James offers a surprising embrace of commercial possibility in his short story "The Great Good Place," highlighting the allure of the commodified authentic for the weary urban resident.[1] The tale depicts a successful English man of letters, George Dane, who is overwhelmed by the products of modern literary life. A steady stream of manuscripts, poems, journals, reviews, and novels pours into his London study each day, pushing Dane to the brink of physical and mental collapse. He is saved, however, by his sudden, magical transportation to the Great Good Place. An idyllic retreat far from the rush of modernity, the place gives Dane the chance to leave behind "the modern madness, [the] mere maniacal extension and motion" (32), and to rejuvenate his aesthetic sensibilities and his inner life. Dane finds the retreat rich in iconic markers of authenticity and tranquillity, and he describes it variously as "the bright country-house" (31), "the sacred silent convent" (31), an "old Italian picture" (33), and "some great mild invisible mother" (38), all united into one lovely and refined package of satisfaction. The place combines nostalgic recompense and aesthetic refinement, blending images evocative of an authentic rural past—the country house, the Italian countryside—with visions drawing on authentic artistic creation—a fine poem, an exquisite piece of music. Dane sinks into the luxury of the retreat, immersing himself in the rejuvenating powers of its pleasures, and welcoming "the representation of a world without newspapers and letters, without telegrams and photographs, without the dreadful fatal too much" (33).[2]

The place may be linked to traditionally noncommercial locations (a monastery, a country house, a mother's lap), but Dane and the other guests must nevertheless pay for their experience. As Dane learns, "payment . . . was definite; it consisted of sovereigns and shillings—just like those of the world he had left, only parted with more ecstatically" (30). While the actual monetary exchange is discreet—guests leave money in their rooms, and it is taken away silently and secretly—money underlies the visit. The arrangements are consistently presented in commercial terms; the guest and the place have a "contract," and "what was offered was guaranteed. [Guests] had no concern but to pay" (32).

Surprisingly, however, James makes explicit that much of Dane's pleasure arises *from* the retreat's commercial nature, rather than in spite of it. Dane is well aware and yet untroubled by the knowledge that he is buying the aesthetic representation of the noncommercial, where satisfaction is intrinsically tied up with the idea that the place is not for sale—and yet available for purchase. The market does not intrude on the aesthetic pleasures, as a reader might expect; it guarantees them, for the commercial nature of the place makes it available, accessible, and most important, controllable. Dane and the other guests may return at will, simply by paying the fees. The retreat may be experienced, altered to suit the needs of the customer, and thus fully and individually possessed. It is a comfort, rather than a disappointment, that "all the sweetness and serenity were created calculated things" (32), for it means that the guests might come again whenever they felt the need, and they might feel in full control of its nature; they might "really call it . . . anything in the world [they] like[d]—the thing for instance [they] love[d] it most for being" (23). Dane and another guest consider with relief that the place is likely to continue because of its profit motive; "it isn't, thank goodness, carried on only for love" (38), but rather because it pays.

The retreat, in fact, bears an uncanny resemblance to the continuous loop of desire and production intrinsic to the modern market. The guests—all of whom are aesthetically refined and sensitive men like Dane and, indeed, like James—seem to create the place through their own desires. As Dane notes, "One's vision seemed less from the facts than the facts from one's vision; . . . the elements were determined at the moment by the moment's need or the moment's sympathy" (34). Knowing its market intimately, the place reflects back to the guests their own sensibilities, perfectly suited to that moment and time. Likewise, the place also *awakens* desire. Dane discusses with another guest the surprise and relief they felt at finding such a place existed. It was just what they wanted and needed, though they themselves could not have articulated this solution before they came; their desire is sparked by the existence of the place. James implies here the feedback loop that sustains the modern market: desire produces product, product produces desire. The Place becomes simultaneously a retreat from modernity and the modern selling of such a retreat.

James himself does not critique the commercial nature of this full-service spa and seems uninterested in exposing the Great Good Place as false or engaged in a bad-faith effort to hide its "real" intent. Dane's choices are an overwhelming modernity that churns out endless literary productions or an alternative modernity that presents a kind of distilled authenticity in a new commercial package. Dane, James implies, is right to embrace this modern solution, and in fact, the place works as Dane's salvation. When Dane "had got his soul again" (35), he finds himself magically transported back to his apartment. To his relief, he discovers all his work has been completed by another capable young man. The rest cure restores Dane fully; he rises from his couch and finds his room seems "disencumbered, different, twice as large. It *was* all right" (42). The commercial retreat, far from being antithetical to the artist, has in fact sustained him. James gives little indication that he himself is scornful of such commercial escapes, recording instead their potential power, both as and for artistic creation.

The Selfridges Revolution

Just nine years later, another American in England discovered the practical applications of the atmosphere James describes. Gordon Selfridge, a self-made millionaire from Chicago, set out to transform British commerce with the opening of Selfridges department store in London in 1909, marking a pivotal moment in British marketing. "London's Greatest Store" perfected the commercial selling of the noncommercial, paradoxically inscribing within its elegantly decorated interior a retail location allegedly unsullied by trade. Visitors on the store's opening day found a luxurious, almost enchanted space, where soft lighting illuminated the vast array of goods from clothes to china to books, where price tags were absent or at least discreet, and where concealed string quartets provided a soothing musical accompaniment for the spectators. In this new commercial environment, the message was that even large-scale stores were free of the taint of the mass market; amid the refined atmosphere the shoppers—or guests, as Selfridges called them—would find an abundance of authentic and exclusive objects, not to be confused with the mass-produced goods available elsewhere. This extraordinary atmosphere marked a dramatic realignment of London's commercial energies, representing one of the first mass-market campaigns to sell a disdain for the mass market.[3]

Selfridges' central marketing strategy turned on a paradox similar to the one Dane discovers in the Great Good Place. This strategy promised to balance the seemingly contradictory desires for an autonomous "authentic" realm apart from the rush of modernity and popular culture, and the desire (or need) to embrace the alluring pleasures, abundance, and flexibility suggested by the modern market. In its broadest form, this approach involved linking places usually considered in opposition to the mass market—the country village, the domestic home, the museum—to the goods for sale. Critically, the strategy also presented the market itself as the best way to obtain the desired noncommercial aura, for the market would provide shoppers access to such purified goods. At Selfridges, on the one hand, the goods and the space were presented as exclusive and refined, defined against the mass market and indeed theoretically not even part of the market itself, existing instead in a purified realm unsullied by conventional markers of commerce; many advertisements implied that the goods at Selfridges were one-of-a-kind objects, in direct contrast with the mass-produced goods available at lesser stores. On the other hand, Selfridges simultaneously invoked the modern pleasures of the mass market: the goods were available to all, and the store would offer shoppers the chance to exchange various styles and to perform various roles within different environments that presented a vast selection of goods. Selfridges was not simply selling notions of the authentic but frankly avowing that this authenticity was commodified, and that this very commodification in turn made the authenticity that much more appealing and available.

Selfridges represented, however, a marked departure from James by dramatically expanding access to this purified realm. In James's story, the Great Good Place is available to a select few; only those men who possess a highly cultured aesthetic sensibility can ever find their way to the Place. At Selfridges, this very exclusivity—often the mark of the high-class shopping experience—was packaged and sold to the more ordinary (read: more middle class) consumer.[4] As one early observer noted, on opening day, the entire public was invited to take part in the glorious refinement of the space:

> The Selfridge idea—that Selfridges exists for the convenience and service of the public—took possession of every one who entered the building, and made every one easy. Music haunted every floor—the music of fiddles and harps.
>
> But if the first and dominating sensation of the thousands of visitors was that of taking part in the inauguration of a public palace of the homely arts, the next sensation was one of admiration at the unexampled perfection of the exhibition itself. Ruskin would have wept for joy at the simple and beautiful arrangement of the interior of Selfridge's. There is nothing ugly from the garden on the roof to the ground floor. Everything is well chosen, in good taste, in harmony with everything else.
>
> Everywhere the thousands of visitors moved in silence on carpets. They were spirited in swift and noiseless lifts from floor to floor.[5]

The hidden music, the hushed and refined atmosphere, and the Ruskin-like arrangements offer a striking parallel to the "quiet footsteps" (James, 21) and "slow sweet bells" (21) set within in "a world of reason and order, of sensible visible arrangement . . . [and] high triumphant clearness" (30) of Dane's retreat. At Selfridges, however, "thousands of visitors" might have access to such refinement, as the store threw open its doors to all shoppers, particularly to another group notably excluded from James's haven: women. Selfridges presented an enormously powerful fantasy with egalitarian possibilities and important gender implications, for the store promised to provide female shoppers a public space of domestic purity, a place where they might remain within a noncommercial sphere and still fully participate in modern commercial exchanges.

Selfridges' urban retreat marks a striking departure from the rural versions imagined by Forster and James and built by Lutyens, Cadbury, and Lever. While most of the models considered in the first chapters set the "authentic" life outside the city—or in a newly imagined Garden City—Gordon Selfridge brought his retreat into the heart of London, directly into an urban, commercial bustle normally considered antithetical to notions of rural serenity or nostalgic authenticity. The rural models were defined largely by their differences from dirty and crowded cities, but Selfridges worked to break down this spatial distinction, drawing, as we will see, equally on images of both country and city life. The store created, in effect, a version of Howard's "third magnet" that combined the best of the country and the best of the city. At Selfridges, however, such a combination did not require a residence in a Garden City; it simply required a trip across town to the massive store at Oxford Street.

Packaging the Authentic

Selfridges transformed the commercial landscape of London both in the unique physical space of the store itself and through an extraordinary marketing campaign. The Selfridges building represented an entirely new trend for London in department store design. Most of the larger stores at the time had started as small conglomerations of shops; even Harrods had flats above its store.[6] Selfridges was one of the first commercial enterprises in England to be built on a large scale, with the whole store designated for one purpose from the beginning. As such, the building could present a concentrated and integrated design. The various architectural elements of the exterior and the large open spaces of the interior created a new showplace that, despite its newness, encompassed quite classical elements. Selfridges represented a physical modernity, a three-dimensional experience in different styles. More than simply an example of modern and traditional elements blended together, Selfridges was a new space, one whose modernity in fact encompassed its play with traditional elements.

A detailed article in the *Times* of 1909, part of a series titled "London Street Architecture," offers an excellent tour of the Selfridges building, as well as a contemporary reaction to its design.[7] The writer's comments address not simply the store itself but also larger questions about what modern architecture and interiors should be. The article begins by citing a central problem with the design of modern stores: "How to invest the front of a building, which is to consist as far as possible of plate glass, with the appearance, as well as the reality, of stability?" Much to the author's dismay, most modern stores reflected a terrible blending of styles, "where a solid-looking brick or stone building rests to all appearance on one story, or even two, composed merely of sheets of plate glass." Selfridges addressed these problems, for "while the proportion of voids to solids is reasonably distributed, and the building itself offers every evidence of solidity, yet its walls are practically of glass." To achieve this effect, the builders used a combination of steel and concrete but clad the steel supports in white Portland stone, leaving "sufficient bulk to satisfy the eye; yet they leave an immense area on the front for glass" (figure 4.1).

Fig. 4.1 Selfridges building, c. 1910
From *HAT-PIC*, SEL Postcard Collection. Reproduced with kind permission from the Selfridges Archive held at the History of Advertising Trust (www.hatads.org.uk).

The effect was a modern building that nevertheless took many design elements from older models of architecture. In part, the building was an amalgamation of classical details. Mammoth Ionic columns rose at even intervals, and the *Times* article commented that it had been inspired by "the old Custom-house at Rome." *Architectural Design and Construction* called it " 'the most imperial building in London.' "[8] Alongside these classical features, however, the exterior was also strikingly modern, with the largest shop windows in the world appearing in between the columns. Behind all this new glass was a series of new spaces, innovative showcases heralding a revolution in window displays that I discuss in greater detail in the next chapter. Surrounded by classical details, the shopper could nevertheless peer into a new world. As another commentator noted, the building represented "the best construction of enlightened modernity and the finest architecture of history."[9]

The layout of the interior space was also distinctly innovative. As the *Times* writer observed, "A shop in London is usually divided into a number of compartments, each walled off from the rest." While fire regulations required some intervening walls, at Selfridges the interior was kept as open as possible, a design that was the very antithesis of the small, dark, and cramped Victorian store:

> The cross-walls have been reduced to the minimum that the law allows, with the maximum of wide openings, arranged to give the longest obtainable vistas in every direction; and all showcases are kept low, so as to allow as wide a view as possible within these limits. The building is amply provided with light on three sides, and there are in addition two open wells for light, with skylights over, within the building itself. The decorations are very simple and practically uniform through all the various departments, and all walls and ceilings are painted white.

This interior was part of a new trend in architecture, and in fact a new trend in the very way space was imagined and configured. As Stephen Kern observes in *The Culture of Time and Space*, new technical innovations such as the use of steel and glass allowed for a much more open structure. The openness of the Selfridges interior anticipates work by architects such as Frank Lloyd Wright, whose "first objective was to reduce the number of . . . separate parts and make a unified space so that light, air, and vistas permeated the whole" (Kern, 187). Distinctions between rooms, and between interior and exterior space, were to be broken down as much as possible.

Selfridges' architectural amalgamation of the modern and the traditional does not indicate a muddled approach but a calculated strategy. What the material space of the store offered shoppers was intriguing: a modern space open enough both physically and metaphorically to allow a range of possible models, models that would include nostalgic appeals to the domestic home, the comfortable familiarity of classical references, and the suggestion of a refined, high-class aesthetic. The modernity was constituted, rather than contradicted, by appeals to authenticity and lay as much in the customers' ability to move among the different commercial appeals as it did in the open, airy interior.

Selfridges launched a campaign to define these open spaces before its customers had even been inside the store. The initial flood of print advertisements to announce the store's opening was unprecedented. Gordon Selfridge hired thirty-eight of the most popular illustrators in London, headed by Sir Bernard Partridge from *Punch*, and commissioned them to create more than a hundred full-page advertisements for eighteen different newspapers, along with half- and quarter-page advertisements. He spent an unparalleled 36,000 pounds to promote his new store before opening day, setting a new standard for London retailers.[10] Using print advertising and a careful series of constructed displays, Selfridges worked to distance its goods from the alleged taint of commerce, promising its "guests" an interchangeable set of lived environments, all with constructed ties to authentic spaces traditionally distinct from retail ventures. Selfridges perfected the nostalgic version of the commodified authentic by presenting the store both as an intimate domestic home and as a village that relied on cottage industry production. Alternatively, Selfridges also developed the originary and aesthetic models of the commodified authentic, insisting that the store was both an established institution and a kind of high-class museum or art gallery, existing solely to provide a one-of-a-kind atmosphere for its guests. Infusing all these environments, however, was the constant refrain that the goods were easy to purchase, plentiful, and available to all; the customers could choose their degree of interaction. Selfridges did not seek to abolish the distinction between a low, commercialized commerce and a high, noncommercial one, or to erase the line between "authentic" goods and mass-marketed ones; the store merely made each side of these distinctions more readily available to a wider audience. By giving customers the chance both to unsettle and reinscribe traditional dichotomies, Selfridges gave shoppers a chance to enjoy both the distinctions and the pleasures of transcending them.[11] These different lived environments had important class and gender implications, for shoppers could select authentic associations that had previously been unavailable to most people, turning authenticity into something fungible and controllable. Selfridges thus worked to move commerce from its tainted position as contaminated "other" into the very heart of British culture. As one advertisement declared, Selfridges was ready to "enter into and take its place in the life of the whole of London, indeed, the United Kingdom, and in its own time of the whole British Empire."[12]

The strategy of Selfridges' advertising campaign can be explored by examining the way it shifted—at least temporarily—commercial space in two very different newspapers, the *Times* and the *Daily Mail*. These papers appealed to two distinct sets of readers and associations, with the *Times* occupying the role of a venerable, established institution and the newly launched *Daily Mail* appearing as a more popular alternative. Selfridges' management carefully studied the readership and demographics of these and other papers, as a document left in Gordon Selfridge's early materials on the store's launch suggests. The *Times* is listed as the most expensive paper, at three pence, with an "upper middle and upper class" readership of about 60,000. By contrast, the *Daily Mail* sold for one-half pence to readers of the "middle and upper middle and lower middle" class, enjoying a circulation of over 900,000.[13] Selfridges' advertisements differed depending on the paper in which they appeared, with these two papers representing the most obvious contrast. On the whole, the *Times* ads tended to be more dignified and less focused on prices, while the *Daily Mail* ads spent more time emphasizing prices and value, as well as the novelty and cutting-edge quality of the products. While Selfridges carefully targeted its advertisements by adjusting its strategy to its audience, intriguingly, even in these distinct papers, it also worked to a common end: to elevate commerce and to blur the line between commerce and the news. In each paper—to different degrees—Selfridges united a sense of fashion and quantity, refinement and accessibility. I draw deliberately on advertisements from both of these papers, exploring the differences between them, but more often exploring the intriguing combination Selfridges offered to readers of all papers.

Authentic Environments I: The Village in the City

The print advertising and the store's policies repeatedly presented Selfridges as a country village in the heart of London, a gathering place for people motivated by more than economic ties. Cadbury and Lever had constructed a nostalgic recreation of past village life in the country, and Gordon Selfridge relied in part on these models, as articles concerning both Bournville and Port Sunlight can be found in the materials he collected as he plotted the store's launch and development.[14] Selfridges, however, was not simply going to move the village into the city; it further promised to produce a country haven in the consumers' own urban homes. Gordon Selfridge first worked to form his staff into a self-sufficient community similar to the model towns, announcing at a staff meeting that the goal was "'not merely to provide the goods of civilization. It is to *be* civilization'" (quoted in Pound, 213). Selfridges provided an urban response to Masterman's lament that "'A village which once fed, clothed, policed, and regulated itself cannot . . . act its own dramas, build its own church, or organize its own work and play.'"[15] Selfridges' staff formed its own community groups, including a popular drama league and athletic clubs. Like small villages across England, Selfridges' employees organized support efforts during World War I: a group of men formed a "House Corps" and actually drilled on the roof and practiced musketry, and employees created the "Selfridges Red Cross Detachment" that met wounded soldiers at the train stations. By almost all accounts, the early employees at Selfridges were well treated, enjoying benefits similar to those found in the model towns, including good wages, opportunities for promotion, pension plans, and a wide array of classes.

At Selfridges, however, the village community atmosphere was not produced mainly for the benefit of the workers; the customer was actively invited to enjoy the sense of village life. Gordon Selfridge himself insisted that the store was a community center, not a shop, declaring, "'My object was to make Selfridges a civic center where friends could meet and where buying was only a secondary consideration'" (quoted in Pound, 254). Selfridges wrapped a sense of absolute novelty in an old-fashioned package. As one early visitor remarked, "Selfridge's is a little world unto itself, and if a visitor falters for a second, he or she is immediately approached by an attendant armed with plans. It is all very wonderful, but all very simple. One might stay a whole day in this new emporium and yet keep in close touch with acquaintances."[16] Another visitor compared shopping at Selfridges to shopping in an old market town, where "soft-carpeted avenues and by-streets of stalls, stands, and counters" might be considered "without anyone suggesting that she makes a purchase."[17] Like a new and improved town elder, the information desk advertised that it could answer any reasonable question on any topic. In 1929, Selfridges even added a traditional country garden on the roof of the store, where the vegetables prepared in the restaurant were grown. The generalized, sentimentalized village aura promised a close-knit community atmosphere, farm fresh produce, and quaint old shopping markets, all in a luxurious urban setting.

The goods themselves were also at times presented as part of an older economic model, available in mass quantities, perhaps, yet still produced in an old-fashioned cottage industry style. An early advertising strategy for Selfridges cast a misty glow over the production process and implied that the goods were made not in factories but the old fashioned way, in small cottage industries that transferred purification to the product and eventually to the buyer. Such a strategy paralleled the home industry section of the Ideal Home Exhibition yet made the goods immediately and easily available to buyers. The cottage industry sales pitch is especially striking in Selfridges' series of article-advertisements that appeared in the *Times* in the weeks before the store opened.[18] These advertisements had the same column format as the news, except the type was spaced slightly farther apart. By mimicking the paper's news stories, the layout emphasizes the continuity between the established and less obviously commercial news of the *Times* and the new news about Selfridges. In one "article," the writer relates "How Selfridge's Gathers Its Goods from All Parts of the World." On romantic journeys, buyers scour the globe, looking for distinctive, original articles, made at home or in cottage industries. The advertisement decries the mass-produced nature of most goods, made by machines churning out identical finished products. This "painful uniformity," however, has been addressed by avid Selfridges buyers; forever "In Search of the Original," they seek goods that "strike a distinctive and individual note." To this end, the buyers try to find the original makers of articles, going "literally off the high road of commerce to penetrate into little known villages, and sequestered districts where manufactures are still carried on in a simple human way by men and women whose workshop is their home and who themselves are artists in their craft rather than artisans." According to the advertisement, peasants in places such as Japan, Germany, and even Britain are still making goods using time-honored methods; crucially, such goods maintain their aura of distinctiveness even when they have left their surroundings. The Japanese articles obtained by the buyers, for example, are "possessed of that touch of personality which the Japanese craftsman loves to put into his work. . . . His work thus embodies his own personality and has a distinction and interest of its own as against the turning out of exact patterns of goods by machinery or in large quantities." Selfridges' shoppers can, as it were, buy this authenticity, located in vague references to peasants, the countryside, home industry, and timeless traditions, and set against the impersonal forces of mechanization, industry, and mass-produced objects. Like Shaw's depiction of a commercialized Irish authenticity, here we see the strategy applied to the authentic "Japanese craftsman," whose allegedly primitive culture brings the customer a suggestion both of the past and of the exotic other. The nostalgic authentic promises that a connection to a village tradition will adhere to an object. These objects are made in the home, by an individual, who creates a commodity that "embodies his own personality" in its very distinctiveness. The goods stand metonymically for the authenticity located in the production process and in the villages themselves, and such objects brought to Selfridges, the advertisement implies, not only can bestow on the store this sense of distinctiveness but can in turn bestow on the shopper's home the sense of authenticity originally located in the village.

By simultaneously advancing and erasing production, Selfridges sought to sell the very kind of authenticity that many saw as antithetical to London's commercial district. The buyer could (allegedly) shop in a capitalist market without taint and could return, with carefully selected purchases, to an earlier mythic past located in an imagined preindustrial world.[19]

Selfridges even introduced the production process directly to his customers, bringing not just the goods but the craftsman himself into the store. In the early years, the store annually offered elaborate exhibitions of "Old-time Industry." On every floor, customers could observe skilled craftsmen actually making the products for sale, an approach that would have been more familiar at an exhibition such as the Ideal Home show than at a department store. A Turkish craftsman wove Oriental rugs, Flemish lace makers in traditional costumes made Brussels lace, and an elderly Scotch crofter sat at an "old time loom" while a "Robust Yorkshire girl" worked on a loom making cashmere. Selfridges, as one commentator remarked, was "just now not only a vast emporium for the disposal of goods, but an instructive workshop affording a striking display of craftsmanship and real artistic skill."[20] Customers could buy every kind of product, and they could also observe (the store promised) authentic production.

Evoking an idealized production process would have been familiar to London shoppers. Selfridges drew on traditions such as the Arts and Crafts Movement, for William Morris, along with a host of precursors and followers, had imagined a similar model of production. Morris, who exposed the actual working conditions of the "peasants" whom Selfridges mythologized, praised the many virtues of carefully crafted goods.[21] What marked Selfridges as a departure, however, was how the store borrowed these "refined" models of commerce, usually by definition separate from the mass market, and deployed them in a structured, mass-market campaign. Such a strategy certainly served an ideological function by hiding the bleak conditions that likely went into producing these goods; as one article heading notes, the Selfridges' buyers "ransack the world" for the products.[22] The strategy also served an intriguing cultural function, however, promising to address the emerging disdain for mass-market production.

By gesturing toward nostalgic models of the country village, Selfridges redefined the commercial landscape by using nonmarket models and at the same time suggested to its guests that they might literally and figuratively buy into such a model. The customer might visit this idyllic town in the position of feudal lord, gather the goods desired before retreating home, and yet avoid any of the guilt or responsibility that might have attached itself to such a position. Alternatively—or simultaneously—the shopper could participate as a valued member of the community, equal to any within the town and invited to share in its bounty, but without the labor such a position might once have required.

Authentic Environments II: The Domestic Home

Not only was Selfridges to be a model town; it was also linked to that perennial icon of noncommercial ties, the private home. Visitors were given small silver keys on opening day, with the wish that they would feel "at home" in Selfridges, while the staff endeavored "in every way imaginable to create and cherish that comfortable sentiment."[23] At the top of the store, elaborate and luxurious rooms of rest awaited the guest: reception rooms, a library, the Silence Room, and the Retiring Room, each with special attendants ready to serve the visitors. Several rooms offered free use of phones and were stocked with paper and writing utensils available at no charge. There were even special rooms for different European guests, decorated in the decor of the visitors' home country and staffed by native speakers so "visitors to town can find themselves a welcome and at home."[24] In this area of the store, material transactions disappeared; the rooms were free and open to all, and no tips of any kind were required or allowed. Just a brief step away, a luncheon hall and a tea garden provided food "in a dainty, home-like fashion."[25] Of course, Selfridges did not re-create the home but presented a vision of a new and improved home, one that had the markers of comforting familiarity yet promised to improve on the reality. As Gordon Selfridge said, his female customers came to the store " 'because it's so much brighter than their homes' " (quoted in Pound, 107). The implication, of course, was that the smart shopper might select goods that would bring the store's atmosphere into the visitor's own residence.

The use of this domestic version of the commodified authentic had two important implications for female customers. First, Selfridges united competing versions of the modern woman. As Rita Felski argues in *The Gender of Modernity*, women at the turn of the century were on the one hand associated with a nostalgic vision of a primitive, preindustrial world separate by definition from the bustling and commercial public sphere. On the other hand, however, a competing vision of women began to emerge in the form of the voracious consumer, caught up in the frenzy of spending.[26] Selfridges deftly combined these images and erased both the contradictions and any negative associations. The careful female shopper at Selfridges could, in effect, remain within the private sphere of the home, surrounded by a domestic atmosphere and homemade products. At the same time, she could still shop, becoming not a mad consumer but a discriminating purchaser, selecting goods that would in turn bring her home closer to the Selfridges model. The woman shopper could also perform the commodified authentic herself, becoming new and fashionable at the same time that she remained (allegedly) noncommercial and thus uncontaminated by trade.

Second, Selfridges offered female shoppers the chance to experience the home from the male perspective. Women might enjoy the Silence Room, the carefully arranged and decorated interior, the sense of service and security—in short, all the classic images of home—but not have to produce the ideal themselves, at least not while they were in the store. This opportunity echoed the exclusive male clubs in London, providing all the amenities of home minus the spouse and children. Selfridges gave women shoppers the chance to sit within the picture of comfort without obligation. As Selfridges understood, misty visions of home derive much of their power from the viewer's lack of responsibility for the scene itself. Adults may be nostalgic for a childhood home, both men and women may be nostalgic for homes they never had, but the fantasy is to be within the scene, the beneficiary of the maternal, homelike comfort, but not to create the comfort oneself. Selfridges allowed women a rare chance to "Feel at Home" without actually having to maintain the home. The modern woman could enjoy the privileges of the modern man.

Authentic Environments III: Cultural Refinement at Selfridges

Selfridges perfected not only a nostalgic form of the commodified authentic but the originary and aesthetic forms as well, casting itself as a venerable, established institution that might serve as a model for later imitations. From the classical design of the building, to the classical and Renaissance motifs in the advertisements, to essays comparing commerce to the "respected professions," Selfridges worked to bring commerce and commodities into a familiar and above all established setting for its shoppers, making the store and its goods seem genuine and somehow above the marketplace. Selfridges sought to change the public perception of trade as a low, almost shameful profession to one with a long and proud tradition. Likewise, shoppers were recast from materialistic consumers snatching up new and gaudy products to calm and dignified guests selecting choice items, and only incidentally and discreetly engaging in actual buying. The initial advertisements in 1909 repeatedly chastise the English public for thinking commerce was simply about making money, regarding business "as no more than a matter of money-getting, as a means only justified by its results."[27] As a second article-advertisement outlines, with headings such as "The Altruism of Business" and "An Institution—Not a Shop," business had "passed beyond that mere money-grubbing stage."[28] Selfridges, the advertisements implied, was there not so much to make a profit as to provide, altruistically, a service to the public, much as established professions such as medicine provided services to their clients.

The early advertisements frequently used generic references to tradition, deploying an amalgamation of ancient, classical, Renaissance, biblical, and even selected Victorian motifs to create a general sense of dignity.[29] Advertisements were often full of columns, stone facades, and men and women dressed either in classical robes or in Renaissance costume. Consider, for example, one of the early advertisements that appeared in the *Times* and many other papers (figure 4.2).[30] The reader sees two kneeling figures, each holding up a corner of Selfridges department store. The two figures, a man and a woman, are endowed with archetypal classical imagery: They are dressed in flowing robes that fall off the shoulder, the man wears a military helmet, and they sit between two Corinthian columns holding up a large stone arch. An idyllic country scene lies between them, and up above the clouds they hold a miniature replica of Selfridges. Unconcerned with the building, they

Fig. 4.2
Selfridges' advertisement, "Confidence and Integrity," 1909
From *HAT-Early*. Reproduced with kind permission from the Selfridges Archive held at the History of Advertising Trust (www.hatads.org.uk).

stare down at a naked child who holds a bunch of grapes and whose line of sight seems to be toward the store. With its classical figures and its "great principles" set in type that suggests the letters are carved into stone, the advertisement works to unite Selfridges with a range of established markers. As if to insist that the underlying motive behind this elaborate picture is not profit, the advertisement declares that the underlying body of the business is "confidence" and "integrity."

Selfridges did not limit this high-class style to papers such as the venerable *Times* but also used such techniques in less expensive newspapers like the *Daily Mail*. Though the opening advertisements in all the papers relied frequently on generic references to venerable traditions, their similar techniques would nevertheless have had different implications for different readers. To the generally higher class readers of the *Times*, Selfridges offered continuity, hinting that commerce, and even a large department store on Oxford Street, might be continuous with their own style (and the "carriage trade" were assured of their own private entrance on Duke Street). To the more middle-class readers of the *Daily Mail*, the advertisements subtly implied an elevation, a promise to provide an exclusive style of shopping but at prices that were nevertheless within reach. Despite pulling in titled visitors for various publicity events, however, Selfridges drew most of its customers from the middle class, including both the upper and lower ends of this group. As cultural theorist Pierre Bourdieu might point out, appeals aimed at an elite consumer were in effect appeals to a middle-class population desiring "cultural capital"—and such appeals in turn ensured the upper classes would continue to favor the more exclusive wares on Bond Street.[31]

By using classical motifs to sell commodities, Selfridges was in part drawing on a long tradition in advertising. As Robert Opie outlines in *Rule Britannia: Trading on the British Image*, the figure of Britannia had been invoked since the eighteenth century to link goods to ideals of antiquity and the strength of the British Empire. Selfridges' difference lies in how these classical motifs were used not to sell one product, or a product already associated with governmental institutions, but to sell a range of products and to sell the image of a store itself. Gordon Selfridge sought to associate his store with so many establishment markers that its newness would no longer be a liability. Shoppers could find what was new and fashionable, the advertisements implied, and yet never leave the comforting and secure paradigms of the British Empire, the British government, and a range of classical icons.[32]

Such advertising techniques represented a marked departure for London stores. For comparison's sake, consider the Selfridges' advertisement alongside another ad that appeared the same month, one from the *Times* run by Debenham & Freebody (figure 4.3). The *Times* advertisement, typical of those used both by

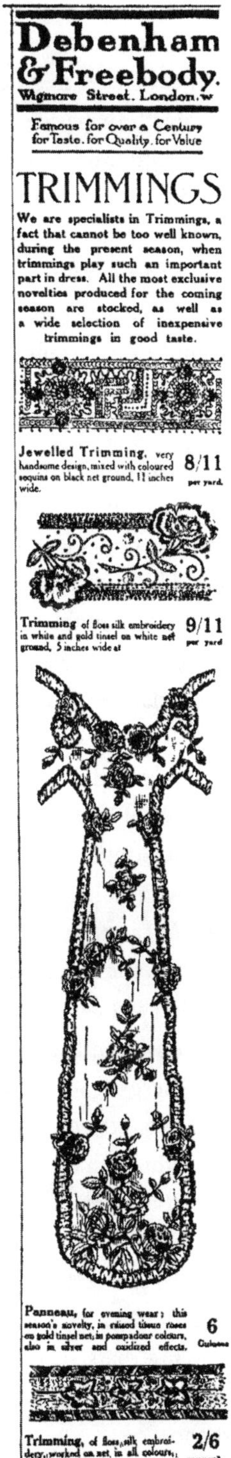

Fig. 4.3
Debenham & Freebody advertisement, "Trimmings," 1909
From *Times*, 22 March 1909, 13.

Debenham & Freebody and other stores at the time, promotes trimmings and reproduces several selections of different styles. Prices are clearly marked in bold numbers, and each article has a short description just underneath or beside it. Advertisements in other papers like the *Daily Mail* were similar in terms of layout, though they often advertised a different class of commodity. The emphasis in such advertisements is on the specific articles that are for sale and the price for which the reader can obtain them; no attempt is made to hide ideas of selling or to make any claims about the mission or character of the store.[33] Selfridges made a clear departure from such advertising, working both to manufacture a refined environment around the store itself and to educate its customers in the new possibilities of commerce.[34]

In addition to classical and Renaissance references, Selfridges also presented the objects for sale as works of art and the store itself as a kind of museum showcase. "'A store,'" declared Gordon Selfridge, "'should be as fine a thing and, in its own way, as ennobling a thing as . . . a museum'" (quoted in Pound, 153). Observers constantly compared Selfridges to a museum or art gallery; as the *Star* noted, Selfridges had a "great classic museum-like building," and the *Daily Express* declared Selfridges was like a "museum or gallery of art." The *Standard* claimed that the opening of Selfridges had turned shopping into "a fine art."[35] Selfridges in fact boasted an actual art gallery on the third floor, and the store presented frequent exhibitions. The advertisement for "Famous Teco Ware" is typical of attempts to bathe not simply the store but also specific commodities in an artistic atmosphere, blending a Morris-like attachment to the handcrafted item with a high-class aesthetic purity (figure 4.4). The ad offers a contrast for the reader between the cluttered, hard-to-read news and the three refined pottery pieces in the advertisements. Teco, declares the copy, is the refinement of Art in Pottery. It cannot be described adequately, but the reader is assured that every piece is dignified and unique, "an embodiment of the genius of a well-known artist." These are works of art in the age of mechanical reproduction, representing not copies but the original objects from which lesser imitations (for sale at lesser stores) might be made. The Selfridges shopper can obtain objects that, in effect, predate any commercial "contamination." The goods are surrounded with the language of art rather than the language of commerce; while this of course remains a commercial strategy familiar to modern readers, it was a new trend for British advertisers. In 1925, Selfridges even extended its established, commercial-free look by removing the sign with the store's name from the front of the building. "'This famous store,'" declared the stationery, "'needs no name on the door'" (quoted in Pound, 190).[36]

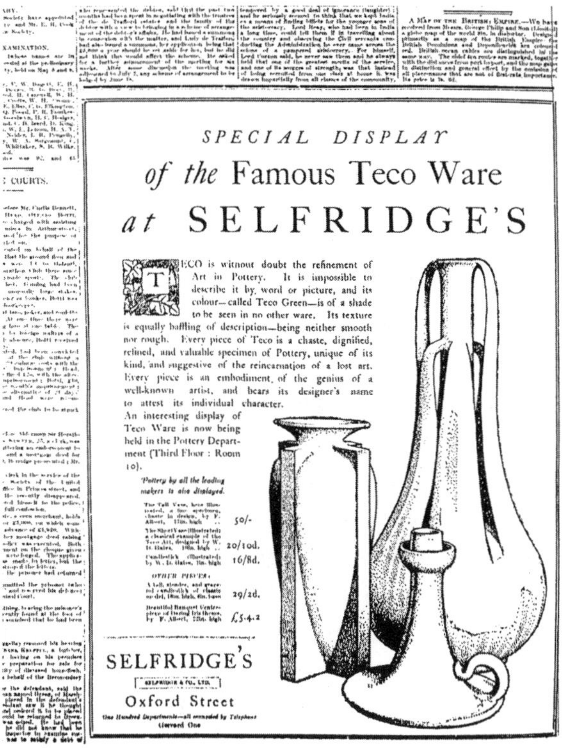

Fig. 4.4
Selfridges' advertisement, "Famous Teco Ware," 1909
From *Times*, 22 May 1909, 4. Reproduced with kind permission from the Selfridges Archive held at the History of Advertising Trust (www.hatads.org.uk).

The authentic environments that Selfridges constructed not only worked to infuse commerce and the mass market into traditionally noncommercial places such as the village, the domestic home, and the museum but also promised to improve on these environments by making them easily accessible to the harried London shopper, and to make aspects of these atmospheres available for purchase. As Gordon Selfridge understood, marketing could do more than advertise a particular commodity; it could promote—and provide—an entire environment. The customer, in turn, was promised access and control, and was trained to recognize the possibilities for reinvention.

Authentic Novelty: An Education in Shopping

Alongside all these efforts to present the goods in environments purified of commercial "contamination," the store simultaneously evoked a more typical mass-market narrative: the goods were plentiful, they were readily available, and they were sold at prices accessible to most buyers. Within the same article-advertisement that claims the goods at Selfridges were made in cottage industries, the writer declares: "Selfridges' will sell nearly everything that any man, woman, or child may require or desire from the day of birth and throughout life—clothes, hats, boots, jewellery, stationery, toys, games, musical instruments, sport requisites, cutlery, glass, china, carpets—but not heavy furniture—household equipments, ornaments, embroideries, pictures, engravings, &c."[37] The store would be a veritable cornucopia of the latest goods. In a similar move, another large advertisement listed Selfridges' many departments, and just a sampling of the goods available in each. The very size of the full-page advertisement suggested the store's vastness, the sheer number of goods that would fit under one roof.[38] The tagline that frequently appeared in the early advertisements, "London's lowest prices—always," further emphasized ready availability. Shoppers might take pleasure in the goods' uniqueness but might simultaneously take pleasure in the goods' abundance.

This cheerful paradox between unique and available goods paralleled the simultaneous move to hide the monetary transaction while acknowledging it. These contradictions may be seen in a long advertisement that presents the script of a short play for the readers. The play takes place in the "Morning-room of Mr. Carew's little house in Mayfair." Mr. and Mrs. Carew have just returned from the Continent to find that their house has been burglarized; with their possessions went all their markers of taste and class. Facing a dinner party that night, the couple is in despair, since their traders are scattered all over town and they could not possibly be reached in time. Turning over a newspaper, Mr. Carew spies an advertisement for Selfridges, and they quickly telephone in an order. Mrs. Carew selects a houseful of goods, all the "best quality," including china, glasses, a clock, and a variety of fruits and flowers. Mrs. Carew dismisses her husband's concern over prices, telling him that "we're getting the best bargain of our lives." The Selfridges assistant assures her that the vases, for example, are "the same things that one buys in the antiquity shops at fancy prices" and that the candle shades are "unique."

The play highlights low prices and gives a clear indication that a whole houseful of goods might be bought at a moment's notice for the specific purpose of constructing the illusion of stable taste and class that the Carews will need for their visitors. The act of buying is at once effaced and foregrounded: the goods are unique aesthetic objects purified of the suggestion that they were ever actually bought, and yet this aura may be purchased with a simple phone call.

Readers are in fact given a performance of how they might perform the Carews' trick. This Janus-faced approach is notable for how readily it changes direction. The very dexterity that Selfridges allows in presenting the latest old goods and the genuine reproduction reflects an irreverent blend of high and low styles; the chance to smooth the gap between different values, and still be free to reinforce this gap, is part of what is so effectively sold.[39] Selfridges may offer commerce in a noncommercial guise—but at the same time it happily exposes this guise not simply as a shopkeeper's trick but as a powerful strategy to possess goods that are both authentic and up-to-date, untainted by commerce and still readily available.

Selfridges' use of the commodified authentic to sell its goods had clear class implications for London shoppers. Selfridges appealed to a rapidly rising middle class and contributed to the emergence of the "middlebrow" culture. As Lawrence Rainey has observed, the term middlebrow actually comes into existence around this time, with its first recorded use in 1904 (3). Middle-class shoppers were offered all the exclusivity implied by the high-class stores on Bond Street, but without the high price tags and snobbish disdain for the nonelite customer that was found there; they were also promised all the spectacle and pleasures of the Oxford Street emporiums, without the negative associations of cheap goods and frenzied shopping. Selfridges' version of the commodified authentic in fact united what appeared to be two contradictory models and made these models available at middle-class prices. The Selfridges shopper might obtain—as the Carews did—a houseful of apparently old stuff, saturated with an instant familiarity that intrinsically promised an erasure of monetary exchange. Such an erasure was usually considered a special purview of high-class dwellings, embodied in the country house or the old urban residences, places where the purchases were made so long ago as to purify them of commercial stain. The commodified authentic, however, cheerfully pricked the sacred bubble surrounding such established places, not only exposing them as constructed environments that were commercial in origin but in the same breath offering this tantalizing high-class erasure to the middle-class shopper. The authentic was of course manufactured, but with the potentially egalitarian result of making high-class models more universally available. Selfridges captured the understandable longing to possess authentic goods—and laid bare the reality that these must be purchased like anything else.

Selfridges' suggestive re-creations of noncommercial environments, and the class and gender mobility such re-creations promised, were literally represented in the store's interior, and a shopper could experience an intriguing geographic hierarchy of monetary associations by simply walking through the store. A shopper might begin in the bargain basement, the lowest floor accessible to the public, where an enormous mass of goods were jumbled together and where low prices were the central theme. She could travel upward to the more exclusive floors, visiting departments where goods were tastefully arranged and price tags were available but not obvious. As the efficient lift whisked her to higher floors, and the carpets became thicker and more luxurious,[40] she could relax in the elegantly decorated lounging rooms, where she might write a letter, read a book, or simply rest. She might enjoy a home-cooked meal in one of the restaurants or, continuing to the roof, simply sit in an English country garden. The farther up she went in the building, the farther away she moved from actual material transactions, where money was exchanged for specific objects. The shopper could, in effect, choose the environment in which she shopped, and by extension select the class and even gender associations she wished to perform. Within the store, the identity of both class and gender might be created and maintained within objects and also elided by their ready exchange within an expanding market of seemingly infinite goods. This sort of mobility was not necessarily liberating, but neither was it necessarily a sinister manipulation. Selfridges presented a new commercial landscape for London, one that used the purity implied in nostalgic laments or markers of high-class taste—a purity usually invoked to place commercialism in the role of contaminated other—as central to a new definition of commerce.

Selfridges' Influence

Selfridges' early marketing strategy was hailed as a revolution. One critic writing for the *Civilian* declared the campaign "a great advance on the methods of advertising," bringing "the highest ideals of art worked out most perfectly by artists of the highest reputation." The *Daily Chronicle* cited the "real genius in the science and art of advertising," and the *Draper* declared the ads constituted an "epoch-making form of publicity."[41] Even commentators who criticized the advertisements, calling the copy "florid" and "high-falutin' nonsense," admitted that Selfridges' campaign marked a distinct shift in marketing.[42] While products and prices continued to dominate advertisements—and Selfridges often followed this model after its initial campaign was over—the campaign offered a clear example of advertising that emphasized an image or lifestyle rather than a particular product and that presented its commercial face through images of noncommercial purity. Selfridges was not the first advertiser to do this, but the store's campaign represented a pivotal moment in the trend.

The initial ads were widely imitated, as several reviewers were delighted to observe. The *Drapers Record* noted how Gimbel Brothers in America seemed to copy the Selfridges ads, relying on similar poses and courtly images and presenting a familiar combination of venerable newness, declaring that "even our novelties and departures are based on the teachings of many years." While some observers disapproved of such ad piracy, as one writer points out, "It is a magnificent tribute to [Selfridges] that their advertising matter has been recognized all over the world as so well worth stealing."[43]

Selfridges most clearly shifted the way other stores advertised in the *Times*. As a typical example, consider two advertisements for Harrods department store. The first, appearing in January 1909, just before Selfridges began its campaign, describes a sale at Harrods.[44] The goods are listed and described plainly, and the prices are clearly marked. No attempt is made to position what is for sale as anything but objects of good quality and value. Two months later, however, after the advertising for Selfridges had started to appear, the ads for Harrods change. In the *Times* of 3 March 1909, Harrods announced the celebration of its Diamond Jubilee, which not coincidentally started the day of Selfridges' opening. In this advertisement, we can find many of the techniques that Selfridges had introduced. Readers are nostalgically reminded that Harrods began as "a tiny Shop" and, at the end of the ad, are sentimentally assured that the old employees at Harrods will be "pensioned off to end their days in comfort." The invocation of the "Jubilee" would have immediately evoked for the London reader Queen Victoria's famous Jubilee, implying Harrods' connection to a "true" England and offering a subtle jab at the American-founded Selfridges. No prices are mentioned in the advertisement, only the beauty and comfort that Harrods' "friends" might enjoy. Grand afternoon concerts would be held in a "specially erected concert hall" with "celebrated operatic and concert artistes" performing every day. "Special fast trains" would whisk customers to the store. Fashion displays, "the most elaborate and artistic conception of its kind London has ever seen," with "each window comprising a distinct colour scheme," would be on view for all visitors. Harrods was not the only advertiser to follow suit. Advertisements for stores such as Dickins and Jones, Debenham & Freebody, and Peter Robinson also began to change their approach to follow the Selfridges model.[45]

The Man behind the Curtain: *Tono-Bungay* and the Tricks of Advertising

Many observers of the time were alarmed, however, at the new commercial strategies that were designed to sell the noncommercial, and the critical impulse to expose schemes like Selfridges' as bad-faith efforts to trick the public was irresistible. In one article on the store, Gordon Selfridge describes the "'harsh criticism'" sent to him from a Wakefield man, who would cut out the advertisements from the papers, "sending a note always with the same wording, 'What do you sell? What do you sell? Why don't you say what you sell in your advertisements?' "[46] *Punch* satirized both the "not for profit" line and the "artistic" advertisements in several cartoons, and other commentators mocked the notion that stores were not about buying and selling. As a critic in the *Bystander* wryly noted:

> Mr. Selfridge . . . in his gracefully worded advertisements, lays but little stress on the commercial side of his gigantic undertaking. We are to look upon Selfridges rather as a pleasant place for a quiet look round than as a mere store. We are to go there as connoisseurs contemplating a choice collection, not as seekers after bargains. Everything is to be done to make our visit pleasant for us, and should anybody desire to acquire any new possessions on a basis of payment, it is rumoured that even that will not be impossible in this remarkable establishment.[47]

The sophisticated irony of this writer reveals his careful understanding of the strategy; he will not be taken in by the noncommercial appearance, he hints, or by any idea that this is somehow not a shop with profit as its central motive.

Novelist H. G. Wells offered an extended version of this critique in his novel *Tono-Bungay* (1909). Published in book form the same year Selfridges opened, his work is an elaborate exposure of advertising in general and attempts to commodify authenticity in particular, presenting the dirty underside of any Great Good Place that marketing might evoke.[48] The main character moves from his early life as the son of a servant at an old country estate to being a business partner with his uncle, the inventor of "Tono-Bungay," an all-purpose tonic that would allegedly cure almost any ailment. The move at first suggests an evolution from the authentic to the inauthentic. At the start of the novel, the boy believes the country estate, Bladesover, represents an authentic England; as he relates, "There came a time when I realized that Bladesover House was not all it seemed, but when I was a little boy I took the place with the entirest faith as a complete authentic microcosm . . . of the whole world" (12). This early faith is gradually replaced by the narrator's growing realization that even Bladesover is a carefully created construct. He later relates that when he returned to Bladesover years later, to find it had been purchased by a wealthy financier, the place seemed shriveled. Fancy new journals and "English new books in gaudy catchpenny 'artistic' covers" had replaced the old brown books, and there were "abundant evidences that her ladyship was playing with the Keltic renascence," the one Shaw so brutally mocked (54).

As the narrator's uncle himself moves up the social scale, he turns from wanting a house full of new things to desiring expensive old ones. The narrator describes how this class of the newly wealthy evolves from "their first crude conception of dazzling suites of the newly perfect" to "a jackdaw dream of accumulating costly discrepant old things" (201). Like Forster's Mr. Wilcox, the narrator's uncle soon decides he needs an old estate in the country, complete with the old traditions. As he remarks, "I'm all for getting that good old English spirit back again. . . . Merrymakings, lads and lasses dancing on the village green, Harvest home. Fairings. Yule log—all the rest of it" (208). Embodying Masterman's lament that wealthy conquerors wanted simply to appropriate rural traditions, the uncle seeks an idealized, easily commodified sense of the past. The narrator and his uncle later produce advertising campaigns for other firms, playing on various ideas of authenticity, creating a storied history for their client Moggs by writing "magazine articles telling of the quaint past of Moggs" and concocting "Moggsiana." For another firm, "we carried their origins back into the mists of antiquity" (174), a strategy that would have been familiar to Selfridges.

The narrator does wonder, however, whether these new industrialists are really changing anything, and whether the aristocrats at the Bladesovers were really any more authentic. "Perhaps," the narrator muses, "always possessions have been Booty, and never anywhere has there been such a thing as house and furnishings native and natural to women and men who made use of them" (203). The new inhabitants at Bladesover, after all, had not destroyed anything worth saving. As the narrator wryly remarks, "One felt that a smaller but more enterprising and intensely undignified variety of stupidity had replaced the large dullness of the old gentry, and that was all" (54). The idea of a stable, "authentic" term that was being covered or erased by commerce is exposed as itself a sham.

Wells ends his novel with the narrator on a barge, moving through London and out to sea. He passes first the "essential London" and the "original England" with its railway stations and warehouses and factories. Then he moves to Blackfriars and Saint Paul's, "the very figure of whatever fineness the old Anglican culture achieved," which has been forgotten and obscured by the steamships and barges and the telephone wires and the traffic. Finally, he reaches London Bridge, and "the old order is altogether dwarfed and swallowed up" and "the dear neat little sunlit ancient Tower of London lying away in a gap among the warehouses . . . that little accumulation of buildings so provincially pleasant and dignified, overshadowed by the vulgarest, most typical exploit of modern England, the sham Gothic casings to the ironwork of the Tower Bridge" (315). Despite his discomfort with idealizing the old order, the narrator implies that the commercial spirit has infected London, the worst example being a sham reproduction of the Gothic, a mere copy of what Ruskin would have deemed the most authentic, spiritual architecture.

In the final moment of the novel, the narrator is caught in a modern dilemma. As the barge moves out to sea, he finds that the central note of the culture is one of "crumbling and confusion, of change and seemingly aimless swelling, of a bubbling up and medley of futile loves and sorrow" (316). Yet even amid these changes, he reserves something he sometimes calls "Science," sometimes "Truth": "But it is something we draw by pain and effort out of the heart of life, that we disentangle and make clear. Other men serve it, I know, in art, in literature, in social invention, and see it in a thousand different figures, under a hundred names. I see it always as austerity, as beauty. This thing we make clear is the heart of life. It is the one enduring thing" (317). Struggling between a sense that all is under siege, subject to change and disintegration, and the belief that there might after all be one thing that endures, the narrator returns to an idea of authenticity, a hope for a stable term that might be purified from the accretions that surround him.

. . .

Read together, James, Selfridges, and Wells reveal critical tensions at the heart of the commodified authentic. We might see the two writers as bringing to clarity two distinct responses to ventures such as Selfridges. Wells represents the unmasker, the critic who seeks to expose the man behind the curtain. The position links Wells to the Shaw of *John Bull's Other Island* and to the culture's general but pervasive fear that the commercial promise will simply leave us gripping a worthless bottle of Tono-Bungay. In James's story, George Dane represents an opposite position, one we might call the reveler. James explores not simply the power of the commodified authentic, as we found in Shaw's *Major Barbara* and in Forster's *Howards End*, but its promised and delivered sensual pleasures. The Great Good Place may be a constructed dream, but this only heightens Dane's delight. If all commercial promises could simply be reduced, as Wells implies in his novel, to trickery—and certainly many of them can—they would not have the power they do. As we saw with the model towns, commodified authenticity must be seen on a continuum, for as James understood, sometimes it delivers.

The brilliance of the commodified authentic as developed by Selfridges is that its pleasures in fact *demanded* that consumers understand the attitudes represented by both James and Wells. Naturally, consumers were invited to believe in the promises of authenticity Selfridges suggested, and as we have seen, visitors did in fact enjoy many of these pleasures, granting them powers often unavailable in their own homes. At the same time that consumers were invited to revel in authenticity, they also had to be adept at unmasking it, for unless they could see it as a construct, they would not, in turn, see it as a commodity. The commodified authentic inspired in consumers the conflicts described by Wells and James, and then promised to resolve them. Ironically, despite all of Wells's narrator's unveiling, it is precisely his final struggle between the sense of modern flux and the sense of "one enduring thing" that the commodified authentic was so adept at encompassing. Amid the sense of urban "crumbling and confusion, of change and seemingly endless swelling," Selfridges reflected a related but reversed image, one that simultaneously promised to turn flux and confusion into abundance, and the search for "one enduring thing" into an easily accessible authenticity. It was a true full-service store, offering both the authenticity and the critique exposing it, achieving the cultural equivalent of a vertical monopoly.[49]

5. "Lustrous behind Glass"

Woolf, Window Shopping, and Authentic Display

This chapter moves from the department store to the individual consumer gaze, examining how constructions of authentic displays became paradoxical sites of modern identity formation. Both in the deliberate productions of authentic spaces and especially in the emerging art of the window display, the consumer was invited to remain suspended between an illusion of authenticity and the appealing promise of easy transformation. Closely connected to strategies of advertising and store design, the new displays offered an iconic representation of a nostalgic, aesthetic, and originary authenticity. As such, they provided a kind of workshop for constructing the self. In these spaces, modern identity became a complex negotiation between the tantalizing allure of an authentic past and the compelling need to create an original, newly authentic self. The attempt to balance this paradox, rather than to resolve it, marked a quintessentially modern experience, one intrinsic to the growth of the commodified authentic and early twentieth-century consumer culture.

Two particular types of authentic display will be considered here: what I call the "tableau of the authentic dead," and the store window display. The tableau of the authentic dead was a carefully constructed arrangement of objects that memorialized a dead person. These displays usually presented the person's "things," the actual objects and clothing used by the deceased. Such displays could be found both in the domestic setting and in the home-based museums that paid homage to an illustrious former resident. There was an emphasis on the authenticity of the objects displayed, but also on the authenticity that the objects produced, suggesting a past moment preserved in the present. Such authenticity was both achingly close to the present-day observer, nestled as it was in a domestic setting, but also forever out of reach. While such tableaux were not technically commercial (though visitors were charged at home museums), they offer an early model of authentic display, one whose intriguing elusiveness would be echoed in the developing art of the display window, but with significant changes. One of the problems with the tableau of the authentic dead was its implication that a past moment—and a dead person—held the authentic, a quality that might be admired or revered in the present but not newly produced. For many living at the turn of the century, the Victorian age threatened to *become* this authentic moment, a past that gave the new century a feeling of belatedness. Commercial culture, however, promised to mend all this, uniting authenticity with accessibility and producing a usable past for the modern consumer.

The second type of authentic display, and the one with which the chapter is largely concerned, was the newly designed store window that began appearing in London in the early twentieth century. These arrangements echoed the tantalizing qualities of the tableaux but made their elusiveness adaptable and obtainable. Inspired in part by the changes introduced by Selfridges, the novel displays deliberately elided the commercial exchange, hiding price tags while emphasizing the enchanting, elegant atmosphere that the few tastefully arranged objects produced. Such displays often re-created an atmosphere of nostalgic, originary, or aesthetic authenticity, an authenticity that was reinforced by the suggestion that it was not for sale. At the same time, of course, consumers were invited to enter the store to obtain for themselves the window's glittering promise. This simultaneous embrace of authenticity and ready availability allowed consumers to sustain a useful contradiction, one that promised to deliver an authentic—and affordable—aura. In addition, consumers were offered parts of the past—aspects of the former tableaux—but aspects that they could select, manipulate, and make their own. A return to a past model could suddenly be a modern move, not so much in the artifact selected but in the *way* such an object was handled and circulated. The past was not to be frozen and worshiped, but to be fragmented, marketed, and incorporated into modern life.

I explore both types of displays through literal examples and through a literary one, Virginia Woolf's early work *Night and Day* (1919).[1] Woolf wrote her novel during World War I but set the story in 1910, the year after Selfridges' opening and the same year *Howards End* was published. Often considered a holdover from the nineteenth century, *Night and Day* in fact narrates the critical transition from the tableau of the authentic dead to a modern version of window shopping. In her younger characters' turn from the appeal of the Victorian tableau to the modern appeals of the urban street scene and its enticing displays, we can read Woolf's own transition from a nineteenth-century novelistic inheritance to more modernist subjects and styles; the transition itself, however, must also be read as modernist, as I will go on to analyze. The novel's shifts reflected not simply Woolf's own experience but the experience of many in her generation. Those coming of age in the early twentieth century had to balance a sense of Victorian authenticity with their own modern position. The novel describes this balance through the authentic tableau and new commercial-like spaces, both of which, in their overdetermined claims of authenticity, suggest the attraction of a venerable nineteenth-century tradition and the emerging attractions of more modern displays. Woolf repeatedly presents the longing for such spaces and objects by constructing stylized scenes of window shopping, where characters stand outside, gazing at a lighted window that promises elegance, authenticity, and romantic fulfillment. Though not typically read as such, the novel finally acts as a powerful narrative of the war, capturing through its later scenes of window shopping the overwhelming urge to preserve the prewar era as an oasis of nostalgic authenticity and security.

The novel's many vacillations between the past and the present have long led critics to ask whether *Night and Day* is essentially a Victorian novel or a nascent modernist one. Such a question implies that what we need to do to dismiss it or to reclaim it is to place the novel within one period or the other. Tainted by the nineteenth century, the novel sinks into anachronism; with hints of the twentieth century, it rises again to assume its rightful, though subordinate, place.[2] Yet this critical tug-of-war echoes the novel's own vexed commitments to both tradition and novelty. Struggling to place the novel in one period or the other misses the fact that the novel's contradictions *are* its modern elements.[3] *Night and Day* is deeply marked by its position on the edge of British modernism, and its struggle both to capture and to question authentic spaces anticipates characters such as Lily Briscoe in *To the Lighthouse*, who stares through the window at Mrs. Ramsay, longing at once to worship and to remake her. *Night and Day* in fact narrates the much larger cultural impulse simultaneously to enshrine and to dismantle various modes of authenticity, depicting the commodified authentic's paradigmatic scene of window shopping, with its complex intersections of desire, authenticity, and skepticism. If we consider *Night and Day* through, as Jennifer Wicke writes in another context, "the lens of consumption," it materializes as a (perhaps unwitting) commentary on modern consumerism, one that reveals the deeply entwined impulses for the authentic and the modern that were themselves part of new advertising techniques and new commercial spaces.[4]

Woolf's scenes of window shopping and authentic tableaux may be fruitfully considered alongside new methods of window displays just before and during World War I. Both the fictional and the actual displays became potent sites for commodified authenticity, sites that were commercial and yet erased signs of their commercialization. These readings and comparisons not only allow a new assessment of *Night and Day*—reclaiming it from charges of historical isolation from the war by showing how its evasions mirrored the culture's evasions—but also define an important transitional moment in the emergence of literary modernism. The window shopper who simultaneously longs to construct an authenticity that would defy its construction—and the commercial spaces that promised to satisfy such a paradoxical longing—offer a critical model for understanding some of the contradictions inherent to modernism, with its vexed commitments to both nostalgia and originality. *Night and Day* may lack literary modernism's more traditional features, such as a fragmented style, yet its very vacillations between an alluring past and the need to redefine and self-create a new future should be seen as an intrinsic part of modernism.

The Tableau of the Authentic Dead

When Ralph Denham first visits the home of Katharine Hilbery in *Night and Day*, Katharine solemnly grants him a tour of the family "relics," ushering him into a small sanctuary just off the main drawing room. The carefully crafted interior displays the personal effects of Katharine's grandfather, the famous nineteenth-century poet Richard Alardyce. In an impressive tableau, the great man's writing table, with an original manuscript still on it, is carefully preserved, along with his quill pen, his spectacles, and even his slippers. An image of nineteenth-century authenticity is produced, on display for the belated present generation. Replete with tastefully displayed "relics" (15), the room presents objects that seem to emit an incandescent aura, creating an aesthetically high atmosphere of calculated authenticity:

> As Katharine touched different spots, lights sprang here and there, and revealed a square mass of red-and-gold books, and then a long skirt in blue-and-white paint lustrous behind glass, and then a mahogany writing-table, with its orderly equipment, and finally, a picture above the table, to which special illumination was accorded. . . .
>
> Katharine waited as though for him to receive a full impression, and then she said: "This is his writing-table. He used this pen," and she lifted

> a quill pen and laid it down again. . . . There lay the gigantic gold-rimmed spectacles, ready to his hand, and beneath the table was a pair of large, worn slippers. . . . She paused for a minute, and then went on, as if these spaces had all been calculated. (15–16)

Set apart by lights that the relics almost seem to produce themselves, these objects taken together promise a richer existence. On the one hand, the scene seems strangely disembodied. What remains of the poet and his generation are a pen, books, a table. Even the portrait reflects only part of a figure. On the other hand, the relics seem tantalizingly close to the poet's actual existence—the slippers are worn, the spectacles lay ready; the scene suggests that he has merely stepped away from his desk for a moment. The poet's "effects" become synecdoches for the poet; together they almost seem to produce the man himself. More important, perhaps, they offer the effect of the poet, an ambiguous aura, combining a sense of "divine friendliness" (15) and his larger-than-life stature; even his everyday possessions now warrant special lights. The scene is arranged to suggest that all these relics might be enough, that objects could in fact hold some essential quality of the dead. Placed correctly, they promise to grant the observer part of the mystical glow itself, though the man and the illustrious past he represents also derive their power from their inaccessibility. The room is indeed calculated space, and Katharine delivers a calculated performance.

The idea that material objects could carry transcendent significance—that they could almost deliver immortality to the owner—had been a pervasive idea in the Victorian era. As we have seen, the rise of commodity culture in the second half of the nineteenth century gave the fetishized commodity unprecedented power. Thomas Richards describes how object-filled rooms could become "transcendent spaces of materiality."[5] The epitome of and even the partial inspiration for such spaces, he argues, might have been Queen Victoria's obsessive memorialization of her husband, Albert. In describing a famous picture of the "Blue Room" where Albert died, Richards notes how Albert's possessions take on overwhelming significance:

> Here the sentimental fascination with transcendence goes hand in hand with the sentimental fascination with the transcendental life of dead matter. The paraphernalia of death, however, do a lot more than preserve Albert's memory by objectifying it monumentally. . . . [S]uch paraphernalia construct an objectified site of contact with another realm. The Blue Room is not only a monument to Albert's memory but an altar to Albert's living presence as enshrined in things. Albert's material body may be dead, but his immaterial presence lives on in this tableau. (100)

Woolf herself, in one of her first published essays, writes about a similar space where a Victorian presence was captured through personal artifacts. She describes a "pilgrimage" to Haworth, the former home and now museum of the Brontës. Of all the things she sees, she is most struck by the preserved relics of Charlotte Brontë, which, much like the objects in the Hilberys' relic room, seem to raise the dead:

> Here are many autograph letters, pencil drawings, and other documents. But the most touching case—so touching that one hardly feels reverent in one's gaze—is that which contains the little personal relics, the dresses and shoes of the dead woman. The natural fate of such things is to die before the body that wore them, and because these, trifling and transient though they are, have survived, Charlotte Brontë the woman comes to life.[6]

Both Albert and Charlotte have been preserved through things, their ghostly presence both material and out of reach.

Similar effects are at work in the relic room of *Night and Day*. The poet is not just memorialized through the objects; his material possessions invoke the poet himself, his "living presence as enshrined in things." The room in *Night and Day*, however, is set in 1910, comfortably past the Victorian era. As such, Woolf's twentieth-century creation of the relic room goes beyond what Richards describes in Victoria's shrine to her husband. Woolf creates an evocative memorial to a poet, but also a memorial to the nineteenth century and its Victorian literary heritage. The illustrious past seems tantalizingly close to Katharine and her parents. Not only are the objects themselves relics, but the scene itself, with all its transcendent suggestion, becomes a relic as well. And these relics offer a heady promise: the poet and even the past might be available in the present through material objects, placed correctly within a room.

The tableau is, however, close to parody. At the same time that Woolf records the attraction, she displays and at least gently mocks the impulse to enshrine the precursor. As Katharine wryly remarks, "I think my grandfather must have been at least twice as large as any one is nowadays" (15). Woolf's own position was similar to Katharine's. She herself faced a daunting Victorian literary heritage, and *Night and Day*, with its marriage plot and linear narrative, is itself a kind of relic, a memorial to a past model that Woolf admires but will move beyond. Woolf depicts in the relic room not only the attraction of a seemingly authentic nineteenth-century tradition but also its dangers for the modern observer, as such attraction threatens to crowd out the present.

The relic room in *Night and Day* is not, of course, commercial space. It is, though, a telling example of reproduced authenticity, in this case, the authenticity of the nineteenth century in general and the Victorian artist in particular. It is authenticity once removed, carefully reconstructed to produce both nostalgic longing and a sense of the originary. Part of the room's allure is how established it seems; it is difficult for observers to imagine that the objects were ever purchased or were ever in a different location. The relic room seems above commodity culture, or, more specifically, before it—before an actual exchange of goods enters the equation. Woolf is careful to emphasize, however, that the space has been deliberately produced and that Katharine presents an orchestrated performance. Despite all the genuine articles, this is authenticity on—and as—display. The room reflects a familiar paradox with a new twist, presenting an authentic aura that suggests the nonconstructed at the same time that it acknowledges its constructed and performative quality—but an aura that is finally and in fact inaccessible. "Lustrous behind glass," the relics are close but out of reach, organized to sustain rather than to satisfy a longing for authenticity. It is this very allure that advertising would try to make accessible to buyers: buy a certain pen and receive not simply a writing implement but the very type of pen used by upper-class British poets, one that might mysteriously bestow aspects of the original owner on the new consumer.[7]

Woolf carefully delineates the dangers of becoming overly invested in this nineteenth-century tableau, presenting Katharine's mother, Mrs. Hilbery, Katharine, and Ralph as three different types of authenticity consumers. Mrs. Hilbery, for example, is a blindly enthusiastic lover of these objects, with a clear belief that authenticity may reside in things. For her, the relics hold enduring significance, becoming almost personified. "'Dear things!'" (22) she remarks, "'Dear chairs and tables! How like old friends they are—faithful, silent friends'" (22). She is the consummate buyer—and seller—of an authentic past, and when Ralph announces his departure, holding out his hand to say good-bye, she tries to persuade him to stay: "'But we've any number of things to show you!' Mrs. Hilbery exclaimed, taking no notice of [Ralph's hand]. 'Books, pictures, china, manuscripts . . .'" (21–22). She is sure that Ralph would merely have to sit in the relic room, and soon he would absorb the atmosphere and would "'write a poem of [his] own'" (22). Mrs. Hilbery fully trusts that the authentic aura is in fact authentic.

Katharine, however, is in effect a shopper who has bought too much. Like her mother, Katharine loves the relics and feels their profound significance, but this very significance threatens to overwhelm the present moment. Sitting in the small sanctuary after dutifully introducing Ralph to all the objects, she falls "for the thousandth time . . . into a pleasant dreamy state in which she seemed to be the companion of those giant men, of their own lineage, at any rate, and the insignificant present moment was put to shame" (16). Katharine believes the promise of the relic room. The objects, presided over by the benevolent gaze of her grandfather's portrait, appear to dwarf any living person or current action. Here, they seem to whisper, lies everything of any importance or significance. Katharine's job is to preserve the collection, getting portraits put under glass and cataloguing new manuscripts and letters that arrive at the house. Taken together, Katharine and her mother reflect a nostalgic worship of the nineteenth century, a stance that Woolf and other modernists would so vehemently reject.

At the opposite extreme of Mrs. Hilbery and Katharine, Ralph declares his modern sensibilities, insisting on his immunity from the appeal of the relic room's authenticity. The very image of the dissatisfied and exacting shopper, he looks over various objects with care, turning over the pages of the first edition "with great decision, as if he were judging the book in its entirety, the printing and paper and binding, as well as the poetry," then "examin[ing] the malacca cane with the gold knob" (18). He declares these objects are mere objects and de-idolizes them. Ralph would hate living among these things, he tells Katharine, which threaten to overshadow the present, for he delights in having no tradition. "'I hate great men,'" he informs Katharine. "'The worship of greatness in the nineteenth century seems to me to explain the worthlessness of that generation'" (20). He wants nothing that implies "'it's all been done for you'" (19). Harbinger of one brand of modernism, Ralph rejects the sense of a weighty, significant past, and indeed any sense of tradition or nostalgia.

The Emerging Art of Window Display

Ralph does not, however, wish to be immune from commodities, and he in fact presents shopping as an antidote to the relic room's authenticity, telling Katharine "almost savagely" that "'you'll never know the pleasure of buying things after saving up for them'" (19). Woolf reveals, though, that what Ralph wants to buy is intrinsically linked to authentic construction such as the relic room displays. As the novel unfolds, Ralph comes to gaze on Katharine with the dreamy idealization with which Katharine and her mother view the family relics, but with an important difference: he hopes to shape the authentic image himself not by inheriting relics but by choosing aspects of Katharine and her lifestyle to desire and possess. Ralph's desire is at once nostalgic—he longs for the venerable authenticity Katharine evokes—and also fully modern, in that he seeks to select and form the authenticity according to his own requirements. For the middle-class Ralph, who lives in a respectable but rather ramshackle house at Highgate, Katharine's upper-middle-class aura, which seems to emanate from Katharine as well as from her well-appointed drawing room, her intellectual father, her cultured mother, and her illustrious ancestors, proves irresistible. After visiting Katharine's home for the first time, Ralph finds himself dreaming about the rest of her house as if he were taking a tour of a model home: "His mind then began to wander about the house, and he wondered whether there were other rooms like the drawing-room, and he thought, inconsequently, how beautiful the bathroom must be, and how leisurely it was—the life of these well-kept people" (28). Ralph's fantasies about Katharine are intertwined with his fantasies about her lifestyle.

The carefully arranged relic room remains inaccessible for Ralph; he cannot grant himself an illustrious past or accomplished ancestors, and of course he declares he would not want to. In his rejection, Ralph in fact gives voice to a central truth about the Victorian tableau of the authentic dead: it cannot be reached. The nineteenth-century past, and a weighty Victorian literary tradition, are gone, and while Ralph's own outsider position allows him to see this more easily, Katharine, Mrs. Hilbery, and even Woolf herself cannot return to this past and are in danger of being captivated by the relic room's venerable but unreachable status. Ralph turns instead to a more modern mode of gazing, one that might allow even the middle-class Ralph to obtain authenticity. If the relic room is authenticity once removed, Ralph takes the next step and becomes the consumer, entering the world of commercial promise, where a constructed authenticity was more widely available. Woolf consistently mediates Ralph's gaze at Katharine through window shopping and the urban street setting. When we bring Ralph's rejection and skepticism together with his paradoxical hunger for authenticity, we come to a uniquely modern scene of window shopping. Throughout the novel, Woolf positions Ralph as a desiring consumer, standing on the sidewalk, longing for the enticing goods on the other side of the glass. As he looks at various store displays, he will suddenly see Katharine, materializing (it would seem) miraculously from his consumer gaze. She seems simultaneously part of a commodified world and yet above it, related to the store windows and yet removed from material transactions. Likewise, as he stands on the sidewalk looking up at Katharine's house, he imagines the drawing room as a place of almost overwhelming distinction, full of light and promise and romance. Ralph's window shopping parallels a related pattern of romance and gazing inspired by new window displays in the early twentieth century, ones that promised an enticing, noncommercial authenticity that was (supposedly) easily obtained through careful purchasing.

Window displays and window shopping—and their connections to modern identity formation—have long been areas of critical interest. Rachel Bowlby, in *Just*

Looking: Consumer Culture in Dreiser, Gissing, and Zola, argues that during the late nineteenth century the shop window replaced the mirror as the site of female identity formation.[8] The new windows offered the consumer different views of possible selves, obtainable for a price. The displays always suggested that the viewer was lacking, producing a never-ending loop of desire, buying, and dissatisfaction. Any sense of a "real" or "stable" identity broke down; as Bowlby writes, "The window smashes the illusion that there is a meaningful distinction in modern society between illusion and reality, fact and fantasy, fake and genuine images of the self" (34).[9] Anne Friedberg, in *Window Shopping: Cinema and the Postmodern*, takes the site of female identity formation a step further, tracing a line from the mirror to window displays to the cinema.[10] Walter Benjamin, Friedberg notes, considered modernity and consumerism through Baudelaire's picture of the distracted, dreamy, male shopper—the *flâneur*—wandering through the Paris arcades. She continues where Benjamin left off, arguing that the rise of the department store allowed for the emergence of a female gazer—the *flâneuse*—who might walk and gaze without social ostracism. *Night and Day* represents a period between the ones considered by Bowlby and Friedberg, a time when the transition from mirror to store window to cinema is still evolving. Ralph is Baudelaire's *flâneur* reimagined by a female novelist. Ralph's window gazing not only is an act of individual identity formation (and he would, in many ways, like to be Katharine himself) but also represents a more general, and less gendered, cultural identity sought by many citizens during the war years: a culture of stability, an established model, a golden promise of permanence. If Bowlby is right that the store window at the turn of the century smashed the illusion between "fake and genuine images of the self," then Woolf portrays the modern subject's longing for a return of this illusion (Bowlby, 34). Ralph searches in places like the relic room and in the modern store window for objects of authentic value, for something that might at once represent the genuine article and yet still be a modern construction. His neo-nostalgic longing reveals not the belatedness of *Night and Day* but a distinctly modern (and indeed modernist) form of identity formation and desire.

Early in *Night and Day*, Ralph is walking through the streets of London, gazing in shop windows on his way to an appointment. As he wanders and gazes, his surroundings become almost dreamlike:

> Late one afternoon Ralph stepped along the Strand to an interview with a lawyer upon business. The afternoon light was almost over, and already streams of greenish and yellowish artificial light were being poured into an atmosphere which, in country lanes, would now have been soft with the

> smoke of wood fires; and on both sides of the road the shop windows were full of sparkling chains and highly polished leather cases, which stood upon shelves made of thick plate-glass. None of these different objects was seen separately by Denham, but from all of them he drew an impression of stir and cheerfulness. (130)

The atmosphere here seems artificially enchanted. The natural light is fading, replaced by green and yellow streams. The objects in the shop windows hold qualities designed to dazzle and hypnotize the gazer—the chains sparkle, the cases are highly polished, the items stand on thick plate-glass, suggesting both visibility and cloudiness. Ralph absorbs the hypnotic atmosphere of these objects, not seeing them distinctly but taking in an impression of light and movement. Ralph's wandering look resembles the "ambulatory gaze" of the modern *flâneur*, described by Friedberg as "the quintessential modern subject, wandering through urban space in a daze of distraction . . . [whose] perceptual patterns—distracted observation and dreamlike reverie—become a prototype for those of the consumer."[11] Ralph's own dreamlike reverie makes him a model of such a subject, gazing distractedly through the streets of London.

Katharine seems to emerge directly from this window shopping. After Ralph has drawn his impressions from the store windows, Woolf writes, "*Thus* it came about that he saw Katharine," as if his reverie itself, inspired by the glittering commodities, has conjured Katharine's presence (130, emphasis added). Katharine seems to Ralph "only an illustration of the argument that was going forward in his mind" (130), an extension, as it were, of his own thoughts. Yet at the same time, she seems absolutely distinct. Separated by "her height and the distinction of her dress" (130), Katharine appears both literally and figuratively above the crowd. Much like the objects set behind glass, she stands apart from the gazers. The very qualities that make up Katharine's distinction in dress and appearance are what might be suggested, reproduced, and sold behind a shop window. It is as if Ralph's Pygmalion-like gaze animates a store mannequin, allowing it to step out of the display to become a mobile commodity, a product of the store windows' glittering promise and Ralph's own imaginings. She materializes, in the most literal sense.[12]

Katharine's appearance has an extraordinary effect on Ralph and his perceptions of his surroundings. As she passes by, "immediately the whole scene in the Strand wore that curious look of order and purpose which is imparted to the most heterogeneous things when music sounds; and so pleasant was this impression that he was very glad that he had not stopped her, after all" (130). Ralph seems to watch Katharine pass in slow motion, a sound track swelling in the background.

Suddenly everything takes on meaning. Just as consumers were mesmerized by small orchestras or piano players in the new department stores, Ralph is captivated by Katharine's appearance, and the first thing he can think of to do, after she walks past, is to keep looking. He is "out of tune for a domestic evening," wanting instead "to walk though the streets of London until he came to Katharine's house, to look up at the windows and fancy her within" (130). Ralph has no desire actually to talk to Katharine; he seems to sense instinctively that the attraction depends on distance. He wants to remain in his position as window shopper, staring at the imaginary image behind glass.

Woolf presents in this complex scene a concentrated analysis of consumer culture in general and of window shopping in particular. She includes the whole transaction—the commodity, the consumer, and the effect of the meeting—and also suggests the reasons behind the display's appeal. The reader sees Katharine (the distinctive commodity), Ralph (the dazed consumer), and the extraordinarily powerful influence Katharine has on Ralph and his perception of the scene. Katharine's distinction and the distance between Ralph and his desired object create Ralph's desire to continue gazing. Like the elegant mannequins in the new store windows, Katharine is at once tantalizingly close and out of reach.[13]

Ralph, of course, does not buy anything or even enter a store, and Katharine is not (at least technically) for sale. Yet the very ambiguity of such scenes, which combine romantic illusion and desire within an urban street setting, connects them in complicated ways to commercialism in London as it was emerging at the time. The scene's dreamy, enchanted quality, never disturbed by any actual purchase, and Katharine's paradoxically combined commodification and transcendence are precisely the attributes achieved by the innovative commercial window displays of London department stores in the early twentieth century. To understand why Woolf might want to recall such displays while describing a meeting of lovers requires that we pause and consider what was distinctive about those windows, and what they represented to the culture that produced them.

Don't Torture the Merchandise: Radical Elegance and the New Window Displays

Between 1910 and 1919, encompassing the years when *Night and Day* is set and the years when it was written and published, window displays in London were being transformed, in large part due to the new approaches in window design at Selfridges. Large shop windows had been introduced in the 1850s, when advances in plate-glass technology had allowed shopkeepers to have large expanses of glass in front of their stores. For the first sixty years, however, little attention was paid to the displays, as most store owners simply crammed as many goods as possible into their windows.[14] In this three-dimensional catalogue method of presentation, owners arranged vast quantities of objects, often in elaborate towers. The trade magazine *Display World* called this method "'torturing the merchandise'" (Wood, 27). Victorian displays could be lavish—recall the tantalizing windows in Dickens's *A Christmas Carol*, for example—but they were rarely carefully composed, and they generally emphasized quantity rather than design.

Starting around 1909, however, the trend moved from these catalogue-type windows to elegant displays that emphasized fantasy and one-of-a-kind commodities, and that de-emphasized both the commercial exchange and the sense of mass production. As with Selfridges' print advertisements, which began to highlight setting, unique products, and elegant images rather than products and prices, many store windows began to present an atmosphere or a lifestyle rather than particular goods at particular prices.[15] This shift occurred less for aesthetic reasons than for economic ones: the new displays were a more effective way to sell things. One of the first innovators of store window displays was Arthur V. Fraser, the display director at Marshall Field and Company in Chicago, who would also prove instrumental in creating new displays at Selfridges. As Leonard Marcus describes in *The American Store Window*, Fraser transformed window design in America:

> At a time when most window displays consisted of dreary parlor scenes or stocky assortments of merchandise, Fraser did windows in an epic style that drew on classical sources of décor and on a highly refined sense of design and composition. He was among the first displaymen to realize the value, when showing fine merchandise, of putting relatively little of it in a window. And although, as Fraser was well aware, his displays made the merchandise in the windows look very expensive (as in fact it usually was) his windows drew large audiences of passersby. As *The Merchants Record* observed: "People do not look in Field's windows for bargains—they look in them for STYLE!" . . . For Marshall Field's very wealthy customers, Fraser's windows may well have resembled the decor of their own homes and apartments or reflected their interests as collectors or travelers. (Marcus, 56)

Fraser used subtle lighting to illuminate different objects or to cast an almost mystical quality over the display. His highly stylized windows were more akin to museum showcases than to typical shop windows of the time. Fraser sold not merchandise but the climate that the merchandise might suggest.

Gordon Selfridge arrived in London after his successful career at Marshall Field's, and he imported many of the ideas that Fraser had developed. In one of his few American hires, Selfridge brought in Edward Goldsman, the display manager at Marshall Field's, to create his new store windows and to reproduce the Fraser style for his London customers.[16] As Alison Adburgham points out in her book *Shops and Shopping*, the new displays were "dramatically different from the crowded windows of Oxford Street into which the cheapest goods were crammed and ticketed to attract the customers in."[17] Goldsman sent his workers to museums, libraries, and historical localities to gather ideas, and he introduced subtle lighting and coordinated colors and arrangements. Displays were carefully constructed, often using classical detailing and elaborately clothed figures, as can be seen in figure 5.1, or displaying a single object or mannequin in a romantic setting. The emphasis was on elegance and refinement, not on buying and selling. Selfridges' windows were also not shuttered at night, as most store windows were, but kept illuminated until late in the evening, inspiring and contributing to the rise in window shopping in London. The trade journal *Merchants Record* pointed

Fig. 5.1 Classical figures. Window display from early years of Selfridges
From *HAT-PIC*, FWD/P/101. Reproduced with kind permission from the Selfridges Archive held at the History of Advertising Trust (www.hatads.org.uk).

out in 1910 that "'merchants realize that . . . hundreds of men and women who are busy all day must do their shopping after dark, and that there has grown up a large class known as 'window shoppers' who study the display windows after supper.'"[18] Gordon Selfridge wanted his windows to become a London attraction. As one advertisement proclaims, "We hope by beautiful setting and study of harmonious colouring to give pleasure to the artistic sense of every passer-by, and to make the 'Window Shows at Selfridge's in Oxford Street' worth a considerable detour to see."[19] The division between the store and everything else was blurring, anticipating the gradual infusion over the twentieth century of commercial culture into ever greater aspects and areas of urban life.

These new modes of selling are at work in Woolf's scene of window watching. The atmosphere, created by artificial lights and glittering objects, places Ralph in the distracted mood that store owners desired to produce in their shoppers. Katharine, separated from the crowd around her, takes the form of a distinctive commodity. Like the string quartets hidden behind the palm trees at Selfridges, the effect of all this on Ralph is to bring a sense of order and beauty to heterogeneous things. And like a good window shopper, Ralph can only wish to stay distracted, to continue to gaze and to desire.

About halfway through *Night and Day*, Ralph again sees Katharine mediated through shop windows, and in this scene, we can read in his gaze the transition from the older model of displays to the newer versions. Sitting in a country restaurant, Ralph becomes agitated with his dinner companion and stands up to stare out the window:

> The people in the street seemed to him only a dissolving and combining pattern of black particles; which, for the moment, represented very well the involuntary procession of feelings and thoughts which formed and dissolved in rapid succession in his own mind. . . . In order to control [his] disorderly race of thoughts he forced himself to read the name on the chemist's shop directly opposite him; then to examine the objects in the shop windows, and then to focus his eyes exactly upon a little group of women looking in at the great windows of a large draper's shop. This discipline having given him at least a superficial control of himself, he was about to turn . . . when his eye was caught by a tall figure walking quickly along the opposite pavement—a tall figure, upright, dark, and commanding, much detached from her surroundings. She held her gloves in her left hand, and the left hand was bare. All this Ralph noticed and enumerated and recognized before he put a name to the whole—Katharine Hilbery. . . . This

> sudden apparition had an extraordinary effect upon him. It was as if he had thought of her so intensely that his mind had formed the shape of her, rather than that he had seen her in the flesh outside in the street. And yet he had not been thinking of her at all. (231–232)

At first, Ralph's vision is scattered and disorderly, confused by the people in the street. He steadies himself by reading the store sign, examining the goods in the store window, and then viewing the shoppers who are doing the same. His cluttered thoughts and his observations of the small window and the specific name on the chemist's shop recall an older model of window shopping, one that relied on selling particular objects. Suddenly, however, the modern moment erupts, and Ralph is jettisoned into a new mode of looking, one where he feels he evokes Katharine by the intensity of his thoughts and desires. He conjures the atmosphere before the particular name of the object, reflecting in fact the very strategy of the new displays. Katharine once again seems to materialize as a distinctive commodity, set apart from her surroundings.

Within this scene, the consumer gaze both overlaps and even seems to produce Ralph's desire for Katharine, and the passage highlights the contradiction within this same hunger. On the one hand, Ralph wants Katharine's aura of distinction; she seems a model for him, apart from the crowd. On the other hand, however, Katharine is linked to the commodity culture. She seems to emerge from Ralph's gaze, an extension of the promise of the objects behind glass. She embodies the originary authentic, attractive because of her prototypical appearance. Part of what the shop windows sell, Woolf hints, is the illusion that the complex web of ideological associations promised by commodities—the sense, for example, of originality, of a "lifestyle," of an established tradition—could be shaped by the consumer and then purchased. The nineteenth century may be out of reach, but Ralph might have something potentially better, or at least more modern: the chance to define his own sense of Katharine's authenticity and to construct it from his own imaginings, much as his consumer counterparts were promised they might do through the new store windows.

Woolf does present in *Night and Day* a critical look at the constructed nature of the shop window's aura, seen through the eyes of the young feminist activist, Mary Datchet: "Now and then [Mary] would pause and look into the window of some bookseller or flower shop, where, at this early hour, the goods were being arranged, and empty gaps behind the plate-glass revealed a state of undress. Mary felt kindly disposed towards the shopkeepers, and hoped that they would trick the midday public into purchasing" (78). Mary sees the gaps, the arranging of goods, the moment before the actual dressing is complete. The shop windows' illusions, which will later work so powerfully on Ralph Denham, are constructed, are tricks to make the public purchase. Mary is the most appropriate character to offer this behind-the-scenes look. A committed activist for the women's vote, Mary forces herself to pursue—painfully, and somewhat against her own inclinations—a life stripped of illusions. She is in love with Ralph Denham and shares his fascination for Katharine, but she is not part of the final arrangement of love matches (Ralph and Katharine, William and Cassandra). She turns aggressively to her work, which Woolf makes clear is a substitute for her romantic desires. Mary also reflects the lower-middle-class character who may be left out of the promises of the commercial culture, representing a class that may more often have to produce, rather than enjoy, the store window displays. Woolf has Mary see the shop window without illusions, forced again to recognize the stark reality behind the romantic facade. Mary's knowledge, however, is presented more as a sober and dispiriting truth than a triumphant knowledge of the "real" way things work. There are advantages, Woolf hints, in "buying into" the dreaminess of a Ralph, despite the blindness it entails.

The construction and implicit promise of such dreaminess, both in *Night and Day* and in the culture more generally, may be clarified by turning to a letter Woolf wrote to her sister, Vanessa Bell, in 1918, the same year she was finishing her novel. The letter reveals a fascinating transformation from actual shopping to Woolf's own idealized vision of commodified authenticity, in this case embodied by her sister. In the first part of the letter, Woolf dramatically tells Vanessa of a terrible shopping excursion:

> I can't describe to you what an agony this afternoon was to me. You know the horror of buying clothes, especially for one forced as I am to keep my underclothes pinned together by brooches. . . . I flung myself into a shop in Holborn. . . . The impropriety seemed to me beyond anything we know. So it went on: I tried shop after shop; and then in a perfectly random way went and bought a wine-coloured black striped coat or dress.[20]

The language seems intentionally overblown. Buying clothes is an agony, a horror, an impropriety. Here we have not the promised vision, the suspended moment of looking that we see with Ralph, but the tiresome process of going from store to store and actually attempting to find something to buy. Like "underclothes pinned together by brooches," it is the disorderly, unglamorous underside of shopping.

Immediately after this description, however, Woolf executes a telling shift. She relates how she has been writing her novel about Vanessa (her sister was the explicit model for Katharine in *Night and Day*): "I've been writing about you all the morning, and have made you wear a blue dress; you've got to be immensely mysterious and romantic, which of course you are; yes, but its [*sic*] the combination that's so enthralling; to crack through the paving stone and be enveloped in the mist" (*L* 2, 232). Woolf leaps from the sordid scene of shopping and actual purchase to the glittering promise of the store window. In Woolf's vision, Vanessa need not buy a dress; she already wears one, taking on the mysterious and romantic quality so seductive to Ralph. Like a dreamy window shopper who is magically whisked from the sidewalk to the enchanted vision before her, Woolf's fantasy is to crack through the material hardness of the paving stone and be enveloped in the ethereal mist. Woolf imagines in Vanessa, and by extension in Katharine, a deliberate exclusion of any act of consumption, presenting only the oasis promised by the finished product. The letter captures the very leap we see Ralph make and the very leap promised to Selfridges' shoppers, that one could skip over the actual shopping and simply obtain the tantalizing vision. It is important to stay alert to the problems inherent in this vision: to the dangers of Ralph's idealization, to insidious marketing techniques, and to Woolf's romantic notions of her sister. It is also important, however, to understand that part of the romanticized promise is not having to do this, not having to leave the mist to be deposited on the material truth of the paving stone.

Woolf translates her romanticized vision of Vanessa into a dressing scene in *Night and Day*, quite likely the very scene Woolf had been describing when she tells Vanessa she had "been writing about you all morning." Near the end of the novel, Katharine is changing her clothes in her room, attended by her younger cousin Cassandra. Echoing Woolf herself, Cassandra stands in awe of Katharine, seeing in her a mysterious and compelling beauty:

> Cassandra, sitting on the bed behind [Katharine], saw the reflection of her cousin's face in the looking-glass. . . . Cassandra was impressed again by Katharine's maturity; and, as she enveloped herself in the blue dress which filled almost the whole of the long looking-glass with blue light and made it the frame of a picture, holding not only the slightly moving effigy of the beautiful woman, but shapes and colors of objects reflected from the background, Cassandra thought that no sight had ever been quite so romantic. It was all in keeping with the room and the house, and the city round them; for her ears had not yet ceased to notice the hum of distant wheels. (344)

This passage is, in many respects, an amalgamation of all the passages I have discussed. Woolf blends here, in Katharine's moving effigy, a fascinating mixture of references. There are echoes of shop windows and dress buying. Cassandra stares not at her own reflection in the glass but at her cousin's, though the ambiguity of which "she" envelops herself in the blue dress leaves open the idea that Cassandra imagines herself in Katharine's place. Katharine's image hints of an ethereal window display, flooded with a blue light that frames the picture, holding not simply a beautiful woman but shapes and colors as well, all centered on the blue dress that surrounds Katharine's form.[21] The image seems to radiate out in ever-expanding circles of connection—the room itself, the house, the city. Cassandra becomes the dazed consumer, transfixed by the seductive image. Yet the scene holds none of the sense of indecency Woolf describes in her own dress shopping. Ideas of purchase or production are evoked (the hum, perhaps, of the distant wheels) but covered with a romantic gloss. Woolf portrays the ultimate promise of the commodity—once the dress is in the home, one might re-create the aura and posses the image reflected in (or behind) the glass.

Compare the blue dress scene with a window display that appeared a few years later (figure 5.2). The designer has created an intimate space. Viewers are invited

Fig. 5.2 Window display for Richard Hudnut, c. 1925
From folder marked "Window Displays" in New York Public Library Picture Collection. Reproduced with kind permission from the New York Public Library Picture Collection.

into a private sanctuary, where they see a woman seated at her dressing table. A sense of production arises from the surrounding jars of lotions and the now empty boxes, but the emphasis is on the elegant finished product: the upper-class woman in a moment of perpetual leisure. A paradigm of looking is established by the woman's position in front of the mirror, staring not at her own reflection but off into the distance. By refusing to have the mannequin look directly in the mirror, the designer leaves a space for the outside viewer to complete the gaze. Viewers are invited to look in the mirror themselves, where they see not their own reflection but that of the elegant young woman they might become. The window shoppers stand in a similar position to Cassandra when she sees the image of Katharine Hilbery fill the mirror rather than her own.

Such scenes of double gazing suggest an important transition. As Friedberg points out, "By the middle of the nineteenth century, as if in a historical relay of looks, the shop window succeeded the mirror as a site of identity construction."[22] Here at the beginning of the twentieth century, the cross section of gazes from mirror to store window is still ambiguous, still in transition. For Woolf and for the artists who created these displays, as well as for the viewers (or readers), such spaces and objects combine several critical elements. The glass becomes both a metaphor for and a material manifestation of the combined accessibility of the goods and the elusiveness of the aura they radiate. The outside gazer could be seduced by the space behind the glass, but it is a willing self-seduction, for the displays by their very manufactured nature make manifest the constructed nature of such a vision, inscribing on the scene the sense of production, even as they work to erase it. Following the gazer, then the glass, then the space and the objects behind it, we achieve a vantage point from which to recognize one tantalizing appeal of modernity: the loop of idealization and desire, connected to a continual dismantling and reconstruction. These displays further encapsulated, as Woolf seems to have recognized, some of the essential paradoxes of her moment and indeed of modernism itself. Modernism too drew its power from contradictory desires: nostalgia for a precommercial and authentic past merging with the hope for a future unencumbered by an outmoded tradition; the appeal of aesthetic elitism, untainted by the tastes of the masses, impossibly united to the antithetical appeal of large-scale production and ready commercial accessibility. The shop windows contrived by Fraser, Goldsman, and Gordon Selfridge, and deployed so tellingly by Woolf in *Night and Day* reflected the contrivers' awareness of these contradictions. In Woolf's case, we can follow that awareness forward to Mrs. Dalloway's early morning shopping trip, or to Lily Briscoe's gaze through the window at Mrs. Ramsay. Of course, window shopping per se is not the exclusive purview of modernism or modernity.

Victorian novelists such as Dickens and Eliot comment on moments of window shopping, as critics such as Andrew Miller have observed.[23] The distinctive modernity and even modernism of Woolf's scenes lies in the ironic awareness she grants to her shoppers: they are willing to be seduced and to acknowledge this seduction, to construct authenticity, and to acknowledge and even celebrate this construction. Woolf's scenes and the commodified authentic offer a now familiar position for the modern viewer, one who is simultaneously aware of and seduced by the vision behind the glass.[24]

War, Windows, and the Nostalgic Vision

Night and Day reflected not only the new commercial energies of the early twentieth century but also the strange realities of window displays during World War I. Woolf wrote her novel during the war, finishing the manuscript on Armistice Day. Over the four years of fighting, window displays functioned in at least two particular ways: they at times reflected the deprivations of war in their emptiness, and they could alternatively defy or evade the war, presenting an image of abundance and tranquillity otherwise unavailable in the urban streets. Woolf uses window shopping in her novel to convey the second of these two functions, erasing the stark realities of the empty windows she sees around her. Reading the novel's window shopping in this historic context reveals the relevance of the novel to the war, and also the particular allure of the commodified authentic during the long years between 1914 and 1918.

At the same time that Woolf is creating the seductive charm of the windows presented to Ralph's gaze, she is recording in her diary the depressing and unsettling emptiness of wartime windows: "The bakers [*sic*] windows now provide almost nothing but little plates of dull biscuits; sections of plain cake; & little buns without any plums. If you see a plum, it is invariably a decoy plum; there are no others" (*D* 1, 112). Anything that would hint at even moderate abundance is a sham. She describes an excursion she and Leonard take in London, echoing the walk and the bus ride that Ralph and Katharine make at the end of *Night and Day*; instead, though, of streaming through the streets as if "victors in the forefront of some triumphal car, spectators of a pageant enacted for them" (*Night and Day*, 502), as her characters do in the novel, the Woolfs pass through bare streets and empty shops:

> Then we took a tram to Kingston & had tea at Atkinsons, where one may have no more than a single bun. Everything is skimped now. Most of the

> butchers [*sic*] shops are shut; the only open shop was besieged. . . . The only abundant shop windows are the drapers. Other shops parade tins, or cardboard boxes, doubtless empty. (This is an attempt at the concise, historic style.) Suddenly one has come to notice the war everywhere. I suppose there must be some undisturbed pockets of luxury somewhere still. (*D* 1, 100)

Woolf in fact creates such pockets of luxury, where windows were still full and radiating promise. Woolf's "historic style" drops out when she imagines the windows within *Night and Day*. Here is an elision not simply of the material transaction but of the war, itself unsettling in its disruption of material plenty.

The elision is disturbing, and many critics have more or less agreed with Katherine Mansfield, who publicly likened the novel to "a ship that was unaware of what ha[d] been happening," and privately noted to John Middleton Murry that the work implied that "the war never has been." Mansfield fervently believed that the war required a totally new style of writing. As she told Murry, "I feel in the *profoundest* sense that nothing can ever be the same[,] that as artists we are traitors if we feel otherwise: we have to take [the war] into account and find new expressions[,] new moulds for our new thoughts & feelings."[25] *Night and Day* seemed willfully naïve, deceitful, and even traitorous. Quentin Bell, Woolf's biographer and nephew, agrees that Woolf leaves out the war in *Night and Day* and implies that she did so deliberately. Just recovering from a severe mental breakdown, Woolf needed to turn away from the war. She wanted, Bell argues, "to see if she could achieve a perfectly orthodox and conventional novel . . . something which would not bring her too close to the abyss from which she had so recently emerged. . . . Deliberately therefore she embarked upon something sane, quiet and undisturbing" (2, 42). In this reading, *Night and Day* becomes a therapeutic work rather than a deliberate lie, one designed to bring Woolf back to sanity by leaving out the historical events that surrounded her.

References to war in *Night and Day* are certainly not as explicit as they are in other Woolf novels—the death of Jacob in the war at the close of *Jacob's Room*, for example, or the shell-shocked Septimus Smith in *Mrs. Dalloway*. Ralph's window watching must be read, however, in the context of window displays during the war. The scene of window shopping, with its promise of authenticity and its cross section of gazes, was an event where tremendous cultural nostalgia might easily be assimilated. The position of an outside observer, standing in the darkness of the street, looking at what seemed a golden space of light, one that combined elements of romance, elegance, and security, and that appeared both achingly close and yet out of reach, was the familiar experience of the window shopper. It was also the metaphoric position of many citizens at the time who began to see the prewar years nostalgically as a place of authenticity and security, elements indeed out of reach during and after the war. *Night and Day* was published just as writers were starting to assimilate what the war would mean—or should mean—for literature. As such, the novel reflects some of the anxieties that seemed most urgent at the time, and not the more familiar responses that began to appear in the literature of the 1920s. In her construction of authentic space behind the glass, Woolf embarked on a strategy of avoidance similar to that conducted by stores such as Selfridges, an avoidance that in fact reflected central cultural tropes from the war years. If *Night and Day* was therapy for Woolf, as Bell claims, it was responding not simply to Woolf's anxieties but to anxieties shared by the larger culture.

In his book *A War Imagined*, Samuel Hynes observes that, during the war years, writers and speakers return repeatedly to two central tropes.[26] The first was that of the world plunging from light into darkness. As Sir Edward Grey said at the start of the war, "'The lamps are going out all over Europe. We shall not see them lit again in our time.'"[27] The second trope centered around the word "civilization." To observers everywhere, the failing light seemed to signal the end of civilization; the war would finish it, and no one knew what would come in its place. While people had different ideas of what civilization meant, "what the mourners felt in common was simply that something of great value, something vaster even than the peace of Europe, had come to an end on August 4, 1914" (Hynes, 3). At the start of the war, Hynes observes, the word "civilization" "appears again and again. . . . One finds it in Parliamentary debates, in newspapers, in private diaries and letters, in reported conversations. Civilization is threatened, is toppling, is mutilated or destroyed; the clock of civilization has been put back" (4). Light, darkness, civilization—these are vague terms, but in 1914, they conveyed the collective sense of danger and loss.

Those in Bloomsbury likewise saw the outbreak of war as threatening civilization and shared the same sense of impending darkness. At the start of the war, Roger Fry laments "'it is over with all our ideas'" (quoted in Hynes, 10). Clive Bell, Woolf's brother-in-law, wrote two essays in 1915, "Peace at Once," and "Art and War," claiming that war would threaten art and urging both artists and nations to "remain civilized" (Hynes, 85). By 1918, Bell was at work on his book *Civilisation*, arguing that the civilized prewar Bloomsbury had been abruptly destroyed by the war. Many in the Bloomsbury group struggled to see how civilization might be defended, though often writing with a sense of ironic resignation. In 1914, several

Bloomsbury members re-formed a play-reading group that had last met in 1909, and Bell records a half-mocking purpose in the minutes:

> I do not know what relationship, if any, this society stands to that older society which was last heard of on January 15 1909. . . . Anyway, in these days of storm and darkness, it seemed right that at the shrine of civilization—in Bloomsbury, I mean—the lamp should be tended assiduously. It has been decided, therefore, to read plays, ancient or modern, English or foreign, tragic, comic, or simply bawdy, at 46 Gordon Square.[28]

With a hint of irony, Bell proposes literature as a light amid the darkness of war and the Bloomsbury group as the heroic tenders of the lamp.

Woolf herself began by turning a half-satirical eye on all the rhetoric concerning the impending collapse of civilization, and its related claim that such civilization represented an authentic past that had slipped out of reach. In a letter to Ka Cox in 1914, she relates that she had "never felt anything like the general insecurity" in those around her, and reports on a trip to London: "Oh Lord! What a lot of talk there was! . . . Clive [Bell] was having tea with Ottoline [Morrell], and they talked and talked, and said it was the end of civilization."[29] The next year, she mocks Clive Bell's incessant talk, urging a friend to buy him a parrot, and "for us all to persuade him that the love of birds is the last word in Civilisation" (*L* 2, 61).

For all her early flippancy, however, Woolf came to use the tropes of light, darkness, and the end of civilization more seriously. After a threatened air raid in 1917, she records soberly in her diary how "the dipping down of the electric lights was taken as a sign of warning: finally, the lights went out, & standing on the kitchen stairs I was deluged with certain knowledge that the extinction of light is in future our warning" (*D* 1, 70). By the end of the war, Woolf compliments Henry James's war book, *Within the Rim*, in a *Times Literary Supplement* review, admiring how James felt called upon to protest the war by an immense and hard-to-define force: "It was everything that he had ever cared for of civilisation, beauty and art threatened with destruction and arrayed before his imagination in one figure of tragic appeal." James, Woolf writes, "makes us understand what civilisation meant to him and should mean to us."[30]

Woolf reimagines these wartime tropes in the climactic scene of window watching near the end of *Night and Day*, when Ralph stares up at the golden drawing room window of the Hilberys':

> Lights burnt in the three long windows of the drawing-room. The space of the room behind became, in Ralph's vision, the center of the dark, flying

> wilderness of the world; the justification for the welter of confusion surrounding it; the steady light which cast its beams, like those of a lighthouse, with searching composure over the trackless waste. In this little sanctuary were gathered together several different people, but their identity was dissolved in a general glory of something that might, perhaps, be called civilization; at any rate, all dryness, all safety, all that stood up above the surge and preserved a consciousness of its own, was centered in the drawing-room of the Hilberys. Its purpose was beneficent; and yet so far above his level as to have something austere about it, a light that cast itself out and yet kept itself aloof. . . . He did not see [Katharine] in body; he seemed curiously to see her as a shape of light, the light itself. (395)

Ralph stands in the metaphoric wasteland of war, stranded in a wilderness, a confusion, and a trackless waste. Across a great divide, he sees the drawing room as a sanctuary and a place of steady light, something that might be called "civilization." Woolf is vague as to what this light of civilization might be, making it a general signifier for all that might be safe and worth preserving. Ralph can imagine and see this light, but he cannot reach it; it remains aloof, tantalizing, casting itself out.

In this carefully constructed scene of window watching, Woolf captures the larger position of wartime observers, who felt an impending darkness closing over what seemed the steady light of the prewar era. As the war came to its bloody close, many found an uncrossable divide had opened between the present and what appeared to be the golden age before the war's beginning.[31] We can see the sense of this divide in Ralph's gaze and in his position. In 1918, when Woolf was writing this passage, she not only sensed the coming division but also anticipated the coming idealization of the past and the accompanying nostalgic stance of many in the postwar society.

Woolf was not the only observer to imagine that a beautifully lighted window might offer some relief from the darkness of battle. Gordon Selfridge himself, who coined the phrase "business as usual" during the war, ensured that his window displays would reflect their prewar glory, giving his customers carefully constructed images of beauty and tranquillity (Pound, 125). For some observers, these displays promised the same sense of safety Ralph garners from watching Katharine's radiant home. The literary magazine the *Academy* observed that the window displays at Selfridges were a welcome relief during the war. The glowing windows were still "'beautifully arranged,'" in marked contrast to

> the death and desolation that reign in the cities on which battle has set its terrible seal. Each beautiful fabric displayed, or product of the lands across

> the ocean, has a new value of its own. It means that looms are working, and factory chimneys smoking; women and children warmed and fed and housed amid the tribulations of war. . . . Without the streets swarmed with placards shouting war sensationalism; stress and the hint of danger were in the air. Within were beauty and order and steady business, nothing feverish in its atmosphere, but a pervading sense of well-being.[32]

Window displays could in fact call on the atmosphere of any number of prominent symbolic sites of civilization: the elegantly appointed drawing room, well-dressed men and women, and classical or even Edwardian settings. Shoppers during the war might see in the window the cultural identity they most wanted: the peaceful and secure glow of an authentic past. Such elision certainly reflects a willful and problematic avoidance of the war, but the very desire to look away also reflected the first reaction of many.

. . .

To close my discussion of window shopping and the commodified authentic, I return again to the idea of performance. The iconic scene of window shopping—where a viewer stands gazing at an authentic vision just behind glass—must be understood in motion, as a carefully orchestrated performance happening both in time and in space. A writer for the *Daily Mail* highlighted this theatrical quality of shop windows: "Each window-frame formed a sort of proscenium for a deep-set scene with a painted background in colours delicately harmonizing with the articles occupying what may be termed the centre of the stage."[33] The viewer could imagine performing within the atmosphere and even playing with a new identity suggested on this stage. The display might promise a temporal shift by representing, constructing, and reproducing part of the past, and it might also work spatially, promising to bring the viewer into contact with another appealing identity, whether in the form of a romantic partner (as we see with Ralph and Katharine), or in the form of an alluring new role for the viewer. Unlike the tableau of the authentic dead, the new displays promised to give the consumer control over the authenticity displayed, offering the chance to perform a new part using various "authentic" markers.

Understanding window shopping as performance in turn allows us to understand how the contradiction imbedded within the commodified authentic might be sustained. Such a scene requires that the viewer learn to perform a paradox, to maintain simultaneously the belief in and the desire for the authentic vision behind the glass, and yet also remain aware that the constructed nature of this vision is the very quality that makes it accessible. The contradiction implied by *performing* the *authentic* reflects this embedded paradox. In a telling dialogue between Ralph and Katharine, Ralph outlines the manifesto that underlies such contradictory yet self-aware seduction, defending his own idealization against Katharine's insistence that he be more realistic:

> [Katharine:] "You come and see me among flowers and pictures, and think me mysterious, romantic, and all the rest of it. Being yourself very inexperienced and very emotional, you go home and invent a story about me, and now you can't separate me from the person you've imagined me to be. You call that, I suppose, being in love; as a matter of fact it's being in delusion. . . . My mother spends her life in making stories about the people she's fond of. But I won't have you do it about me, if I can help it."
>
> "You can't help it," [Ralph] said.
>
> "I warn you it's the source of all evil."
>
> "And of all good," he added.
>
> "You'll find out that I'm not what you think me."
>
> "Perhaps. But I shall gain more than I lose."
>
> "If such gain's worth having."
>
> They were silent for a space.
>
> "That may be what we have to face," he said. "There may be nothing else. Nothing but what we imagine." (381–382)

Certainly Woolf exposes a familiar idealization, that of a male lover for an objectified female (with the critical difference that here the object talks back and insists on redefinition). Woolf also presents, however, the possibility that the imagination might be all we have; there is no unconstructed "authentic" object or place, only the authenticity that we construct. Ralph's insistence that he maintain his authentic vision of Katharine, while clearly seeing the constructed nature of such a vision, aligns him with the modern window shopper; both must obtain authenticity by knowing it as performance (or it becomes unavailable) yet seeing it as authentic. Ralph's modernity is implicit not simply in his willingness to admit the constructed nature of his vision but in his insistence on sustaining a sense of authenticity within this construction. The figure of the outsider, who desires an authentic, often romanticized ideal, who realizes the constructed and often commodified nature of such a promise, and yet is still willing to be seduced by it, not only suggests characters such as Woolf's Ralph and Forster's Margaret but also anticipates later figures such Leopold Bloom, Lily Briscoe, and the twenty-first-century shopper, to whom I turn in my conclusion.

6. Conclusion

Modernist Excursions

Over the course of the twentieth century, the commodified authentic became more than a marketing technique—it became a marketing climate. This pervasive strategy not only shaped how particular commodities were sold but also influenced the emergence of the larger concept of lifestyle design. It arose both in urban and in rural settings, often offering the rural to the urban, the urban to the rural. Its development paralleled the spread of consumer culture from the stores, to the streets, to the home, to the media. Analyzing the growth of the commodified authentic in its many guises and locations—from the design of homes to the design of communities, in the country and in the city, in the stores and in the advertisements, in the architecture and in the literature—reveals its enduring force in the development of modernity.

As I have explored, the commodified authentic makes additional appearances and accrues additional significance in the development of literary modernism. Since the commodified authentic was in part a transitional strategy, one formed to entice consumers both bewildered and excited by the shift from the nineteenth century to the twentieth, the strategy has been best understood through commercial ventures and literary works that emerge in this transitional period, rather than through later high modernist texts. Nevertheless, after considering modernity and modernism from this earlier view, we can also fruitfully move forward to high modernist works to see how the landscape has shifted.

As discussed in chapter 1, in the past two decades the critical stance that viewed modernism as an elitist endeavor that eschewed commerce, mass culture, and past traditions has given way to more inclusive readings that expose modernism's intimate connections to advertising and commodity culture, as well as its surprising alliances with issues of nostalgia and authenticity. The commodified authentic allows us to unite these old and new readings of modernism, as this commercial strategy by definition encompassed both the desire for commercial purity and the embrace of commercial possibility. The originary wish to "make it new," the nostalgic urge to look back in longing, and the aesthetic impulse to keep art untainted by commerce merged with each other, blending into a variety of new forms, both commercial and literary. The commodified authentic provides a model for understanding some of the contradictions *of* modernism as inherent *to* modernism. It is not simply that modernists have contradictory impulses toward tradition and originality, toward the past and entirely new futures, toward commerce and the dream of a cultural space outside the marketplace; it is that modernism itself is about the vacillations among these various contradictions, its definition arising as much from this movement as from the extremes themselves.

Several concise excursions into high modernist texts will reveal how the study of the commodified authentic might further recalibrate our understanding of modernism and the market. Three scenes that depict three different kinds of shopping, from D. H. Lawrence's *Women in Love*, James Joyce's *Ulysses*, and Virginia Woolf's *To the Lighthouse*, suggest how the issues surrounding the commodified authentic that I have examined in earlier works became defining features of modernism itself. Lawrence takes the radical critique and skepticism seen in Wells and Shaw of attempts to market authenticity and forges this rejection into a modernist aesthetic. Joyce creates a playful, parodic response to the selling of the country-house aura, a response that reveals how the paradoxical stance required by the commodified authentic parallels the stance Joyce requires of his readers. Woolf presents a response somewhere in between those of her two male counterparts, demanding of both character and reader a rejection and a wider acceptance. Taken together, these three scenes confirm that the union of—and the contradiction between—authenticity and its production lies at the heart of both modern marketing and modernism itself.

Excursion One: D. H. Lawrence, *Women in Love*

Lawrence's *Women in Love* (1920) would at first seem a rejection of many of the commercial/authentic blends explored within this study.[1] Lawrence's characters repeatedly observe the sordid industrialization of modern life, often viewing commercial enterprises as the drivers of mechanical repetition. The idea of a benevolent businessman on the Cadbury line, as embodied by the patriarch Thomas Crich, is literally and figuratively killed off in the book, as the dying Crich sees his attempts at a kinder, gentler coal-mine ownership eclipsed by the Nietzschean will of his eldest son, Gerald. In the town in which the book's main action takes place, Beldover, industry is the traditional blot on the landscape, the town center an electric and vulgar parade of shops, and the country outskirts teeming with outworn examples of a dying way of life. The Criches' country home, Shortlands, masks (unsuccessfully) the industry that produces it, as the house and its surrounding features "hid the colliery valley beyond, but did not quite hide the rising smoke" (23).

Yet within the novel, the pervasive atmosphere of rejection links to many of the tensions that the strategy of commodifying authenticity sought to address. Lawrence evokes, for example, the powerful nostalgia that ideas of "home" at various class levels produce in his modern characters, a nostalgia that is always followed at once by a dismissal of home as an empty or confining past tradition. At the lower-middle-class level, Gudrun feels "nostalgia" for her childhood home, a feeling she quickly rejects as she recalls "how utterly cut off it was, how hideous and how sickeningly mindless" (116). Later, she imagines a more luxurious picture of "marriage and a home" that echoes an iconic scene in twentieth-century advertising: "a rosy room, with herself in a beautiful gown, and a handsome man in evening dress who held her in his arms in the firelight, and kissed her. This picture she entitled 'Home'" (376). Despite these occasional (and often ironic) longings, the characters repeatedly declare that the idea of home is an outworn creed; as Birkin remarks, "'One should avoid this *home* instinct. It's not an instinct, it's a habit of cowardliness. One should never have a *home*'" (352), and the two women, returning to their childhood home, weep not over the past, as they tell Birkin, but that "'it ever *was*'" (374). Even the aristocratic model of country living, represented by the Georgian estate Breadalby, is evoked only to be discarded, as can be seen in this typical passage of Birkin's musings on the house:

> He was thinking how lovely, how sure, how formed, how final all the things of the past were—the lovely accomplished past—this house, so still and golden, the park slumbering its centuries of peace. And then, what a snare and a delusion, this beauty of static things—what a horrible, dead prison Breadalby really was, what an intolerable confinement, the peace! (97)

This kind of oscillation between nostalgia and rejection in part led to the growing success of nostalgic forms of the commodified authentic, which as its very strategy sought to address both the longing for the past and the need to craft past models into new forms. Lawrence's characters, though, dismiss the idea that material objects might somehow address these tensions. As Birkin remarks, "'We have an ideal of a perfect world, clean and straight and sufficient. So we cover the earth with foulness; life is a blotch of labour, like insects scurrying in filth, so that your collier can have a pianoforte in his parlour, and you can have a butler and a motor-car in your up-to-date house . . . it is very dreary'" (55). While the commodified authentic as a marketing technique would surely have been rejected by both Lawrence and his characters, Lawrence nevertheless gives voice to the very tensions that fueled its rapid growth.

To escape this cycle of nostalgia and its dismissal, the characters at times turn to originary and aesthetic appeals. Birkin, for example, locates in his ambivalent admiration of "primitive" African art a sense of originary energy. At other moments, Lawrence's characters explore the possibilities of blending a kind of aesthetic authenticity with industrialism. As one character proclaims, "'Since industry is our business, now, then let us make our places of industry our art—our factory-area our Parthenon. . . . Art must *interpret* industry'" (424). Likewise, the characters note a mocking awareness of the self-fashioning of "authentic" modes of life. Gudrun remarks to her sister, "'You'll find that the really chic thing is to be so absolutely ordinary, so perfectly commonplace and like the person in the street, that you really are a masterpiece of humanity, not the person in the street actually, but the artistic creation of her'" (51). Yet all these responses are finally incomplete, as Lawrence locates the condition of modern life as a struggle to form—and the impossibility of forming—some kind of future within these different appeals.

Toward the end of his novel, Lawrence presents a shopping scene that encompasses all these impulses, defining modernism in part through a violent rejection of commerce, of authenticity—in its originary, nostalgic, or aesthetic forms—and of any attempt to unite them in the unholy alliance of the commodified authentic. Two of Lawrence's central characters, Ursula and Birkin, wander down to an outdoor market for a typically bleak excursion: "There was a jumble market every Monday afternoon in the old market-place in town. Ursula and Birkin strayed down there one afternoon. They had been talking of furniture, and they wanted to see if there was any fragment they would like to buy, amid the heaps of rubbish collected on the cobblestones" (354). Like commercial wasteland shoppers, they hope to find a "fragment" amid all the "rubbish." The marketplace itself is far from a quaint old-fashioned icon, composed instead of "a mere bare patch of granite sets" framed by "meager houses" and a large blank hosiery factory (354). The civic project in this space, the "crowning monument," as the narrator wryly calls it, is a set of public baths in new redbrick alongside a clock tower. This dismal atmosphere, where the ineffective and generic improvements only add to the bleakness, extends to the town's inhabitants; they "seemed stumpy and sordid," on the same continuum with the dirty air and the "many mean streets" (354) that extend out from the market.

The scene mocks the offerings of a Selfridges or a Bournville, leaving little room for nostalgic authenticity. Ursula, however, at first seeks an authenticity not of objects but of people. Despite the atmosphere, "Ursula was superficially thrilled when she found herself out among the common people" (354). One can catch the half-sneering, half-admiring tone of the narrator at this thrill, at Ursula's nostalgic evocation of a group that might, presumably, really be living at the heart of things. Ursula's nostalgia does not involve thinking these "common people" are idyllically happy. She "excitedly" watches a young couple looking at an old mattress; the man is "down-at-heel and dejected," the woman is pregnant, "secretive" and "anxious" (354). The thrill for Ursula seems to come from finding them primitive, raw, somehow closer to the animal form. She—or perhaps the narrator—repeatedly imagines, for example, that the man is a "creature," a "dark-eyed, silent rat" (358). Her excitement, colored by Lawrence's subtle distaste for and attraction to this excitement, comes as it might from an anthropologist observing the fascinating habits of an (allegedly) primitive people.[2]

Much to their surprise, Ursula and Birkin do find a fragment worth buying: "It was an arm-chair of simple wood, probably birch, but of such fine delicacy of grace, standing there on the sordid stones, it almost brought tears to the eyes. It was square in shape, of the purest, slender lines, and four short lines of wood in the back, that reminded Ursula of harp-strings" (355). Despite its beauty, the chair has lost part of its allure to time. As Birkin remarks, " 'It was once . . . gilded,' " and a wooden square has been crudely attached where previously a cane seat had granted " 'perfect lightness and unity in tension' " (355). Still, they like the chair enough to buy it. Once the purchase is made, Birkin and Ursula begin to attach a variety of larger meanings to this old/new commodity. Birkin first sends up a nostalgic and aesthetic elegy:

> "So beautiful, so pure! . . . It almost breaks my heart." They walked along between the heaps of rubbish. "My beloved country—it had something to express even when it made that chair. . . . When I see that clear, beautiful chair, and I think of England, even Jane Austen's England—it had living thoughts to unfold even then, and pure happiness in unfolding them. And now, we can only fish among the rubbish-heaps for the remnants of their old expression. There is no production in us now, only sordid and foul mechanicalness." (355)

Birkin imagines a golden age, represented by the old chair—a relic of temporal density, and an object that would not be out of place in a corner at Howards End. Underlying Birkin's lament seems to be one from the novelist: Birkin cites a literary representation of England produced by Austen, who reflects an older model of novel writing no longer available to the modernist. Birkin seems sunk in modern despair, a "foul mechanicalness" the only possible mode of production.

The nostalgic moment is not sustained, however; authenticity is not permanently embedded in this chair. Ursula quickly moves to debunk Birkin's glossy view of the past: "'*Really*, I don't think so much of Jane Austen's England. It was materialistic enough, if you like. . . . I hate your past. I'm sick of it. . . . I believe I even hate that old chair, though it *is* beautiful. It isn't *my* sort of beauty. I wish it had been smashed up when its day was over, not left to preach the beloved past to us. I'm sick of the beloved past'" (355–356). Ursula denies that there was some golden non-materialistic era, though she does not find the current time any more palatable. "'I hate the present,'" she declares, "'but I don't want the past to take its place'" (356).

Birkin then swings violently in the other direction with Ursula. They both end up rejecting the chair and decide that not only do they not want old things, they "don't want things at all," no furniture, no house, no "definite place." Birkin declares the nostalgic, originary, and aesthetic forms of authenticity to be intolerable: "'If you have a Tudor house and old, beautiful furniture, it is only the past perpetuated on top of you, horrible. And if you have a perfect modern house done for you by Poiret, it is something else perpetuated on top of you. It is all horrible'" (356). For Birkin and Ursula, there is no haven, no place or time where goods might safely generate authenticity. They end up giving the chair to a couple expecting a baby, though they have trouble explaining to the bewildered and suspicious pair why they are making this offer.

If Woolf's *Night and Day* presents a willing self-seduction, Lawrence's scene reveals both the seduction and the violent awakening. Here, ideas of authenticity and its rejection are consciously presented as various poses, different modes at Lawrence's disposal. It is Ursula and Birkin who almost automatically take on the task of assigning meaning to the chair. Like cynical, jaded marketers, they spin a variety of contradictory associations around the object, only to dismiss them all. Deeply dissatisfied with their shopping experience, they wish to divorce themselves from the entire commercial transaction and walk away without the item they purchased.

The attitudes of Ursula and Birkin suggest a rejection that for many years was seen as one of the defining features of modernism. Although the jumble market is far from the mass-market shopping spectacle of a Selfridges, closer to what today would be considered the more "authentic" choice of the open-air market, the couple eschews any commercial answer to their search. In part, they depict the stereotypical modernist avoidance of commerce (one revised considerably in recent years); there is, however, another way that this scene is quintessentially modernist, one that emerges when considering the examples of the commodified authentic in this book. Lawrence presents the continual exchange of various critical positions. His modernist characters are like pinballs jettisoned from point to point, careening first toward a nostalgic authenticity, only to spring back in favor of a new, modern vision, and just as quickly bouncing violently away from such a point and declaring a desire not to play. Despite their repeated refusals, the characters still move among these points, their modernist position in fact defined by their movement.

Ursula and Birkin thus become unmaskers of attempts to commodify authenticity, and in this role, a line may be traced back to Shaw and Wells, and forward to Lawrence and to many contemporary critics. The characters embody the distaste one feels at being taken in, at finding one's self believing in the commercial promises that have become the contemporary climate. Throughout the novel, the characters struggle to discover what to do next, what to put in place after their sweeping denouncements, and they remain committed to an elaborate dance of disenchantment and dismissal. Such a dance reflects an important critical response to commodity culture in general, and to attempts to commodify authenticity in particular, a critique that derives its energy from continual fluctuation between a recognition of an authentic appeal in its various forms, and a rejection of any attempts to reify a material object as a possible location of that appeal. For Lawrence, modernism becomes vacillation, not to be defined by a longing for the past or an embrace of the future, but a form that requires that his characters never settled in any particular place or stance for long, a vacillation that the commodified authentic acknowledged. The commodified authentic itself became a kind of material fluctuation, promising to deliver, rather than to resolve, the very tensions that Lawrence so eloquently details. That Lawrence's characters (and likely Lawrence himself) would reject such commercial solutions does not negate the fact that they were, in part, designed precisely to appeal to the vacillations that Lawrence describes.

Excursion Two: James Joyce's *Ulysses*

The second excursion involves a Joycean version of the Ideal Home Exhibition, a section in *Ulysses* (1922) that both borrows and re-creates the strategies the marketers of the commodified authentic were learning so well.[3] Joyce's intimate ties to commerce and advertising have been brilliantly analyzed in recent years by critics such as Jennifer Wicke, Garry Leonard, and Thomas Richards, but another relationship emerges when moments in Joyce are considered through the prism of the commodified authentic.[4] Joyce not only drenches his prose in the nostalgic, originary, and aesthetic forms of this strategy; he uncovers and deploys the modernist implications behind these forms, asking that his readers sustain the same paradox that marketers were crafting, and turning this paradox into a new prose style. If Lawrence's approach to the commodified authentic is to demand a continual rejection and redefinition in order to destabilize its power, Joyce's strategy involves a different kind of movement, one that shifts so quickly from critique to unmasking to understanding to re-creation that it simultaneously evokes, dismantles, and evokes again appeals to various forms of authenticity, celebrating authenticity's allure and its inevitable constructedness.

In "Ithaca," appropriately the homecoming chapter, Joyce brings his unconquered hero back to Eccles Street, where Joyce investigates what it might mean to create an ideal home, or an "abode of bliss," through both commercial and imaginative means. The chapter contains the three final references to the "Plumtree's Potted Meat" advertisement that has reappeared throughout the book, and these references—read together with the narrator's creation midchapter of Bloom's ideal home in the country—offer a Joycean construction and deconstruction of attempts to market ideas of "home." From the first use of the advertisement in chapter 5, "Plumtree's" has served as a painful reminder for Bloom of his own disordered home:

> *What is home without*
> *Plumtree's Potted Meat?*
> *Incomplete.*
> *With it an abode of bliss.*
> (5.144–147)

Most obviously, the advertisement within the novel offers a crude association for Bloom to Molly's adultery, and the "meat" of Blazes Boylan that had filled Bloom's absence in the marital bed; the advertisement floats through Bloom's head throughout the day, especially when he is asked a question about Molly that forces him to think of Blazes. At other moments in the novel, Bloom is reminded that as Henry Flower (and as Bloom) he has "no fixed abode," that his very home is threatened. The advertisement itself relies on a vague sense of nostalgic authenticity, promising the perfect home to consumers of Plumtree's. Originary claims appear as well, for on the label of the meat tin the consumer is urged to "beware of imitations," implying Plumtree's meat is the first, the model, the prototype (17.604).

Throughout the novel, both Joyce and Bloom expose the advertisement's hyperbolic and ridiculous promises. If the claims of the commodified authentic must be seen on a continuum, as I explored in chapter 2 with Bournville and Port Sunlight, then the Plumtree ad is at the farcical end; the idea of potted meat making a home complete or turning it into an abode of bliss is obviously absurd, the claim and the product bearing no relationship with one another. As an adman, Bloom objects to the advertisement on several levels, from its empty promise to its unsavory placement under the obituaries in the newspaper. Thus, it would seem that the Plumtree's jingle is evoked to be dismissed. By the time the advertisement reappears in chapter 17, however, it offers in fact a much more complicated set of references to the home—and by extension to the commodified authentic—than might initially appear.

The first reference to Plumtree's in the Ithaca chapter arises in the list that the (pseudo)scientific narrator gives concerning the contents of Bloom's kitchen shelf:

> On the middle shelf a chipped eggcup containing pepper, a drum of table salt, four conglomerated black olives in oleaginous paper, an empty pot of Plumtree's potted meat, an oval wicker basket bedded with fibre and containing one Jersey pear, a halfempty bottle of William Gilbey and Co's white invalid port, half disrobed of its swathe of coralpink tissue paper, a packet of Epps's soluble cocoa . . . (17.302–307)

Within this pedantic and supposedly objective list of the narrator, Joyce presents particular items with an emotional and highly subjective punch. In particular, the empty pot of meat speaks again to Molly's affair, set as the pot is beside the remains of the basket from Boylan to Molly, presumably the same basket that the reader had seen Boylan sending earlier in the novel. The reader has now been trained to associate the empty pot of Plumtree's with the adultery (as Bloom has done so all day), and to see it as a sign that Bloom's abode is "incomplete" in many ways. Just as Bloom had earlier commented on the placement of the Plumtree advertisement on the newspaper page, here Joyce's placement of the advertising reference changes how the reference is read. Note, too, Joyce's own dexterous dismantling and reconstruction of the ad itself. As I discussed, Bloom, Joyce, and the reader have all dismissed the ad's claims repeatedly by this point in the novel. Yet Joyce then reinstantiates the advertisement's promises. Here, the empty pot of Plumtree's potted meat in fact denotes a home that is incomplete, for in Bloom's daylong absence, Boylan has literally eaten the meat at Bloom's house and figuratively potted his meat within Molly. In Joyce's hands, the advertisement signifies. The continuous motion of Joyce's approach is critically important. He unmasks the advertisement on numerous levels, suggesting that its claims, whether to a nostalgic version of home or as a "model" from which imitations might be made, are false, yet at the same time he reanimates the advertisement, granting it greater significance because Bloom himself has determined that significance, as the ad becomes a kind of mnemonic for Bloom's memory of Molly's affair. Joyce demonstrates through his flux the paradox of creating and simultaneously questioning notions of authenticity and meaning.

In the next reference to Plumtree's in chapter 17, Joyce provides another model for constructing authenticity, this time by exploring the marketing cycle. As the narrator informs the reader, Bloom is thinking about advertising and its possibilities, specifically in respect to placement and layout. The narrator explores a range of advertisements that stimulate Bloom's thoughts; the potted meat ad, though, is listed under the "Such as never" question, implying that this advertisement does not interest Bloom. The narrator reproduces the entire Plumtree's jingle quoted earlier and then traces the potted meat back to its origins:

> Manufactured by George Plumtree, 23 Merchants' quay, Dublin, put up in 4 oz pots, and inserted by Councillor Joseph P. Nannetti, M. P., Rotunda Ward, 19 Hardwicke street, under the obituary notices and anniversaries of deceases. The name on the label is Plumtree. A plumtree is a meatpot, registered trade mark. Beware of imitations. Peatmot. Trumplee. Moutpat. Plamtroo. (17.600–605)

Here the narrator gives a rundown of how and where Plumtree's meat is manufactured, and where the advertisement will be placed. Joyce again implies the emptiness of the original ad, but he also offers a mini–marketing cycle, from product to advertising to manufacture to advertising strategy. He hints how products are made and how they are marketed; how meaning arises and shifts and reforms. He can both mock the advertisement and take it seriously, show meaning both constructed (and as a construct) and how it might literally be re-formed by language—or even by changing letters and sounds.

Bloom may dismiss Plumtree's promise to make a house "complete," but the narrator claims that Bloom begins to dream of his own "Abode of Bliss" shortly after the chapter's second Plumtree passage. The scientific narrator presents the readers with a utopian domestic fantasy, one that echoes the language that might be found in a *Daily Mail* Ideal Home Exhibition catalogue or a pamphlet for a house in a Garden City:

> to purchase by private treaty in fee simple a thatched bungalowshaped 2 storey dwellinghouse of southerly aspect, surmounted by vane and

> lightning conductor, connected with the earth, with porch covered by parasitic plants (ivy or Virginia creeper) halldoor, olive green, with smart carriage finish and neat doorbrasses, stucco front with gilt tracery at eaves and gable, rising, if possible, upon a gentle eminence with agreeable prospect from balcony with stone pillar parapet over unoccupied and unoccupyable interjacent pastures and standing in 5 or 6 acres of its own ground. (17.1504–1512)

The language here draws from at least two different commercial sources; first, the narrator evokes a kind of commercial epic catalogue, featuring a conglomeration of objects, from the dwellinghouse with its porch to the door brasses to the stucco front. Blending within these objects is a second source: advertising copy in the overblown language of the real estate brochure, selling an authentic country life that is "connected with the earth," promising "a gentle eminence with agreeable prospect." On one level, the narrator creates the circular flow of the commodified authentic, moving seamlessly from objects to the aura they evoke and back to the objects. He captures and produces the climate of commercially available authenticity, one that hints both at a venerable past with its "thatched bungalow" and also at a sleek, modern future. On another level, Joyce presents a prototypical experience of modernity, the consumer-as-Bloom and the consumer-as-reader experiencing the tantalizing allure of advertising's promise at the same time that they experience its inevitable disappointment. Finally, Joyce's presentation itself suggests a new literary strategy, turning a Victorian novel's obsession with things into the art of advertising and presenting the modernist result. Joyce crafts his parody of the advertisements and this country house fantasy into a new model, capturing how the hapless but strangely self-aware consumer shapes, and is shaped by, the commodified authentic.

The narrator also suggests one of the promises of commodity culture, the dream that anyone—even an outsider like Bloom—might literally buy into a kind of ideal English country lifestyle, despite not having the family connections or the history to do it the old-fashioned way. Crucially, the narrator does not describe Bloom as inheriting this ideal domestic house. The fantasy is "not to inherit by right of primogeniture, gavelkind or borough English" (17.1499), and the narrator claims that Bloom does not picture a "baronial hall" (17.1502). He does not, in other words, seem to imagine an upper-class life, nor does he fantasize about achieving this domestic vision through bequest, a symbol of familial continuity. Like Woolf's Ralph, the narrator has Bloom purchasing his old home, "by private treaty in fee simple" (17.1504). What had for so long been out of reach, the advertisements promised, could now be available to all, but it required a simultaneous belief in the authenticity and a belief that this very authenticity could be newly constructed. Joyce displays how this union might happen, mimicking the implied flow from advertisement to purchasing. The house's "oval flowerbeds in rectangular grassplots" are planted with "crocuses, polyanthus, sweet William, sweet pea, lily of the valley (bulbs obtainable from sir James W. Mackey (Limited) wholesale and retail seed and bulb merchants and nurserymen, agents for chemical manures, 23 Sackville street, upper)" (17.1554–1559). Similar to the second Plumtree reference in the chapter, the narrator offers a commercial cycle; language here moves from the idyllic descriptions, to the commercial catalogue, to the actual source of the flowers. Much as Joyce depicts the process of writing as he himself writes, he shows the process of construction behind the idyllic scene.[5]

The narrator presents Bloom as the satisfied shopper within this domestic picture, designing through carefully chosen clothes the image of the perfect country gentleman:

> In loose allwool garments with Harris tweed cap, price 8/6, and useful garden boots with elastic gussets and wateringcan, planting aligned young firtrees, syringing, pruning, staking, sowing hayseed, trundling a weedladen wheelbarrow without excessive fatigue at sunset amid the scent of newmown hay, ameliorating the soil, multiplying wisdom, achieving longevity. (17.1582–1587)

The narrator crafts a country gentleman by dressing him—the wool garments and Harris tweed and useful garden boots make up the country vision, as he describes Bloom engaging in sentimentalized garden pursuits with little strain. He pictures Bloom emerging at the end of the day to watch the landscape, noting in sweet melancholy how the land's sterility contrasts with the "agreeable cottagers' fires of smoking peat turves" (17.1598–1599).[6] The passage ends with advertising's vague and implicit promise that by some alchemic process, the right clothes will produce this vision, allowing Bloom to improve the soil and grow in wisdom. The narrator simultaneously constructs this tantalizing vision (and hints at its absurdity) and then reveals its impracticality by listing all of Bloom's unlikely schemes for getting the money that would bring such commodities within reach.

The narrative voice in the chapter removes the novel from Bloom's direct consciousness, acting as a filter that makes it impossible to determine Bloom's own thoughts. In many ways, the scientific, objective language might be considered the antithesis to advertising language, with its reliance on metaphor, on suggestiveness, on image, on empty promises. Yet as becomes clear in the "allwool garment" construction of the English gentleman, even this scientific language can participate in advertising strategy. The apparently objective language blends into the enticing promises of marketing and advertisement, as Joyce shows that the description one might consider more "authentic" in terms of accuracy in fact becomes difficult to separate from the meaning that swirls (and does not swirl) around advertising.

The vision of Bloom's ideal home culminates in a final evening meditation on the perfect advertisement. The narrator describes Bloom's supposed dream of creating "some one sole unique advertisement to cause passers to stop in wonder, a poster novelty, with all extraneous accretions excluded, reduced to its simplest and most efficient terms not exceeding the span of casual vision and congruous with the velocity of modern life" (17.1770–1773). The dream recalls several forms of marketing—the display poster, the shop window that draws the gaze of the viewer, and the new sleek newspaper ads that Bloom has been trying to canvass all day. In all these forms, the modern advertisement has been (as shown throughout this book) stripped of "extraneous accretions." Bloom is here at once pictured as buyer and seller, consumer and adman; the description of Bloom's country home moves from advertisement to commodity to shopper, from the creation of the promotional material to the final purchase. The ideal advertisement, like Joyce's prose, would be "congruous with the velocity of modern life." Joyce not only presents a critique and a commentary on the commodification of authenticity; he also demonstrates a peculiarly modernist response. To read Bloom's ideal home in all its richness, one must see parody flow into understanding, mockery blend with attraction. Joyce crafts his critique into a new literary form, turning contradiction into art.

Joyce's play with home construction and with notions of authenticity is epitomized in the final reference to "potted meat" in the chapter. As Bloom climbs into bed at the end of a very long day, the narrator describes what he encounters: "New clean bedlinen, additional odours, the presence of a human form, female, hers, the imprint of a human form, male, not his, some crumbs, some flakes of potted meat, recooked, which he removed" (17.2123–2125). Here again, the narrator's objective, scientific descriptions of the various objects Bloom encounters—and does not encounter—are infused with emotion. In particular the potted meat, long associated with Boylan's sexuality and the affair, are presented as literal evidence of the earlier tryst. This final encounter with potted meat may be read pessimistically; Bloom removes the meat, hinting the bed will (no longer be) an "abode of bliss" with all the sexual suggestiveness of that phrase. The adultery itself and Bloom's inability to have sex with Molly reveal a home that is broken, that is incomplete. And yet, it is equally possible to argue that this is a moment of triumph for Bloom. He removes the meat, which is recooked and old and merely flakes and crumbs, almost as if he is dismissing Boylan from the bed; he is asserting, potentially, his own right to his bed, his own right to define his "abode." These individual readings, however, are not as important as their number, for the very fact that this advertisement jingle may now be interpreted in so many ways reflects Joyce's mobility of expression and interpretation within the novel. For Bloom and for Joyce, a radical self-fashioning of the home is possible: an insistence that the home is to be created, is protean, is capable of being transformed and constructed, is not to be fixed. And yet within this mobility lies still the elegiac longing to come home, to return to some kind of permanence that must nevertheless be questioned and remade even as it is desired. Joyce captures here the heart of the paradoxical promise of the commodified authentic—that one might construct the very authenticity that both celebrates and belies its constructedness.

Excursion Three: Virginia Woolf, *To the Lighthouse*

The final excursion brings us to a scene that might not at first appear to be commercial at all: Lily Briscoe's attempts to paint as she stares through the window at Mrs. Ramsay sitting with her son, James, in Woolf's *To the Lighthouse* (1927).[7] Woolf presents a scene that recalls Ralph's window shopping in *Night and Day* and that had and has, in multiple variations, been produced throughout the twentieth century. A viewer, standing outside, sees a lighted place of authenticity, embodied perhaps in a domestic image (a kind-looking woman engaged in a domestic task such as knitting or cooking, children at her feet), or in an image of radiant, untouchable beauty. As we stare into televisions, into magazines, into newspapers, we find countless advertisements that reproduce such a vision, tantalizing us with the promise that just through the window lies all that we might desire, lies our chance to bring the image into our own lives. Woolf not only captures this extended moment of gazing but also imagines a possible response for Lily, for her readers, and even for consumers more generally.

Woolf opens the first section of the novel, "The Window," with the domestic moment that Lily observes between Mrs. Ramsay and James. Mrs. Ramsay knits the famous brown stocking while James sits at her feet, cutting out pictures from the Army and Navy Stores' catalogue. As the section unfolds, readers see the variety of gazes that fall on Mrs. Ramsay, in particular the artistic gaze of Lily Briscoe, who tries to paint a picture that will capture the image of mother and child. As Lily stands outside the window looking in, she imagines a previous moment, a night when Mrs. Ramsay had come to her room, and she herself was in the child's position, sitting at Mrs. Ramsay's feet. Lily finds in Mrs. Ramsay and the setting an almost indescribable authenticity, some way that she holds truth or creates reality that Lily struggles to define:

> Was it wisdom? Was it knowledge? Was it, once more, the deceptiveness of beauty, so that all one's perceptions, half-way to truth, were tangled in a golden mesh? or did she lock up within her some secret which certainly Lily Briscoe believed people must have for the world to go on at all? . . . Sitting on the floor with her arms round Mrs. Ramsay's knees, close as she could get . . . she imagined how in the chambers of the mind and heart of the woman who was, physically, touching her, were stood, like the treasures in the tombs of kings, tablets bearing sacred inscriptions, which if one could spell them out, would teach one everything, but they would never be offered openly.[8]

Close as Lily is, she imagines getting closer still, pressing into secret chambers where she might find some enduring answer. Lily seeks to discover the central authentic quality of Mrs. Ramsay, both for herself and for her painting. Like Katharine Hilbery, Lily remains deeply attached to Victorian icons, but she also hopes she may represent such icons through a new form of art rather than seeking to become like them herself. Lily desires both to understand the authenticity Mrs. Ramsay represents and to be able to reconstruct it on her own terms.

Mrs. Ramsay reflects several versions of authenticity we have considered. Most powerfully, perhaps, she represents a tantalizing domesticity. As she knits her stocking, child at her feet, surrounding by worn but comfortable furniture, she might be the spokesperson for a domestic version of nostalgic authenticity that so many feared was threatened by an encroaching modernity. Committed equally to motherhood and to marriage, Mrs. Ramsay reflects and anticipates a long line of similar scenes, stretching before and after the novel, reproduced in advertisements and commercials. She also reflects, however, versions of originary authenticity. Part of what makes Mrs. Ramsay so enticing is her one-of-a-kind quality. As Mr. Bankes tells her, "'Nature has but little clay . . . like that of which she moulded you'" (29). She seems both to Lily and to Mr. Bankes to be iconic, her physical beauty radiating out to suggest a kind of luminous uniqueness. The seemingly mundane details of a woman sitting in a wicker armchair transform in Lily's eyes into a kind of hushed, sacred space, an "august shape," "a dome" (51).

On the surface, it would seem that Mrs. Ramsay in fact embodies everything that is *not* commercial, not the mass market, not the artificial spectacle, but the real thing, outside commodity culture. To understand the link to commercialism, it is necessary to approach the scene from outside of high modernism, to trace, as this book has attempted to do, the way this very image of authenticity and noncommercial suggestion was at the heart of so much commercial strategy. Woolf may not be purposefully mimicking the techniques of commercial culture, but the importance of this scene to the discussion of the commodified authentic lies in the way advertising techniques harnessed and attempted to package various forms of Mrs. Ramsay–like authenticity. Reading this odd scene of window gazing in fact allows us to read with greater clarity our own contemporary moment.

Part of Mrs. Ramsay's allure is her ability to shine through the mundane details of modern life and, indeed, to transform those details, and this quality links her to the experience of current advertising. Woolf, in a sense, presents another marketing cycle: the transformation of the discrete commodities that James cuts out of the catalogue into the elaborate authentic climate around and within Mrs. Ramsay. Mr. Bankes is struck by the incongruity of Mrs. Ramsay amid ordinary surroundings. As he speaks to her on the telephone about the thoroughly modern and mundane subject of train times, "He saw her at the end of the line very clearly Greek, straight, blue-eyed. How incongruous it seemed to be telephoning a woman like that" (29). The prose flows from the sublime to the trivial: "The Graces assembling seemed to have joined hands in meadows of asphodel to compose that face. He would catch the 10:30 at Euston" (29). Mrs. Ramsay is both domestic goddess and alluring supermodel, raised above the trivialities of daily life, tantalizingly close but out of reach. Her uncanny ability to transform her surroundings, to provide an oasis of calm and beauty in the midst of the ordinary, finds its unlikely parallel in advertising as it was emerging at the time, and as it remains: the commercial oasis offered by Selfridges' newspaper advertisements, elegant and simple against the surrounding clutter of articles; a lighted store window that presents a compelling contrast to the noise and bustle and stark realities of urban streets; a television commercial that flickers into vision after the tangle of news, promising an escape through commercial satisfaction. Like a window shopper who might gaze longingly through the glass, Lily gazes in on Mrs. Ramsay, hoping that something "in there" holds a mysterious but powerful answer, some way to bring meaning out of chaos.

Woolf's scene also suggests a model for resisting the enticing authenticity of a Mrs. Ramsay and the commercial images she parallels. Lily must stay outside the scene to have her vision, and this distance allows for criticism. Lily is not a blind admirer of Mrs. Ramsay. She may gaze with longing, but she also resists her and what she represents. On the night Lily remembers, when Lily places her head on Mrs. Ramsay's lap, Mrs. Ramsay insists that "they all must marry," that "there could be no disputing" that "an unmarried woman has missed the best of life." Lily wants to "urge her own exemption from the universal law; [to] plead for it; [for] she liked to be alone; she liked to be herself; she was not made for that." And as "she had laid her head on Mrs. Ramsay's lap" she "laughed and laughed and laughed, laughed almost hysterically at the thought of Mrs. Ramsay presiding with immutable calm over destinies which she completely failed to understand" (50).[9] Rejecting Mrs. Ramsay's plans, Lily, of course, paints a picture instead, and her artistic response has been of continued interest to critics. What Lily also offers, here at the end of the third excursion, is another distinctive modernist response to authenticity's construction. When Lily returns more than ten years later to finish her painting, she sets her easel in the same spot, but Mrs. Ramsay is no longer there at the window. Finding or even believing in the authenticity that Mrs. Ramsay represented seems no longer possible, that sort of belief having been a casualty of the war and the twentieth century. Yet the fact of absence does not end the longing for a return, despite the knowledge that such a return is not possible or even fully desired. Lily feels profoundly the initial allure of Mrs. Ramsay and all she represents. She also feels the intense need to resist this allure, threatening as it does all that Lily hopes to achieve. The modernism of the scene certainly in part lies in Woolf's technique, in Lily's abstract painting, and in the depiction of postwar society. Yet another critical part of Woolf's modernism lies in the flow between Lily's attraction and her rejection. To survive the contradiction, she must ignore neither the allure nor the importance of resistance; she must, instead, incorporate the contradiction into her own art, her art becoming, in a sense, both a way to resist and a way to acknowledge—and indeed reproduce—the allure.

Ironically, marketers offer a similar (though perhaps perverse) version of this creation. Capturing the tantalizing pull of authenticity in all its many forms, marketers turn the authentic into objects, into images, and into carefully constructed spaces. Now infinitely more flexible than the image of Mrs. Ramsay, fully capable of morphing into various forms of pleasure or appeal, the commodified authentic promises to allow the viewer full access to the appeal, but without the drawbacks. This is, after all, authenticity once removed, and what it lacks in actual authenticity (goes the promise), it makes up for in suppleness and availability.

Commodity culture has thus far proved stronger than any critique, and as we have seen, part of what makes the commodified authentic in particular such a powerful strategy and so resilient even after sustained criticism is that it demands its own critique. It demands that we unmask it and see it as constructed, for unless we do, we cannot imagine that we could obtain it for ourselves. To understand the commodified authentic, we must understand, as Lily does, the powerful appeal of the authentic vision at the same time that we resist it, at the same time that we acknowledge its construction.

. . .

In the course of writing this book, I was repeatedly struck by the endurance of the commodified authentic as a marketing strategy. All the commercial examples discussed—Bournville, Port Sunlight, Letchworth, Selfridges, Lutyens' homes, *Country Life* magazine, and the Ideal Home Exhibition—continue to thrive, in part because of their continued ties to authenticity and commerce. Admittedly, such ties have shifted over the years. Selfridges in London, for example, remains an attraction both through its status as a venerable old store and through its aggressive new shift to marketing itself as a hip retail presence.[10] Even outside these examples, however, the commodified authentic meets us at every turn, from the endless commercialization of British heritage to the continual selling of English country life. What I have attempted to do in this book is not to excuse the often crass and manipulative nature of such endeavors but to suggest that their power lies in an ability to present a usable past in a modern package.

The puzzle of authenticity itself—hardly a revered concept among twenty-first-century academics—continues to be an elusive concept. A few years ago, I gave a talk on the commodified authentic at the Modern Language Association's annual conference, and I received an interesting question: Wasn't I assuming, or at least implying, that there was no such thing as authenticity itself, that it was all simply a marketing trick? It is easy, in fact, to assume all authenticity in the twenty-first century has become a kind a simulacra, that the continuous move to commodify authenticity has, in fact, resulted in the emptying of the term.

I am, of course, on dangerous ground. Defining the authentic precisely is difficult and a potential minefield. When the question is simply to distinguish an actual artifact from a reproduction, the task is perhaps easiest. An expert can, for example, tell an "authentic" nineteenth-century farm tool from its copy in the twentieth. Historical reproductions can also be assigned "authentic" labels; a living-history museum that whitewashes the past and erases its painful elements will be deemed less "authentic" than the one that presents the past in all its gritty details. In this case, "authentic" takes the meaning of "accurate." When authenticity gets commodified, however, the case is far muddier. As I discuss in the previous chapters, the commodified authentic must be seen on a continuum, with more and less "authentic" versions. In general, the commodified authentic is often viewed as more successful the more skillfully it hides its commercial origins, as many higher class versions of the commodified authentic do; the expertly but deliberately distressed piece of furniture may appear more "authentic" than the mass-marketed versions of an English country cottage, though both are versions of the commodified authentic. There may, in fact, be advantages in style and quality to the higher class models, but one should be cautious, as

Pierre Bourdieu reminds us, that questions of class are not masquerading as questions of taste.

An important difference exists, however, between the authenticity of an object associated with one's own history and one that simply looks as if it has such a connection. My grandmother's old watch, worn by use, and valued by me because of its history and its visible connections to past events—the dent, for example, where I dropped it as a teenager—holds more significance for me than any other watch, new, antique, or simply made to look old. Such authenticity can accrue on any object, from a beautiful old chair, to a plastic purse, to a ceramic gnome, and arises from the object's personal connection over time with the owner. My claim in this book is not that authenticity does not exist, but that (1) the division between the authentic and the nonauthentic is often not clear-cut, and can change over time, (2) not everyone has the opportunity to have weathered original furniture, and thus demands for authenticity can at times hide a kind of class snobbery, and (3) the faux-distressed object might in fact have both personal and cultural value in itself, though admittedly this may be different than that offered by a personal heirloom.

Examining the commodified authentic forces us to ask difficult questions about authenticity and marketing. They form, at times, an unholy alliance, one that can distort history and present a crass imitation of something valuable. Historically, in early twentieth-century Britain, the alliance also served as a potentially liberating, playful, mobile hybrid, one that helped ease the difficult transition from the Victorian age to the modern one. Our position both as consumers and as critics should always be one of suspicion and attraction, of remaining alert to the dangers of the commodified authentic while recognizing its possibilities.

Notes

Chapter 1: Introduction

1. Commonly attributed to Oscar Wilde; an unsourced quotation.

2. The term "mass market" is a controversial one. I use it deliberately in places where I mean to refer to the historic disdain for products sold in mass on the popular market.

3. The commodified authentic developed somewhat differently in the United States, a far younger country where the hunger for the old and the desire for the authentic held a special appeal, but where the emphasis on spectacle and the spectacular was far more in evidence. While there is still significant overlap between the British and American versions of the commodified authentic, the American version lies outside the scope of this book. For more on the development of advertising and consumer culture in America, see William Leach, *Land of Desire: Merchants, Power, and the Rise of a New American Culture.*

4. Virginia Woolf, "A Sketch of the Past," in *Moments of Being*, 147.

5. Henry James, "The Great Good Place," in *The Complete Tales of Henry James*, vol. 11, 31–32.

6. Critical theory stretching back to Marx has acknowledged the role of the glorified commodity in Britain and the cultural values that can adhere to objects. As Marx famously observed, in the nineteenth century goods had come to exceed their use value, becoming commodities that were fetishized, transcendent, and even "mystical." The power of the commodity to produce such auras, however, relied (and relies) not on the individual object but on the way this object circulated within the culture. Understanding the power of a given commodity naturally requires understanding it as only one part of a larger discourse of cultural formation and exchange. If we view, for instance, examples of the commodified authentic as single objects—a "fake" weathered piece of furniture, a dress advertised as a return to Renaissance values—they become easy to dismiss as bad-faith efforts to dupe unwary consumers. See Karl Marx, *Capital*, vol. 1, 163–177.

7. Alun Howkins, "The Discovery of Rural England," in Robert Colls and Philip Dodd (eds.), *Englishness: Politics and Culture 1880–1920*, 62–88. See also Martin Wiener, *English Culture and the Decline of the Industrial Spirit, 1850–1980*, for a highly negative view of the

English attachment to rural England. Also, George K. Behlmer and Fred M. Leventhal (eds.), in *Singular Continuities: Tradition, Nostalgia, and Identity in Modern British Culture*, offer a useful summary of the heritage debate and its critics, from Wiener to later revisions.

8. No study concerning authenticity, modernity, and modernism would be complete without reference to Walter Benjamin's influential essay "The Work of Art in the Age of Mechanical Reproduction," in *Illuminations*, 217–251. Well known but often misread, Benjamin's essay explores the author's ambivalent assessment of authenticity and aura in relation to art, as Benjamin seems to lament the loss of authenticity brought about by mechanical reproduction at the same time that he sees political and cultural possibilities in such loss. Benjamin's idea of "aura" is touched on at several places in this work, and his very ambivalence toward authenticity is itself an instructive model for both the possibilities and the dangers of the commodified authentic.

9. See note 11.

10. Andreas Huyssen, *After the Great Divide: Modernism, Mass Culture, Postmodernism*. Huyssen goes on to argue that it was the avant-garde that embraced mass culture as constituting its very aesthetics. Fredric Jameson, "The Politics of Theory: Ideological Positions in the Postmodernism Debate," 64. The positions of both critics on modernism and material culture are more nuanced than these frequently cited passages suggest.

11. See, for example, Lawrence Rainey, *Institutions of Modernism: Literary Elites and Public Culture*; subsequent references to this book will be cited parenthetically in the text; Thomas Strychacz, *Modernism, Mass Culture, and Professionalism*; John Xiros Cooper, *Modernism and the Culture of Market Society*; and Edward P. Comentale, *Modernism, Cultural Production, and the British Avant-garde*. Also, see the excellent collection of essays in Kevin J. H. Dettmar and Stephen Watt (eds.), *Marketing Modernisms: Self-Promotion, Canonization, and Rereading*; and Ian Willison, Warwick Gould, and Warren Chernaik (eds.), *Modernist Writers and the Marketplace*. For a later consideration, see Catherine Turner, *Marketing Modernism between the Two World Wars*.

12. Lawrence Rainey has recently provided a penetrating assessment of the selling of *Ulysses*, a text marketed specifically *as* an exclusive, noncommercial venture (*Institutions of Modernism*, 42–76). See also Rachel Bowlby, "Walking, Women, and Writing: Virginia Woolf as *Flâneuse*," in Isobel Armstrong (ed.), *New Feminist Discourses: Critical Essays on Theories and Texts*, 26–47; and Jonathan Freedman, *Professions of Taste: Henry James, British Aestheticism, and Commodity Culture*. Jennifer Wicke's work remains the essential source for incisive analysis of modernism's ties to advertising and marketing; see *Advertising Fictions: Literature, Advertisement, and Social Reading*; and "Coterie Consumption: Bloomsbury, Keynes, and Modernism as Marketing," in Dettmar and Watt, *Marketing Modernisms*, 109–132.

Running alongside and often overlapping these efforts are critical works that reassess the divisions between high and low moderns, both by bringing renewed attention to neglected (read: low) writers and by skillfully showing how each category overlapped and indeed influenced the other. See, for example, Maria DiBattista and Lucy McDiarmid (eds.), *High and Low Moderns: Literature and Culture, 1889–1939*; Lynne Hapgood and Nancy L. Paxton (eds.), *Outside Modernism: In Pursuit of the English Novel, 1900–1930*; and Ann L. Ardis, *Modernism and Cultural Conflict, 1880–1922*.

More generally, consumer culture and advertising have a vast number of critics, only a few of whom I discuss here in relation to modernism. See, for example, the work of the Frankfurt school, including Max Horkheimer and Theodor Adorno, *The Dialectic of*

Enlightenment, as well as Roland Barthes's *Mythologies*. See also Stuart Ewen's *Captains of Consciousness: Advertising and the Social Roots of the Consumer Culture*.

13. Svetlana Boym, in *The Future of Nostalgia*, gives both a history of nostalgia and a subtle reflection on some of its possibilities, focusing on Russian and Eastern European examples. David Lowenthal offers an encyclopedic work on the past and nostalgia in *The Past Is a Foreign Country*. Authenticity receives continual attention from a range of theorists. See, for example, Lionel Trilling's series of lectures in *Sincerity and Authenticity*, which presents a cultural history of the two terms and argues that authenticity has replaced sincerity as the modern ideal. See also Charles Taylor's philosophical assessment in *The Ethics of Authenticity*. As instructive as all these works are, they do not engage at length with the commercialization of authenticity and nostalgia.

14. Relations between modernism and authenticity have been explored, for example, in a recent cluster of articles in *Modernism/modernity*, guest edited by Debra Rae Cohen and Kevin J. H. Dettmar, 14, no. 3 (September 2007). The Modernist Studies Association sponsored peer seminars on modernism and authenticity at both the 2003 conference in Birmingham, UK, and the 2005 conference in Chicago.

15. Various critics offer insightful analyses of the dangers of commodifying nostalgia and authenticity, as well as the invention of traditions and the heritage industry more generally. Hobsbawm and Ranger examine how government-sponsored revivals of national "traditions" were largely nationalist projects that invented traditions never practiced; see Eric Hobsbawm and Terence Ranger (eds.), *The Invention of Tradition*. Richard Terdiman finds that from the nineteenth century on, a commodified nostalgia endangered memory itself; as the mode of production for commodities became hidden, commodities began to challenge memory and to make it inauthentic; see Terdiman, *Present Past: Modernity and the Memory Crisis*. See also Wiener, *English Culture and the Decline of the Industrial Spirit, 1850–1980*, summarized above. Jean Baudrillard takes this to its pessimistic extreme, finding no authentic memory or real object but only a world of simulacra, a "hyperreality" of self-referential signs; see *Simulacra and Simulation*. For more critiques of the heritage industry, see David Lowenthal, *The Heritage Crusade and the Spoils of History*; Patrick Wright, *On Living in an Old Country: The National Past in Contemporary Britain*; and Robert Hewison, *The Heritage Industry: Britain in the Climate of Decline*.

Raphael Samuel, while detailing some of the darker sides of attempts to commodify nostalgia, urges a more nuanced approach, suggesting that rather than envisioning a single-minded plot, we might "think of the invention of tradition as a process rather than an event"; see *Theatres of Memory: Past and Present in Contemporary Culture*, vol. 1, 17.

16. Jon McKenzie, *Perform or Else: From Discipline to Performance*, 15.

17. Richard Schechner, *Performance Studies: An Introduction*, 19. For more on performance studies, see also Schechner's *Performance Theory*; Henry Bial, *The Performance Studies Reader*; and Jane Milling and Graham Ley (eds.), *Modern Theories of Performance: From Stanislavski to Boal*. Judith Butler, of course, remains the diva of performativity, especially in regard to gender; see *Gender Trouble: Feminism and the Subversion of Identity*.

Chapter 2: The Past Is a Present Country

1. Howard's scheme was instrumental in launching the first Garden City at Letchworth, and his ideas continued to influence England's town planning efforts well past World War II. Howard's work has been documented in many sources. For a reprint of Howard's

book, see the carefully annotated Routledge edition, with commentary by Peter Hall, Dennis Hardy, and Colin Ward. Two books on the growth of the Garden City are fundamental: Walter L. Creese, *The Search for Environment: The Garden City, Before and After*, and the excellent volume by Standish Meacham, *Regaining Paradise: Englishness and the Early Garden City Movement*; see also Kermit C. Parsons and David Schuyler (eds.), *From Garden City to Green City: The Legacy of Ebenezer Howard*; and Robert Fishman, *Urban Utopias in the Twentieth Century: Ebenezer Howard, Frank Lloyd Wright, and Le Corbusier*.

2. Howard himself was more utopian than nostalgic, and he often found himself irritated by the more conservative, backward-looking bent of many who were attracted to the Garden City Movement. See Meacham, *Regaining Paradise*, 68–69.

3. A. R. Sennett, *Garden Cities in Theory and Practice*, vol. 1, 3.

4. C. F. G. Masterman, *The Condition of England*, 191.

5. For a history of housing reform efforts in the nineteenth century, see John Burnett, *A Social History of Housing: 1815–1970*; Martin Doughty (ed.), *Building the Industrial City*; and works on housing reformer Octavia Hill, including Robert Whelan (ed.), *Octavia Hill and the Social Housing Debate*.

6. For a longer discussion of the housing concerns and utopian ideas of William Morris and John Ruskin, see M. H. Lang, *Designing Utopia: John Ruskin's Urban Vision for Britain and America*.

7. Small-scale literal versions of these literary utopias were attempted by William Morris and Edward Carpenter, among others. Several critics have explored the development of nineteenth- and twentieth-century utopian experiments, including Phillip E. Wegner, *Imagined Communities: Utopia, the Nation, and the Spatial History of Modernity*; Kishan Kumar, *Utopia and Anti-Utopia in Modern Times*; Gregory Claeys, *Citizens and Saints: Politics and Anti-politics in Early British Socialism*.

8. I discuss such exhibitions in chapter 3.

9. See Elizabeth M. Cadbury, "George Cadbury: A Paper Read on September 29th, 1929, at the Jubilee Celebration of the Removal of the Works from Bridge Street to Bournville in 1879" (*BCA-CF*, MS 466-41-8-68, 1929), 1.

10. I do not attempt here a full history of Bournville or Cadbury Brothers, which may be found in other sources. For an early history of Cadbury Brothers that includes information on the village itself, see Iolo A. Williams, *The Firm of Cadbury: 1831–1931*; subsequent references to this source will be cited parenthetically in the text. A more recent and thorough history of Bournville is Michael Harrison's *Bournville: Model Village to Garden Suburb*. Both Meacham and Creese include sections on Bournville; see Meacham, *Regaining Paradise*, 11–43, and Creese, *The Search for Environment*, 108–143. For more information on the architecture at Bournville, see W. Alexander Harvey, *The Model Village and Its Cottages: Bournville*; subsequent references to this source will be cited parenthetically in the text. An early history of both the firm and the village may be found in T. B. Rogers (ed.), "Memories of Bridge Street and Early Bournville," *Bournville Works Magazine* 8 (1909): 325–340.

11. In practice, however, Bournville was largely controlled by Cadbury Brothers and its concerns.

12. Industrial profits had long sustained the country lifestyles of the wealthy; philanthropic causes used contributions from industry to ameliorate housing conditions, and model villages were built throughout the nineteenth century by wealthy industrialists. Cadbury, however, blended industry with housing reform not simply by using industrial profits

but by creating a community where modern factory production was an intrinsic part of the model community.

13. Deed of Foundation, Bournville Village Trust (1900), 1.

14. *The Bournville Village Trust: An Account of Its Planning and Housing Schemes in Suburban and Rural Areas* (Bournville: Publication Department, c. 1938), 20.

15. Edward Cadbury, *Experiments in Industrial Organization*, xvii; subsequent references to this source will be cited parenthetically in the text.

16. Comments from "a Somerset clergyman," quoted in C. F. G. Masterman, *The Condition of England*, 191.

17. *Bournville Village Trust: An Account of Its Planning*, 5.

18. *Bournville Village Trust*, pamphlet (Birmingham: Cond Brothers, 1927), 5. Bournville, of course, could not avoid the provisions for bye-law streets—Bournville had to follow the rules for street width as well as Birmingham—but the designers did everything possible to provide variety and to avoid the monotonous stretches found in the industrial city.

19. J. H. Whitehouse, "Bournville: A Study in Housing Reform," *Studio* (1901–1902): 170–171, quoted in Creese, *The Search for Environment*, 111.

20. As I discuss at length in the next chapter, the picturesque cottage has a long architectural history in Britain, emerging before the late nineteenth century. Bournville's architectural novelty lay in uniting this tradition with industry.

21. Most of the public buildings united an architectural expression of tradition and past eras with modern layout and conveniences. The public schools, for example, were built with some Gothic detailing, though Cadbury insisted that "every effort [be] made to embody the latest improvements" (Harvey, *The Model Village*, 14). Another building, the appropriately named Ruskin Hall, built in 1902, was "a center for the intellectual and artistic life of the village"; in 1911, it also became the School of Arts and Crafts (*Bournville Village Trust: An Account of Its Planning*, 46). Like the school, the building offered a Gothic design with a broadly sloping roof and casement windows. Here again, Bournville combines a sense of the past with an insistence on contemporary development.

22. *Bournville Village Trust*, 27.

23. *The Bournville Village Trust: An Account of Its Planning*, 47.

24. Meacham, *Regaining Paradise*, 22.

25. George Cadbury Jr., *Town Planning, with Special Reference to the Birmingham Schemes*, 89.

26. Elizabeth Cadbury also noted in 1942 that "many of the social amenities, that we now take for granted, did not exist 50 years ago, such as Old Age Pensions, Health Insurance, Unemployment Benefits, [and] Hospital Contributory Schemes" ("How Did the Garden Grow?" Personal memoir of George Cadbury [*BCA-CF*, MS 466-72, 1942], 3).

27. W. J. Ashley, preface, in Edward Cadbury's *Experiments in Industrial Organization*, xiii.

28. The Cadbury advertisements in the *Electro Register* from the early years of Bournville, located at the Cadbury archives at Birmingham Central Library, reveal a continuous emphasis on the purity of the product, with nationalist undertones that reassured consumers that the cocoa was made with "no foreign substances." The advertisements also frequently drew on nostalgic images, such as offers for special tins of cocoa that were printed with sentimental scenes of old-looking buildings at Bournville. Another recurring advertisement displayed the cozy interior of an inn, with a mother and her child enjoying a steaming mug of cocoa, and the copy above them declaring, "Good Old English Cocoa of

the Good Old English Days" (*BCA-CF*, MS 466/10, 1904–5, and MS 466/11, 1906). As I discuss in chapter 4, Selfridges department store would perfect this kind of nostalgic selling, and it would further suggest such an atmosphere in the material space of the store itself.

29. In her biography of Yeats's wife, George, Ann Saddlemyer notes that George and the Cadbury daughters had attended school together, and that Mrs. Emmeline Cadbury (married to Richard Cadbury's son William) enthusiastically supported the efforts of the Cuala Industries. See *Becoming George: The Life of Mrs. W. B. Yeats*, 333.

30. Disney reverses this process, evolving from the reproduced Main Street, U.S.A., at Disneyland, to a reconstruction of the same street at Disneyworld, and then to the construction of its actual model town, Celebration, U.S.A.

31. See Jean Baudrillard, *Simulacra and Simulation.*

32. W. L. George, *Labour and Housing at Port Sunlight*, 4; subsequent references to this source will be cited parenthetically in the text. In the same vein, the company's magazine *Progress* declared, "It is one of Mr. Lever's vital principles to decline to pose as a philanthropist. He wishes the world to be convinced that it pays for large employers of labour to spare no pains and no expense in providing their workers with healthy and beautiful homes and pleasant surroundings" (*Progress* 1 [1899]: 44).

Longer histories of Port Sunlight may be found in numerous sources, including Creese, *The Search for Environment*, 108–143; Meacham, *Regaining Paradise*, 11–43; and Edward Hubbard and Michael Shippobottom, "Architecture," in *Lord Leverhulme: Founder of the Lady Lever Art Gallery and Port Sunlight on Merseyside, Exhibition to Mark the Golden Jubilee, 1930–1980* (London: Royal Academy of Arts, 1980), 149–199. See also T. Raffles Davison, *Port Sunlight: A Record of Its Artistic and Pictorial Aspect*; subsequent references to this source will be cited parenthetically in the text.

33. W. H. Lever, "Prosperity Sharing v. Profit Sharing in Relation to Workshop Management," *Birkenhead News*, 24 November 1900; reprinted in *The Buildings Erected at Port Sunlight and Thornton Hough* (Cheshire, 1905), 47.

34. Lord Leverhulme, *The Six-Hour Day and Other Industrial Questions*, 54.

35. Ibid., 54.

36. W. H. Lever, "Land for Houses: A Paper Read before the North End Liberal Club, on Tuesday, October 4, 1898"; printed in *Birkenhead News*, 8 October 1898; reprinted in *The Buildings Erected at Port Sunlight and Thornton Hough* (Cheshire, 1905), 33.

37. W. H. Lever, "The Buildings Erected at Port Sunlight and Thornton Hough" (paper presented by W. H. Lever at meeting of the Architectural Association, London, 21 March 1902); reprinted in book of same title (Cheshire, 1905), 19.

38. Lever, "Land for Houses," 34.

39. Lever, "The Buildings Erected," 10, 12.

40. Ibid., 12.

41. "A London Journalist's Impressions," *Progress* 1 (October 1900): 550.

42. Lever, "The Buildings Erected," 27.

43. Ibid.

44. Both Creese and Meacham link Thornton Hough to the quickly constructed old-looking village at the Royal Jubilee Exhibition in Manchester in 1887. See Creese, *The Search for Environment*, 127ff., and Meacham, *Regaining Paradise*, 36–37. I discuss such exhibitions in relation to the *Daily Mail*'s Ideal Home Exhibition in chapter 3.

45. "The Poetry of an Old Soap-Box," *Progress* 1 (March 1900): 262.

46. See the death and birth statistics in Cadbury's *Experiments in Industrial Organization*, 284–285, and George's chapter "Some Results" in *Labour and Housing at Port Sunlight*, 143–166. Certainly Bournville and Port Sunlight had their critics, and Lever came under special fire for many of his actions. For an interesting account of the early days of Port Sunlight and the problems of restricting the village to Lever's workers, see Andrew Knox, *Coming Clean: A Postscript after Retirement from Unilever*, 1–16. For an account of Lever's failed scheme to develop the Hebrides, see Nigel Nicolson, *Lord of the Isles: Lord Leverhulme in the Hebrides.*

47. While quite different than Howard's imagined Garden City, Bournville and Port Sunlight were frequently categorized as Garden Cities in later years. For example, H. E. Johnson refers to "the Garden City of Bournville" in "George Cadbury, 1839–1922," memorial number of the *Bournville Works Magazine* (*BCA-CF*, MS 466-226, 1922), 15.

48. See, for example, "Commentators' Introduction," by Peter Hall, Dennis Hardy, and Colin Ward, in Ebenezer Howard, *To-morrow: A Peaceful Path to Real Reform*, 2.

49. Howard, *To-morrow: A Peaceful Path to Real Reform,* title page; subsequent references to this source will be cited parenthetically in the text.

50. A vast literature exists on both Barry Parker and Raymond Unwin, and I do not attempt here a complete history of their work at Letchworth. See, for example, Dean Hawkes (ed.), *Modern Country Homes in England: The Arts and Crafts Architecture of Barry Parker*; Walter L. Creese (ed.), *The Legacy of Raymond Unwin: A Human Pattern for Planning*; and Mervyn Miller, *Barry Parker and Raymond Unwin*, and his work *Letchworth: The First Garden City.*

51. Their offices, built in 1907, now house the First Garden City Heritage Museum.

52. Raymond Unwin, *Town Planning in Practice: An Introduction to the Art of Designing Cities and Suburbs*, 12.

53. Ibid.

54. *Letchworth Citizen*, 13 May 1913, 5; quoted in Meacham, *Regaining Paradise*, 103.

55. W. H. Gaunt, "A Few Notes upon a Recent Essay on Architecture," *The City*, September 1910, 109; quoted in Meacham, *Regaining Paradise*, 107.

56. For an account of Adams's efforts on behalf of Letchworth and the Garden City Movement, see Michael Simpson, *Thomas Adams and the Modern Planning Movement: Britain, Canada, and the United States, 1900–1940*, 9–40.

57. "Letchworth Garden City" pamphlet, *LGC-Gen P*, January 1909, 4.

58. See *Letchworth Garden City in Fifty-five Pictures* (London: Halton House, 1911), and "Letter Card" pamphlet (no date or publication information), both in *LGC-Gen P.*

59. "Letchworth: A Town in the Country" pamphlet (Letchworth: Letchworth Printers Ltd., c. 1929), 1, in *LGC-Gen P.*

60. Ibid., 3.

61. Sutherland Lyall mentions "instant thatch" in *Dream Cottages: From Cottage Ornée to Stockbroker Tudor, Two Hundred Years of the Cult of the Vernacular*, 18.

62. From Shaw's letter to Edward Rose, 14 December 1899, *Collected Letters*, vol. 2, 118; hereafter abbreviated as *CL*, followed by the volume and page number.

63. From an unpublished letter from Shaw to Howard's son, A. C. Howard, 25 May 1928, in Hertfordshire Archives and Local Studies (DE/Ho/F22/2). Shaw actually bases a character

in *Heartbreak House* on Howard. See Michael Holroyd, *Bernard Shaw: 1918–1950—The Lure of Fantasy*, vol. 3, 16.

64. Nicholas Grene offers a brief but insightful introduction to Shaw's connection to the Garden City Movement. See "The Edwardian Shaw, or the Modernist That Never Was," in Maria DiBattista and Lucy McDiarmid (eds.), *High and Low Moderns*, 135–147.

65. Letter from Shaw to Gilbert Murray, 7 October 1905, *CL* 2, 566.

66. The production histories of *John Bull's Other Island* and *Major Barbara* both reflect the attempt to produce commercially viable plays that were still artistically bold and modern. As critic Jan McDonald outlines, the plays were produced at the Court Theatre, a short-lived but critically important venture that ran from 1904 to 1907 and was dominated by Shavian drama. As McDonald points out, "Shaw was part of a commercial enterprise at the Court, however enlightened that commercialism might be" (273). Shaw recognized that the Court Theatre had to be financially viable to remain artistically viable, and he portrays an interesting exploration of this idea in *Major Barbara*, as I explore further later. See Jan McDonald, "Shaw and the Court Theatre," in Christopher Innes (ed.), *The Cambridge Companion to George Bernard Shaw*, 261–282.

The actual publication of these early plays reflected a similar delicate balance. Shaw worked carefully to position his own plays in particular and modern drama in general to a reading public that was growing rapidly. As critic Katherine Kelly details, "Shaw aimed to fashion his plays as 'high' art by giving his published scripts the material look and poetic weight of fiction and poetry" (25). Borrowing ideas from William Morris, whose Kelmscott Press had reintroduced the idea of bookmaking as an artistic form, Shaw created a certain "look" for the new volumes, one that quickly became associated with his works (Kelly, 42) but that also tied the plays to the already accepted look and feel of volumes of novels and poetry. The plays were "high" art but were designed as high to appeal to a larger group of consumers. See Katherine E. Kelly, "Imprinting the Stage: Shaw and the Publishing Trade, 1883–1903," in Innes, *The Cambridge Companion to George Bernard Shaw*, 25–54.

67. Quotations from *John Bull's Other Island* taken from Dan Laurence (ed.), *The Bodley Head Bernard Shaw: Collected Plays with Their Prefaces*, vol. 2; hereafter cited as *CP*, with volume and page number.

68. For a full description of Shaw's discussions with Yeats about *John Bull's Other Island*, see Norma Jenckes, "The Rejection of Shaw's Irish Play: *John Bull's Other Island*," 38–53.

69. Bernard Shaw, "Preface for Politicians," in *Complete Plays with Prefaces*, vol. 2, 443.

70. Bernard Shaw, *Our Theatres in the Nineties*, vol. 2, 33. It should be noted that Yeats and Lady Gregory, like Shaw, also sought to dispel Irish stereotypes and to "show that Ireland is not the home of buffoonery and easy sentiment"; see Lady Gregory's *Our Irish Theatre*, 9.

71. Broadbent's exploitation of Rosscullen may be linked to recent critical discussion of cultural tourism and the issues of authenticity it raises. Such discussions are beyond the scope of this chapter, but for more information, see Barbara Kirshenblatt-Gimblett, *Destination Culture: Tourism, Museums, and Heritage*, and Chris Rojek and John Urry (eds.), *Touring Cultures: Transformations of Travel and Theory*.

72. Bernard F. Dukore, "Shaw's Big Three," *Shaw: The Annual of Bernard Shaw Studies* 4, 38.

73. *Our Theatres in the Nineties*, vol. 2, 33.

74. Shaw's exposure of Haffigan and Broadbent may be read as an attack on any attempts to sell a falsely romanticized image of Ireland. While far more sophisticated, W. B. Yeats and

Lady Gregory's work to return to a true version of Irish culture, to recover Celtic traditions and to revitalize Celtic myth, met with little sympathy from Shaw, or later from Joyce. For a discussion of Shaw, see Jenckes, "The Rejection of Shaw's Irish Play: *John Bull's Other Island*," 38–53.

75. Numerous critical works have been written on the invention of traditions and the heritage industry more generally. See note 15 in chapter 1 for a summary.

76. Quotations from *Major Barbara* taken from Dan Laurence (ed.), *The Bodley Head Bernard Shaw: Collected Plays with Their Prefaces*, vol. 3; subsequent references to the play will be cited as *CP* and by volume and page number.

77. While presented as a spiritual or moral crisis for Barbara, her reluctance to have her realm invaded by commercial profits—especially profits that in fact cause some of the miseries she sees in the shelter—reflects a larger set of discourses that look both backward to the Victorians and forward to the moderns. Through Barbara, Shaw gestures toward the Victorian aversion to trade as a shameful and contaminated arena, represented here in an especially virulent form, and the related, if incipient, modernist desire to create an aesthetic apart from the contamination of the market or mass culture. Like Barbara, at certain times both sides have had for different reasons an emphatic desire to establish and protect a space outside the marketplace, one that might be morally and aesthetically pure. These mythic, commercial-free cultural locations, such as the Victorian private sphere, have been usefully exposed by modern critics such as Mary Poovey, Leonore Davidoff, and Catherine Hall; on the modernist side, critics such as Jennifer Wicke, Jonathan Freedman, Kevin J. H. Dettmar, and Stephen Watt have likewise corrected the idea that literary modernists were somehow above commerce, as I discuss in greater detail in chapter 1. As critical as these corrections are, however, the *fantasy* of a commercial-free space still persevered. See Mary Poovey, *Uneven Developments: The Ideological Work of Gender in Mid-Victorian England*; Leonore Davidoff and Catherine Hall, *Family Fortunes: Men and Women of the English Middle Class, 1780–1850*; for modernist critics, see notes 11 and 12 in chapter 1.

78. *Morning Post*, 29 November 1905; reprinted in T. F. Evans (ed.), *Shaw: The Critical Heritage*, 44–146.

79. Beatrice Webb, diary entries, 29 November and 2 December, 1905, in Barbara Drake and Margaret I. Cole (eds.), *Our Partnership* (1948): 314; reprinted in Evans (ed.), *Shaw: The Critical Heritage*, 147–148.

80. Sir Oliver Lodge, "*Major Barbara*, G. B. S., and Robert Blatchford," *Clarion*, 29 December 1905, 734–735; reprinted in Evans (ed.), *Shaw: The Critical Heritage*, 160–162.

81. Martin Meisel, "Shaw and Revolution: The Politics of the Plays," in Norman Rosenblood (ed.), *Shaw: Seven Critical Essays*, 106–134.

82. Michiyo Ishii, "Two Political Implications of Shaw's *Major Barbara*," 31; Nicholas Grene, "The Edwardian Shaw, or the Modernist That Never Was," in DiBattista and McDiarmid, *High and Low Moderns*, 141.

83. Harold Bloom, "Introduction," in Harold Bloom (ed.), *George Bernard Shaw's Major Barbara*, 11.

84. From a letter from Shaw to Edward Rose, 25 September 1899, *CL* 2, 103. Shaw was far from seeing such industrial towns as a panacea for social ills. As he notes in a letter to Thomas Demetrius O'Bolger, who wrote to complain about *Major Barbara*, "If, in dealing with Undershaft, you demonstrate that the social problem will never be solved by the Henry Fords and the Leverhulmes [founder of Port Sunlight], well and good: I shall heartily

endorse your conclusion." It was not his intention, suggests Shaw, to propose that idealistic industrial leaders would be sufficient to combat poverty. See Bernard Shaw, *CL* 3, 629.

85. Much as Bournville and Port Sunlight are best understood as living performances of the commodified authentic, so Shaw's plays must be considered as a kind of performance of this type of performance. Physical, literal performances were, for Shaw, one of the most effective ways to be active in social change, producing a greater effect than mere words alone. As he wrote in a letter to Gilbert Murray, it is not enough "to hold aloof in a superior attitude and beat the air with words" (*CL* 2, 565).

Chapter 3: Buying Time

1. Sutherland Lyall traces the history of the vernacular movement in *Dream Cottages: From Cottage Ornée to Stockbroker Tudor, Two Hundred Years of the Cult of the Vernacular.* Malcolm Kelsall presents an overview of the country house tradition in *The Great Good Place: The Country House and English Literature.* For an excellent volume on the country house during the late Victorian and Edwardian age, see Gavin Stamp and André Goulancourt, *The English House 1860–1914: The Flowering of English Domestic Architecture*; most subsequent references to this work will be cited parenthetically in the text. While now somewhat dated, Raymond Williams's *The Country and the City* remains a valuable guide to Britain's historic representations of city and country life. More recently, Deborah Cohen has offered a fascinating historical reading of British interiors and consumers in *Household Gods: The British and Their Possessions.*

2. See Stamp and Goulancourt, *The English House*, 29. Around 1910, there was a surge of books published on the country house and continual cries against its dissolution, including W. Shaw Sparrow, *The English House: How to Judge Its Periods and Styles*, and Basil Oliver, *Old Houses and Village Buildings in East Anglia, Norfolk, Suffolk and Essex.*

3. Forster's nostalgia has engendered understandable critical discomfort. He has been accused of celebrating a willfully naïve image of Britain summarized by Jeremy Tambling as "agricultural, non-industrial, pre–motor car" (2) and of embracing an "archaism and nostalgia" that denies the intensifying problems of modern life by Paul Delany (78). Tambling links Forster's inability "to move out of nostalgia" to Forster's slighting of gender issues and to his failure "to become incisive about the enormity of British rule in India" (10). For Delany, Forster's pastoralism blinds him to encroaching problems of modernity; fed by Forster, literature might "waste away on its vegetarian diet" (78). See Jeremy Tambling, *E. M. Forster*; and Paul Delany, "'Islands of Money': Rentier Culture in *Howards End*." Lois Cucullu has explored how Forster's idealized Hellenism offers a fantasy of an all-male sexual and literary tradition, with women writers outside the exclusive circle. In these readings, Forster's nostalgia becomes a blind for various agendas, a deliberate evocation of a golden era strategically eliding social realities. See Lois Cucullu, "Shepherds in the Parlor: Forster's Apostles, Pagans, and Native Sons." A few critics, however, do evaluate Forster's nostalgia enthusiastically; Judith Weissman, for example, discovers in the mythic space of Howards End "the beginning of a radical new economic order that can subvert the Wilcoxes and their empire" (444); see Judith Weissman, "*Howards End*: Gasoline and Goddesses." As should become clear, I steer a course between condemning Forster's nostalgia and accepting it.

4. Peter Inskip, *Edwin Lutyens*, 27; subsequent references to this work will be cited parenthetically in the text.

5. As discussed in chapter 2, this book considers the commodification of nostalgia in two ways, and the blurring of these definitions is deliberate. First, the term refers to the packaging and selling of a nostalgic image—here the commodification of an idyllic country home referential of the past, where time itself seems to move differently. Second, I consider the way commercial ventures and monetary transactions—the very things that the idyllic image attempts to erase—produce and support these images.

6. Forster's descriptions of Howards End were inspired by Rooksnest, Forster's boyhood home. See Forster's "Boyhood Recollection of Rooksnest."

7. Daniel Born, "Private Gardens, Public Swamps: *Howards End* and the Revaluation of Liberal Guilt," 142; subsequent references to this article will be cited parenthetically in the text. The function of the house in *Howards End* has a long critical history. Lionel Trilling argues that the house is "the symbol for England" (118); Wilford Stone agrees and further considers Howards End as representing a disturbing "feminine sanctuary" (265). Born offers an insightful correction to the discussion of the houses in the novel, considering the real estate of *Howards End* in material rather than symbolic terms. See Born, above; Lionel Trilling, *E. M. Forster*; and Wilfred Stone, *The Cave and the Mountain: A Study of E. M. Forster*.

8. I use the term "commerce" to delineate a range of values and activities associated with Forster's Mr. Wilcox. By commerce, I refer to the evolving economic order in the Edwardian age—spurred by the explosion of trade both in England and from imperial interests—as opposed to money made the old-fashioned way, by aristocratic landholders. Forster links commerce to urban London, to the motorcar and the accompanying increase in the speed of life, and to overly cheap or opulent houses. Money from commerce, however, was becoming inextricably linked to the production of nostalgic space, as Forster knew, and as the vernacular architects (whose clients made their money in trade) were discovering.

9. All quotations from Forster's novel taken from *Howards End*, edited by Paul B. Armstrong; subsequent references to this work will be cited parenthetically in the text.

10. By 1910, pianos were continuously advertised both as a middle-class status symbol and as the glowing center of family life. The popular artist Goodman painted sentimental domestic scenes, with women and children in idyllic country or domestic settings.

11. Jameson's writing on *Howards End* has become central to discussions of modernism and imperialism, and the way "traces of imperialism" (64) may be found in Western modernist writing. Jameson explores how writers like Forster, unable to grasp the loss or suffering imperial power produces elsewhere, unknowingly register that loss spatially. For Forster, empire comes roughly to correspond to London malaise, commercialism, Mr. Wilcox, motorcars, and so on, but Forster is, according to Jameson, incapable of recognizing how "the other pole of the relationship, what defines [Mr. Wilcox] fundamentally and essentially in his 'imperial' function—the persons of the colonized—remains structurally occluded, and cannot but so remain" (58). I do not disagree with Jameson's reading, though I explore other aspects of Forster's engagement with commercialism. Jameson, "Modernism and Imperialism," in *Nationalism, Colonialism, and Literature*.

12. Stephen Kern, *The Culture of Time and Space: 1880–1918*; subsequent references to this book will be cited parenthetically in the text.

13. Stephen Bernstein, "Modernist Spatial Nostalgia: Forster, Conrad, Woolf," 41. The spirit of modernity certainly resides at Howard End from the start of the novel, however. Mrs. Wilcox's idyllic country image acts as a foil to the motor-car-driving, commercially oriented members of her family.

14. Trilling, *E. M. Forster*, 118.

15. Despite Forster's seeming protests to the contrary, he actually makes a move similar to "artistic crews" such as the new architects. As at Bournville, Port Sunlight, and Letchworth, Forster and the architects wished to distinguish *their* representations of authenticity from what they saw as less-sophisticated renderings, between a real nostalgic atmosphere and a sham one.

16. Kevin J. H. Dettmar presents a compelling analysis of Leonard Bast's efforts to gain "cultural capital" (14), reading Forster as sympathetic to Bast's situation. See "Bookcases, Slipcases, Uncut Leaves: The Anxiety of the Gentleman's Library."

17. Critics often cast this tension as a crisis in liberalism. Trilling observes the discomfort of the liberal intellectual who is "obscurely aware how dependent is his existence upon the business civilization he is likely to fear and despise" (*E. M. Forster*, 125). Peter Widdowson argues that the novel accurately predicts "the crisis of liberal-humanism in the twentieth century" (*E. M. Forster's Howards End*, 114). Born notes a similar tension between culture and capital, but he finds that the final failure to reconcile, or even acknowledge, these connections does not reflect a failure of liberalism but instead serves as a warning to liberalism itself, "that it cannot relax if it is to remain functional" ("Private Gardens, Public Swamps," 159). Delany sees the tension as intrinsic to those in the "rentier culture" who can live off investment income (See "'Islands of Money'"). This chapter restates this central tension as one between nostalgia and commerce and suggests that the connection between the two reveals not a guilty secret but a frank acknowledgment of their symbiotic relationship.

18. Jon Hegglund, in his insightful article "Defending the Realm: Domestic Space and Mass Cultural Contamination in *Howards End* and *An Englishman's Home*," is the first critic to link Forster's *Howards End* with the Arts and Crafts Movement, and he includes Lutyens and the vernacular architecture movement under this heading. Rather than a touchstone of authenticity, Howards End is "constructed to appear older than it is" (405), an architectural example of houses such as Munstead Wood. While Forster distinguishes between the pure, timeless world of Howards End and the fast-paced and corrupt urban life, the house is "already infected by the mass culture it seeks to exclude" (400), an infection that "deconstructs the idea of the English house as a space opposed to urban mass culture" (401). Hegglund's insights are constructive and valuable, though I read the link between architecture and commerce (rather than mass culture) not to indicate a contamination of the country house but as an engaged meditation on the difficult terrain of commodified nostalgia. See, too, Peter J. Kalliney's excellent reading of *Howards End*, Garden Cities, and imperialism in *Cities of Affluence and Anger: A Literary Geography of Modern Englishness*.

19. All quotations from Muthesius taken from *The English House*, edited by Dennis Sharp; subsequent references to this work will be cited parenthetically in the text. Although not translated into English for seventy-five years, Muthesius's work is still a central reference on British domestic architecture at the turn of the century. Stamp and Goulancourt, for example, rely heavily on Muthesius.

20. See also Stamp and Goulancourt, *The English House*, 25. Muthesius perhaps overstates the innovative quality of the Domestic Revival. Numerous critics have pointed out that an idealization of rural life and an interest in picturesque cottages have a long tradition in British culture (see, for example, Williams, *The Country and the City*). This nostalgia, however, does not always arise from identical sources. As Alun Howkins suggests, assuming

the rural ideal is unchanged over time "underplays the very real differences of social formation surrounding the production of texts" (63). Howkins argues that there is a marked surge in "Englishness" in the late nineteenth and early twentieth centuries, one that arises in part from the fear of urban contamination and a turn away from the excesses of the industrial revolution. See Alun Howkins, "The Discovery of Rural England."

21. See Inskip, *Edwin Lutyens*, 9, 11.

22. Gertrude Jekyll, "Country Homes, Gardens Old & New: Orchards, Surrey. The Residence of Mr. William Chance," *Country Life* 10 (31 August 1901): 272; subsequent references to this "Orchards" article will be cited parenthetically in the text.

23. Jekyll's description is echoed in a whole range of *Country Life* articles on Lutyens, praising him for both his naturalness and simplicity, and his originality of design (that nevertheless evoked a sense of the old). See, for example, the description of "Little Thakeham," *Country Life* 26 (28 August 1909): 292; and of "Nashdom," *Country Life* 32 (31 August 1912), 296. Muthesius and the architects likewise implied that the English Domestic Revival was not only more aesthetically pleasing but morally superior as well.

24. Examples of time-play drawn from Inskip, *Edwin Lutyens*, 27–28; and Lawrence Weaver, *Houses and Gardens by E. L. Lutyens* (Suffolk: Antique Collectors' Club, [1913] 1987), xxx.

25. Quoted in Stamp and Goulancourt, *The English House*, 39, from *Home and Garden*, 1900.

26. It is worth noting that Lutyens himself was sometimes criticized, both by his contemporaries and by later commentators, for producing sham-nostalgic effects. Sir Robert Lorimer, for example, disliked Munstead Wood for its "induced antiquity" (Inskip, *Edwin Lutyens*, 27), and more recently, Inskip has noted that some of Lutyens's houses were "so dependent on fantasies of a make-believe world that they lack that spontaneity of the direct solution" (*Edwin Lutyens*, 29). Stamp and Goulancourt proclaim Lutyens "the master at the art of instant age" (*The English House*, 39), but they go on to claim that while Lutyens was playing a sophisticated intellectual game, other architects "were trying to fake antiquity" (39). Authenticity is, of course, largely in the eye of the beholder.

27. Quoted in Stamp and Goulancourt, *The English House*, 39. Stamp, Goulancourt, Inskip, and others attribute this quotation to Lutyens, though Weaver quotes the original writer as Walter Pater, from *Notre Dame d'Amiens*. See Weaver, *Houses and Gardens*, xxx.

28. An excellent history of the *Daily Mail*'s Ideal Home Exhibition may be found in Deborah S. Ryan, *The Ideal Home through the 20th Century*. I gratefully acknowledge my debt to Ryan for an introduction to the exhibition's early history (9–59). I have drawn most quotations in this section from articles and advertisements in the *Daily Mail* about the first three exhibitions: 9–24 October 1908; 8–23 April 1910; and 12–27 April 1912. I have also consulted Wareham Smith's biography, *Spilt Ink*.

29. Alfred Harmsworth, later Lord Northcliffe, had started the *Daily Mail* in 1896, targeting specifically a middle-class and lower-middle-class audience.

30. "Ideal Home Exhibition," *Daily Mail*, 14 October 1908, 3.

31. "Ideal Home," *Daily Mail*, 16 April 1912, 7.

32. Exhibitions had long been a familiar feature in Britain. Since the Great Exhibition of 1851, England had hosted many such shows; in 1908 alone, it was possible to visit the Franco British Exhibition at the White City, the *Daily Mail* British and Irish Lace Exhibition, and many others. Reproductions of houses and even entire villages were part of many of these

shows. The Ideal Home Exhibition was the first, however, to focus entirely on the home and thus serves as the best example for the chapter (see Ryan, *The Ideal Home*, 13, 21).

33. "Ideal Home," *Daily Mail*, 9 April 1910, 7.

34. "Ideal Home Exhibition: The Making of a Home," *Daily Mail*, 16 October 1908, 3.

35. "Building, Decorating and Furnishing a House: Lessons at Olympia," *Daily Mail*, 12 April 1912, 3. Olympia was the name of the building that housed the exhibition.

36. "The Science and Art of Home Making," *Daily Mail*, 22 April 1912, 5; Forster, *Howards End*, 5.

37. "A Tudor Village: Old Time Shops and Shopping at Olympia," *Daily Mail Ideal Home Supplement, Daily Mail*, 9 April 1910, II.

38. "Notes from Exhibitors," *Daily Mail*, 20 April 1910, 13.

39. See "Review of Exhibits: Seventh Notice," *Daily Mail*, 16 October 1908, 3. Also "Review of Exhibits: Tenth Notice," *Daily Mail*, 22 October 1908, 10.

40. "Review of Exhibits: Third Notice," *Daily Mail Ideal Home Supplement, Daily Mail*, 12 October 1908, II. Ryan also uses part of the quotation; see *The Ideal Home*, 32.

41. "The Art of Home-Making," *Daily Mail*, 28 September 1908, 3.

42. "What Is the Ideal Home?" *Daily Mail*, 20 August 1908, 8.

43. "The Daily Mail Ideal House," *Daily Mail*, 11 April 1912, 3. The booth was sponsored by the Knebworth Garden Village, located about thirty-five minutes from London.

44. "Ideal Home Shopping," *Daily Mail*, 20 October 1908, 4.

45. Another interesting blending involved the national exhibits. A range of different countries arranged their own displays, the most notable being the vast Dutch Village of the 1912 exhibit. These national arrangements often suggested a blending of time and space, both exoticized and primitivized, suggesting to the English viewer that to leave England was not only to go to a different place but often, because of the allegedly less developed nature of the country, also to go back in time.

46. This democratization would not, however, have included the working class. As Ryan points out, most people in the working class would not have been able to afford the entrance fee for the early shows (*The Ideal Home*, 28).

47. See "Review of Exhibits: Eighth Notice," *Daily Mail*, 19 October 1908, 2; Forster, *Howards End*, 41.

48. For example, Delany faults Forster, finding he clings in the end "to archaism and nostalgia while failing to engage the contemporary passions of the ordinary citizen" ("'Islands of Money,'" 78). Born, however, finds that the fault lies with Margaret and her sister, and that the ending is Forster's warning to a complacent liberalism ("Private Gardens, Public Swamps," 159). Michael Levenson offers a compelling way out of such debates in his insightful reading of the novel as one of varying modes, what he describes as "the elasticity of experience in this novel" (101); Forster moves among the claims of individuals and the needs of the many, among the possibilities of the imagination and its symbolic functions, and among the political and economic limits of the society, "contracting and expanding according to changes in mood and mode, offering visionary historical prospects to those who recede from history, exiling the individual and then placing high responsibility upon that exile who might at any moment be asked to signify the community and symbolize its future" (101). Levenson, "Liberalism and Symbolism in *Howards End*," in *Modernism and the Fate of Individuality*.

49. Questions concerning Forster's nostalgia often become entangled with a larger question that has dominated Forster criticism: In what ways is Forster a Victorian realist or

an early modernist? These questions about Forster's place in literary history are interesting, but the danger is that such debates create dichotomies that reinscribe the critical tendency simply to transmit nostalgia into the "bad" category. Although there are exceptions, critics tend to praise the aspects of Forster that they label as "modern" and condemn those that seem nostalgic. Instead of viewing Forster's nostalgia as a mask for a dangerous conservatism or as the cloak of an incipient modernism, we can instead consider his nostalgia, and its radical relationship with commercialism, as itself shaping—rather than hiding or ignoring—definitions of modernism.

50. See P. N. Furbank, *E. M. Forster: A Life*, 264–269.

51. Recollection of Sandy Campbell, "Mr. Forster of King's," *Mademoiselle*, June 1964, 80–81, 120–124; quoted in J. H. Stape (ed.), *E. M. Forster: Interviews and Recollections*, 113–114.

52. Recollection of Frank Hauser, "A Late Debut: E. M. Forster on Stage," *Grand Street* 4 (Autumn 1984): 145–148; quoted in Stape, *E. M. Forster*, 130–131.

53. Recollection of Lady Faith Culme-Seymour, "Memories of E. M. Forster," quoted in Stape, *E. M. Forster*, 87.

54. Recollection of L. P. Wilkinson, "E. M. Foster: The Later Years," from a lecture to the English Association at the Alliance Hall, Westminster, 21 October 1972; in Forster papers, King's College, Cambridge, quoted in Stape, *E. M. Forster*, 162.

55. I will return to such a stage set of authenticity in my discussion of the relic room in Woolf's *Night and Day* in chapter 5.

56. Anne Billson, "Our Kind of People," *New Statesman and Society*, 29 May 1992, 32–33; reprinted in Paul B. Armstrong (ed.), *Howards End*, 467–468. Also Andrew Higson, in *English Heritage, English Cinema: Costume Drama since 1980*, explores at greater length the history of the heritage film in Britain, and in particular offers an insightful case study of the film *Howards End* and its marketing.

Chapter 4: The Vanishing Act of Commercialism

1. Henry James, "The Great Good Place," in *The Complete Tales of Henry James*, vol. 11; subsequent references to this story will be cited parenthetically in the text.

2. Several theorists have offered readings of this story, though none along commercial lines. For example, Krishna Baldev Vaid reads the Great Good Place as a mystical place of inner stillness and the payments as only symbolic; see *Technique in the Tales of Henry James*, 201–207. Both Leon Edel and John Bradley consider the homoerotic undertones of the story; see Leon Edel, *Henry James: The Treacherous Years, 1895–1901*, 240–242; John R. Bradley, "Henry James's Permanent Adolescence," in *Henry James and Homo-Erotic Desire*, 49. Adeline R. Tintner reads the dreamlike Great Good Place as "a kind of memorial to Burne-Jones" (399); see "Henry James and the Symbolist Movement in Art."

3. In this chapter, the term "Selfridges" refers not simply to the store itself but to the larger phenomenon of Selfridges that encompassed the advertisements, window displays, and store design, as well as the atmosphere created by this larger discourse. I have removed the apostrophe from the store's name to avoid confusion. The owner of the store is always referred to as Gordon Selfridge.

I should note that furniture stores, most notably Whiteley's, did anticipate some of Selfridges' displays, offering in the 1880s opulent and luxurious showrooms and elaborately designed store windows. See Deborah Cohen, *Household Gods: The British and Their Possessions*, 44. Selfridges, though, expanded on these displays and brought such techniques to a much broader audience and to a much larger variety of commodities. When Gordon Selfridge opened his store, he followed some of Whiteley's designs, and he agreed he would not sell heavy furniture so as not to compete with Whiteley's.

4. Thorstein Veblen, in his well-known work *The Theory of the Leisure Class* (1899), coined the phrase "conspicuous consumption" and argued that consumer spending among the middle class was largely driven by a desire to emulate the upper classes, what he termed "pecuniary emulation." Not surprisingly, this theory has been developed and complicated by many critics. For example, Lori Anne Loeb, in her work *Consuming Angels: Advertising and Victorian Women*, argues that late Victorian middle-class consumption was actually driven more by hedonistic impulses. I find that Selfridges created a commercial space that allowed middle-class shoppers to traverse different models of consumption, allowing them both to obtain markers of high-class culture (à laVeblen) and at the same time redefine such markers on their own terms.

5. "New Era of Shopping," *Daily Express*, 16 March 1909, *HAT-BB*, 11.

6. For a history of Harrods, see Tim Dale, *Harrods: The Store and the Legend.*

7. "London Street Architecture: Selfridges," *Times*, 12 March 1909, 11.

8. Quoted in Reginald Pound, *Selfridge: A Biography*, 206.

9. "The Opening of Selfridges," *Black and White*, 20 March 1909, *HAT-BB*, 1.

10. For more information on the early campaign, see Pound, *Selfridge: A Biography*; T. R. Nevett, *Advertising in Britain: A History*; and Gordon Honeycombe, *Selfridges: Seventy-five Years, The Story of the Store 1909–1984*; subsequent references to all three books will be cited parenthetically in the text. See also A. H. Williams, *No Name on the Door: A Memoir of Gordon Selfridge*; Williams worked for Gordon Selfridge in various capacities for many years.

Diane Erika Rappaport offers the only rigorous analysis of Selfridges to date, in her excellent chapter "'A New Era of Shopping': An American Department Store in Edwardian England," in *Shopping for Pleasure: Women in the Making of London's West End*, 142–177. She too observes that Selfridges offered "a blend of elite and mass culture" (166), although she inadvertently repeats Pound's mistaken claim that Selfridges took out no initial advertising in the *Times* (Rappaport, 159; Pound, 60).

11. Thomas Richards has argued that from the time of the Great Exhibition of 1851, commodities were typically set on pedestals, under lights—both literally and figuratively—hiding any sense of production in favor of the final, seemingly ahistorical product. Commodities so represented could sell the ideology of England, from its imperial fantasies to its moral codes; see *The Commodity Culture of Victorian England: Advertising and Spectacle, 1851–1914*, 4, 40. By glorifying commodities and hiding production, sellers could distance a product from a sense of everyday use or from mundane suggestions of actual work; even the sense that such objects were for sale could be obscured. Advertisements, as Jennifer Wicke has pointed out, can form an "aesthetic space" around these objects, which could in turn "put the actual act of commercial exchange under a unique form of erasure"; see *Advertising Fictions: Literature, Advertisement, and Social Reading*, 70, 83. Selfridges was one of the first advertisers in Britain to exploit fully the "not for sale" aura surrounding the shop goods, and exploit it in a fully realized, mass-market, campaign.

12. Selfridges' advertisement, "London's Greatest Store: Its Ideal and Principles of Business," *Times*, 24 February 1909.

13. *HAT-GS.*

14. Ibid.

15. Comments from "a Somerset clergyman," quoted in C. F. G. Masterman, *The Condition of England*, 191.

16. "Scenes at Selfridge's," *Standard*, 16 March 1909, *HAT-BB*, 52.

17. "Woman" column, *Star*, 30 March 1909, *HAT-BB*, 55.

18. Selfridges' advertisement, "London's Greatest Store: How Selfridge's Gathers Its Goods from All Parts of the World," *Times*, 26 February 1909.

While these article-advertisements were new, Honeycombe is a too enthusiastic booster of Selfridges when he declares that they "looked and sounded like no advertisement ever seen before in England" (172). My research in the *Times* reveals that such article-advertisements had already started to appear when Selfridges began its campaign.

19. As at the Ideal Home Exhibition, intrinsic to many of these displays were the alleged "primitive" qualities of the foreign culture. Places outside of England—from Wales to Turkey—were presented as embodying a kind of charming premodernity, separate from London both by space and by time.

20. "A West End Exhibition," *Drapers Record*, 4 September 1909, *HAT-BB*, 123; "Novel Enterprise: Articles in the Making at Selfridge's," *Evening Standard*, 31 August 1910, *HAT-BB*, 131d.

21. See, for example, Morris's lecture "How We Live and How We Might Live," given to the Hammersmith Branch of the Socialist Democratic Federation at Kelmscott House, 30 November 1884. In this lecture, Morris goes on to argue that the leisure to make such goods might be obtained by proper use of machinery. Reprinted online on the William Morris Internet Archive, www.marxist.org/archive/morris/index.htm.

22. Selfridges' advertisement, "London's Greatest Store: How Selfridge's Gathers Its Goods from All Parts of the World," *Times*, 26 February 1909.

23. "Shopping Palace," *Daily Chronicle*, 15 March 1909, *HAT-BB*, 8. Selfridges' advertisement, "Visitors' Day," *Times*, 19 March 1909.

24. "An International Hostel," *Review of Reviews*, April 1909, *HAT-BB*, 73. See also "The New White City," *Daily Mail*, 22 March 1909, *HAT-BB*, 16; and "A Novel Feature of London's New Emporium," *Daily Graphic*, 16 March 1909, *HAT-BB*, 14.

25. Selfridges' advertisement, "Visitors' Day," *Times*, 19 March 1909. This domestic model was encouraged not simply among the guests but among the employees as well. One of the expressions among the staff was "I'm home," meaning the sales target had been met for the day; bonuses were then given out in what Selfridges called " 'a little family ceremony' " (quoted in Pound, 182–183). Gordon Selfridge declared at a press dinner that it was "their intention to make the place a business home for the 1200 young people engaged in it"; "Electricity in Business," *Standard*, 16 March 1909, *HAT-BB*, 52.

26. See especially Felski's chapters "On Nostalgia: The Prehistoric Woman" (35–60) and "Imagined Pleasures: The Erotics and Aesthetics of Consumption" (61–90) in *The Gender of Modernity*.

27. Selfridges' advertisement, "London's Greatest Store: Selfridges and Its Origin," *Times*, 23 February 1909, 4.

28. Selfridges' advertisement, "London's Greatest Store: Its Ideal and Principles of Business," *Times*, 24 February 1909, 4.

29. A discussion of advertising in Britain is hardly complete without a reference to perhaps the most famous nineteenth-century advertisement, "Bubbles," for Pears' Soap, which

used a painting by Sir John Millais of a small boy blowing bubbles to advertise its product (see Nevett, *Advertising in Britain*, picture insert between pages 82 and 83). Selfridges was a retailer, rather than a manufacturer like Pears, and thus the advertisements from the two companies belong in different categories. Nevertheless, Selfridges through its ads not only could promise that a particular product could produce a particular atmosphere but also could invite the customer to enter such an atmosphere within its store.

30. This advertisement appeared in the *Daily News*, *Paris Mail*, *Evening News*, and the *Star* on 16 March 1909; it appeared in the *Times* on 17 March 1909.

31. The use of various aesthetic markers to sell goods is, of course, a technique quite familiar to most readers of advertisements today, and the subject of much critical debate. Pierre Bourdieu, for example, in his well-known work *Distinction: A Social Critique of the Judgment of Taste*, exhaustively analyzes the consumption of cultural goods in French society, including art, music, food, and political and entertainment choices. Jonathan Freedman has brilliantly considered the work of Henry James and its relationship to the complex negotiation between British aestheticism and commodity culture; see Freedman, *Professions of Taste: Henry James, British Aestheticism, and Commodity Culture*.

32. In 1918, Gordon Selfridge even produced a mammoth work, *The Romance of Commerce*, outlining the glorious history of commerce and tracing its origins back to antiquity.

Gordon Selfridge continued these classical associations in a telling and long-standing series of weekly essay-advertisements. For many years, he either wrote or commissioned newspaper columns on general themes concerning commerce and business. About 500 words each, and similar to the article-advertisements produced during the opening campaign, these essays were written in a sermonizing, elevated, and rather florid style. They were always signed "Callisthenes," after a classical figure reputed to be the nephew of Aristotle and the first "press agent" for Alexander the Great (Honeycombe, 172). Reaction to these quasi editorials was mixed; some critics found them overbearing and self-satisfied, while other readers applauded their traditional style. Whatever their quality, the essays achieved wide cultural capital; they were quoted in sermons, reprinted in periodicals such as the *Harvard Business Magazine*, and used as models of writing in schools (Pound, 219; Honeycombe, 172). In 1916, Chapman and Hall even published a collection of these essays entitled *The Counsels of Callisthenes* (London: Chapman and Hall, 1916). For more information on the Callisthenes articles, see Honeycombe, 171–174.

33. Of course, Debenham & Freebody was an established store, in business for more than a century, and thus had little need to tie itself to a larger tradition.

34. Gordon Selfridge had used similar techniques in his former Marshall Field's advertisements as he did for his Selfridges' opening. In contrast, a few years after the opening, many Selfridges' advertisements reverted to the older-style advertisements that emphasized prices and the objects for sale. Nevertheless, the advertisements used in Selfridges' opening, and the selling techniques practiced at the store, shifted the commercial environment of London.

35. "'Selfridges,'" *Star*, 15 March 1909, *HAT-BB*, 54; "New Era of Shopping," *Daily Express*, 16 March 1909, *HAT-BB*, 11; "Carnival of Shopping," *Standard*, 18 March 1909, *HAT-BB*, 53.

36. At every opportunity, Selfridges was linked to what was already established. An advertisement that appeared in the store's opening weeks even claims precedence for Selfridges' displays. The lavish fruit and flower arrangement, for example, was not really new,

but had, "in its details, been duplicated in various shops in London for some years past" (Selfridges' advertisement, "Selfridge's Oxford St.," *Times*, 20 March 1909, 8). In a dexterous sleight of hand, the rhetoric positions the new Selfridges as the original model, which the past displays have copied.

37. Selfridges' advertisement, "London's Greatest Store: How Selfridge's Gathers Its Goods from All Parts of the World," *Times*, 26 February 1909, 4.

38. Selfridges' advertisement, "Selfridges Oxford St.," *Times*, 20 March 1909, 18.

39. We can see here the starting elements of what Raphael Samuel, in his book *Theatres of Memory*, calls "retrochic," the postmodern blending of old styles with the new. Retrochic, relates Samuel, "differs from earlier kinds of period revival in that what it does is parodic. It is irreverent about the past and only half-serious about itself. . . . Retrochic, in this view, involves not obsession with the past but an indifference to it: only when history had ceased to matter can it be treated as a sport" (95). Retrochic lacks the sentimentality or the high seriousness associated with the Victorians, "is untroubled by the cult of authenticity," and is happy to "blur[] the distinction between originals and re-makes" (112). While Samuel assigns retrochic to post–World War II society, Selfridges offers at least a glimmer of what Samuel describes. See *Theatres of Memory: Past and Present in Contemporary Culture*, vol. 1.

40. See "At the Stores," *Star*, 16 March 1909, *HAT-BB*, 54.

41. "The New Art Era in Business Advertising," *Civilian*, 20 March 1909, *HAT-BB*, 7; "Shopping Palace," *Daily Chronicle*, 15 March, 1909, *HAT-BB*, 8; "Hints to Advertisers," *Draper*, 27 March 1909, 373, *HAT-BB*, 19.

42. "The Symbolism of Selfridge," *Advertising World*, April 1909, 574–579, *HAT-BB*, 62.

43. "A Much 'Cribbed' Design," *HAT-BB*, 170.

44. The two advertisements I describe can be found in the *Times*: "One Week Sale," 8 January 1909, 8; "Diamond Jubilee," 3 March 1909, 5.

45. The influence of Selfridges is evident in the Cadbury advertisements of 1911 that I considered in chapter 2; many of the advertisements in the *Daily Mail*, however, continued to emphasize prices and products.

46. Quoted in "Criticising Mr. Selfridge," *Evening News*, 19 March 1909, *HAT-BB*, 28.

47. "A Week of Shopping," *Bystander*, 17 March 1909, *HAT-BB*, 5.

48. References to *Tono-Bungay* are cited parenthetically in the text. Ironically, the subtitle for the novel's serialized edition was "The Romance of Commerce," the same name that Gordon Selfridge would give his own book nine years later.

Tono-Bungay has received a modest amount of critical attention. Perhaps the most cited piece is David Lodge's assessment of the novel as an example of the "Condition of England" tradition; see *Language of Fiction: Essays in Criticism and Verbal Analysis of the English Novel*. More recently, William Kupinse has offered an economic reading, examining the "waste-driven system of value" (52) that dominates the novel; see "Wasted Value: The Serial Logic of H. G. Wells's *Tono-Bungay*." Philip Griffin considers the ambiguous symbol of the destroyer X2 at the end of *Tono-Bungay*; "'X2': The Final Chapter of *Tono-Bungay*." For an exploration of the intersections of imperialism, commerce, and modernity, see Benita Parry, "*Tono-Bungay*: Modernisation, Modernity, Modernism, and Imperialism, or The Failed Electrification of the Empire of Light."

49. I am grateful to my colleague John Grammer for suggesting the term "vertical monopoly."

Chapter 5: "Lustrous behind Glass"

1. Subsequent references to *Night and Day* will be cited parenthetically in the text.

2. *Night and Day* itself has long been considered a relic, and not a sacred one. Critics have dismissed the novel both because it never decisively breaks with spaces such as the relic room and because the novel seems a holdover from the realist tradition. As Katherine Mansfield complained in 1919, the novel was a throwback: "We had not thought to look upon its like again." Quentin Bell spoke for a generation of critics when he labeled the novel "a conventional story," and even Woolf's most recent biographer, Hermione Lee, points out that the book's structure "was not formally experimental." See Quentin Bell, *Virginia Woolf: A Biography*, vol. 2, 171; Mansfield quotation from her review in the *Athenaeum*, 26 November 1919; Hermione Lee, *Virginia Woolf*, 369.

More recently, a few critics have reassessed *Night and Day*'s position as a novelistic relic, reclaiming it by revealing its overlooked modern and even postmodern qualities. Susan Merrill Squier, for example, analyzes the work as a new kind of city novel, while Helen Wussow finds the language of war embedded in the novel's prose. In perhaps the most sensitive assessment of *Night and Day* to date, Alex Zwerdling argues that the book's traditional elements are challenged by the newly mapped power relations within the novel, which are never fully resolved. Woolf's first novel, *The Voyage Out*, has been the subject of similar debates about its Victorian and modernist elements. See Susan Merrill Squier, "Tradition and Revision: The Classic City Novel and Virginia Woolf's *Night and Day*"; Helen Wussow, "Conflict of Language in Virginia Woolf's *Night and Day*"; Alex Zwerdling, *Virginia Woolf and the Real World*.

3. In discussing both Woolf and Forster in this book, I want to encourage a new way of relating these authors, one that avoids placing them in a zero-sum relationship. Too often when they are assessed together, Forster becomes a point of resistance for Woolf, a touchstone of the traditional to set against Woolf's modern tendencies. Malcolm Bradbury, for example, writes, "[Forster], it seemed, still respected the old novel; [Woolf] wrote the 'new' one, the insubstantized novel. He was an Edwardian, she a 'modern,' who came later to fiction, in a different spirit"; *The Modern British Novel*, 181. In these readings, if Forster is a late Victorian, then Woolf is a modernist; if Forster is granted a place at the modernist table, then Woolf has left to join the postmodernists. Alternatively, when Forster's symbolism and narrative experimentation in a work such as *Passage to India* are read alongside Woolf's more domestic settings, Forster is cast as the roaming male modernist, with Woolf appearing as the epitome of a kind of feminine modernity. Woolf and Forster also seem intertwined because they read and wrote about each other's work and often defined themselves against each other. Certainly the differences between the two authors are constructive, but their fates need not be so closely united. By introducing *Night and Day* into the larger discussion of authenticity and commerce, we can see how Woolf considers within an urban setting issues similar to those we found in Forster, as well as in Selfridges.

4. Jennifer Wicke, *Advertising Fictions: Literature, Advertisement, and Social Reading*, 122.

5. Thomas Richards, *The Commodity Culture of Victorian England: Advertising and Spectacle, 1851–1914*, 100; subsequent references to this work will be cited parenthetically in the text.

6. Virginia Woolf, "Haworth, November, 1904," in *The Essays of Virginia Woolf*, vol. 1, 7.

7. Woolf understood the allures of such originary objects. She comments in her diary of 1918 about her own prototypical pen, the one that had belonged to her mother: "Here I am experimenting with the parent of all pens—the black J. *[T]he* pen, as I used to think it,

along with other objects, as a child, because mother used it; & therefore all other pens were varieties & eccentricities" (*D* 1, 208). The pen becomes the model against which all other pens must be compared.

8. Subsequent references to Bowlby's *Just Looking: Consumer Culture in Dreiser, Gissing, and Zola* will be cited parenthetically in the text. Bowlby traces the rise of the department store, window displays, and the commodity in nineteenth-century culture and links this to the rise of literary naturalism, an emerging mass-market readership, and the perceived split between culture and commercialism; see also Bowlby, "Walking, Women, and Writing: Virginia Woolf as *Flâneuse*." Bowlby offers a more general introduction to shopping in the twentieth century in her now classic *Carried Away: The Invention of Modern Shopping*. See, too, Andrew Miller, who examines the Victorian novel and the window display in *Novels behind Glass*.

9. Bowlby's insistence that art forms influenced industry as much as the reverse parallels my own argument that commercial ventures did not simply appropriate modernist tenets but were in fact influenced by them. Bowlby also discusses the democratic ethos of the new department store, which allowed women of different classes to experience similar shopping pleasures. I considered a related trend in Selfridges in the previous chapter.

10. Subsequent references to Friedberg's *Window Shopping: Cinema and the Postmodern* will be cited parenthetically in the text. Friedberg considers how alterations of time and space by new technologies such as film have affected postmodernity. Both the opening of shopping malls and the cinema's development of the mobilized eye brought the gaze itself to the center of capitalist society, influencing postmodern conceptions of space and time. See, too, Liz Conor, *The Spectacular Modern Woman: Feminine Visibility in the 1920s*.

11. Anne Friedberg, "Les Flâneurs du Mal(l): Cinema and the Postmodern Condition," 420–421.

12. Reginald Abbott observes a similar moment in *Mrs. Dalloway*. Abbott argues that *Mrs. Dalloway* offers an "acommodity aesthetic," where characters might "shop[] without spending and consume[] without commodities" (209). Clarissa stays above commodity culture, herself a "genuine article," the icon on which to base new styles. I likewise find spending is elided in *Night and Day*, but I argue that Woolf's focus away from material transactions is not a denial of commodities but a reiteration of how commodities were actually presented in London department stores. See "What Miss Kilman's Petticoat Means: Virginia Woolf, Shopping, and Spectacle."

13. Ralph, of course, is walking near the Strand, not on Oxford Street where Selfridges was located. Woolf does write specifically of Oxford Street and its atmosphere in "Oxford Street Tide," where she contrasts the "sublime rites" (16) of shopping on Bond Street with the "too blatant and raucous" (16) buying and selling on Oxford Street. By 1932, when Woolf published her article, Selfridges was much less focused on hiding the commercial exchange and more content to highlight prices and bargains.

14. See Friedberg, *Window Shopping: Cinema and the Postmodern*, 65; Leonard S. Marcus, *The American Store Window*, 17–18; Gordon Honeycombe, *Selfridges: Seventy-five Years, The Story of the Store, 1909–1984*, 165; and Barry James Wood, *Show Windows: 75 Years of the Art of Display*, 27.

15. See Marcus, *The American Store Window*, 18.

16. See Honeycombe, *Selfridges*, 166 and following, for a longer account of the store windows at Selfridges.

17. Alison Adburgham, *Shops and Shopping: 1800–1914, Where, and in What Manner the Well-Dressed Englishwoman Bought Her Clothes*, 275.

18. Quoted in Marcus, *The American Store Window*, 18–19.

19. Selfridges' advertisement, "Selfridge's by Night," appeared in the *Daily Chronicle*, the *Daily Graphic*, and the *Daily Mail* on 20 March 1909. See *HAT-Early.*

20. From Woolf to Vanessa Bell, 22 April 1918, in *The Letters of Virginia Woolf*, vol. 2, 232; subsequent references to Woolf's letters will be cited parenthetically in the text by volume and page number.

21. The blue dress also recalls the "long skirt in blue-and-white paint lustrous behind glass" (*Night and Day*, 5) in the relic room, which is likely a traditional portrait of a woman, but which is described almost as a modernist work, a fragment of a woman hanging behind glass. Cassandra gazes on Katharine in the blue dress scene as she might gaze on an object of art.

22. Friedberg, "*Flâneurs*," 422. This relay of looks continues, Friedberg observes, as "the shop window was displaced by the cinema scene" ("*Flâneurs*," 422). For Friedberg, the window displays were the still-life prototypes of the cinema: "The window frames a tableau, placing it behind glass and making it inaccessible, and arouses desire. Cinematic spectation, a further instrumentalization of this consumer gaze, produced paradoxical effects on the newfound social mobility of the *flâneuse*" (422). The movement in *Night and Day* from the window displays to Katharine's live-action mobility—complete with a sound track swelling in the background—anticipates this same transition.

23. See Miller, *Novels behind Glass*.

24. The emphasis on technique in the new window displays also paralleled the growing concern with technique in literary modernism. Rather than, as it were, cramming the novel full of realistic details, fin de siècle writers and modernists began to focus on the single aesthetic object or moment, and ideas of color or texture or effect. *Night and Day* is not itself notable for its technical modernism, for the kind of stylistic features such as stream of consciousness or the nonlinear narratives of Woolf's later work. The scenes of window shopping in this early novel, however, suggest a new modernist atmosphere conveyed through a realist representation.

25. Ship quotation from Mansfield's review of the novel in the *Athenaeum*, 26 November 1919; private comments from Mansfield's letter to Murry, 18 October 1920, in *The Collected Letters of Katherine Mansfield*, vol. 3, 82.

26. See Samuel Hynes, *A War Imagined: The First World War and English Culture*, 3; most subsequent references to this source will be quoted parenthetically in the text.

27. Quoted in Hynes, *A War Imagined*, 3. The original source of the quotation is unclear, though as Hynes points out, Grey does cite the remark in his memoirs. See Hynes' notes, 470–471, for a full description.

28. Quoted in Lee, *Virginia Woolf*, 261. From the "Play Reading Book" in the papers of Clive Bell at the King's College, Cambridge; quoted by permission of the Society of Authors, literary representatives of the Estate of Clive Bell.

29. *L* 2, 51; also quoted in Hynes, *A War Imagined*, 4.

30. Virginia Woolf, "'Within the Rim,'" in *The Essays of Virginia Woolf*, vol. 3, 22–25.

31. As Hynes points out, "men and women after the war looked back at their own pasts as one might look across a great chasm to a remote, peaceable place on the other side" (*A War Imagined*, xi).

32. Quoted in Reginald Pound, *Selfridge: A Biography*, 130.
33. "The Shopping Carnival," *Daily Mail*, 16 March 1909, *HAT-BB*, 15.

Chapter 6: Conclusion

1. References to *Women in Love* will be cited parenthetically in the text.

Critical discussion of Lawrence and commodity culture has focused on Lawrence's own interests in advertising and promoting his work, and the material conditions under which those works were published. See Joyce Wexler, "Selling Sex as Art," in *Marketing Modernisms: Self-Promotion, Canonization, and Rereading*; and John Worthen, "D. H. Lawrence and the 'Expensive Edition Business,'" in *Modernist Writers and the Marketplace*. Lawrence's own status as a central modernist is in question; Michael Bell offers a useful analysis of Lawrence's position in "D. H. Lawrence and the Meaning of Modernism," in *Rethinking Modernism*.

2. My argument here implies an underlying link between primitivism and authenticity. Modernists' fascination with "the primitive" has been well documented, and this search for origins overlaps with the desire for nostalgic and originary forms of authenticity. The mass-marketed selling of the "primitive" that we might associate with a Pier One aesthetic does not, however, seem to emerge in force until later in the century.

3. James Joyce, *Ulysses*, edited by Hans Walter Gabler; references to this work will be cited parenthetically in the text by chapter and line number.

4. See Jennifer Wicke, *Advertising Fictions: Literature, Advertisement, and Social Reading*, especially chap. 4, as well as four other essays by Wicke on Joyce and advertising or commodity culture: "Joyce and Consumer Culture," in *James Joyce*; "Enchantment, Disenchantment, Re-enchantment: Joyce and the Cult of the Absolutely Fabulous"; "Modernity Must Advertise: Aura, Desire, and Decolonization in Joyce"; and "'Who's She When She's at Home?' Molly Bloom and the Work of Consumption." Garry Leonard offers a comprehensive analysis in his book *Advertising and Commodity Culture in Joyce*. See, too, Thomas Richards, *The Commodity Culture of Victorian England: Advertising and Spectacle, 1851–1914*, especially chap. 5; Garry Leonard and Jennifer Wicke also edited a special double issue on Joyce and commodity culture for *James Joyce Quarterly*, 30, no. 4 and 31, no. 1 (1993). For an examination of the novel's material history, see George Bornstein, *Material Modernism: The Politics of the Page*, 118–139. Catherine Turner also considers the publication history of *Ulysses* in *Marketing Modernism between the Two World Wars*.

5. Daniel P. Gunn argues that Joyce uses advertisements to parody his own techniques; see "Beware of Imitations: Advertisement as Reflexive Commentary in *Ulysses*."

6. Bloom dreams of being a "resident magistrate" (17.1610). Magistrates, as Don Gifford describes, were "popularly portrayed as living the ideal life of the hunting-shooting-fishing country gentleman." See Don Gifford, *Ulysses Annotated*, 591.

7. In general, critics approaching Woolf and commodity culture have focused on *Mrs. Dalloway*, with its explicit scenes of shopping. See, for example, Reginald Abbott, "What Miss Kilman's Petticoat Means: Virginia Woolf, Shopping, and Spectacle." Abbott includes a short discussion of *To the Lighthouse* in his article, focusing on the role of the Army and Navy Stores' catalogue; I discuss this article further in note 12 of chapter 5. Also Jennifer Wicke, "*Mrs. Dalloway* Goes to Market: Woolf, Keynes, and Modern Markets."

8. Virginia Woolf, *To the Lighthouse*, 50–51; subsequent references to this novel will be cited parenthetically in the text.

9. Unlike Mr. Bankes, who can coolly and passionately admire Mrs. Ramsay's allure, Lily knows she is not supposed simply to gaze and to admire but, in her turn, to reproduce the domestic scene she sees.

10. Selfridges' new store in Birmingham, with its ultramodern design, emphasizes this new spirit.

Selected Bibliography

Abbott, Reginald. "What Miss Kilman's Petticoat Means: Virginia Woolf, Shopping, and Spectacle." *Modern Fiction Studies* 38, no. 1 (1992): 193–216.

Adburgham, Alison. *Shops and Shopping: 1800–1914, Where, and in What Manner the Well-Dressed Englishwoman Bought Her Clothes*. London: Barrie and Jenkins, 1989.

Ardis, Ann L. *Modernism and Cultural Conflict, 1880–1922*. Cambridge: Cambridge University Press, 2002.

Barnes, Julian. *England, England*. New York: Vintage Books, 2000.

Barthes, Roland. *Mythologies*. Translated by Annette Lavers. New York: Hill and Wang, 1972.

Baudrillard, Jean. *Simulacra and Simulation*. Translated by Sheila Faria Glaser. Ann Arbor: Michigan University Press, 1994.

Behlmer, George K., and Fred M. Leventhal, eds. *Singular Continuities: Tradition, Nostalgia, and Identity in Modern British Culture*. Stanford, CA: Stanford University Press, 2000.

Bell, Michael. "D. H. Lawrence and the Meaning of Modernism." In *Rethinking Modernism*, edited by Marianne Thormählen, 132–148. New York: Palgrave Macmillan, 2003.

Bell, Quentin. *Virginia Woolf: A Biography*. 2 vols. New York: Harcourt Brace Jovanovich, 1972.

Bellamy, Edward. *Looking Backward, 2000–1887*. Edited by John L. Thomas. Cambridge, MA: Harvard University Press, 1967. First published 1888 by Ticknor and Company.

Benjamin, Walter. "The Work of Art in the Age of Mechanical Reproduction." In *Illuminations*, edited by Hanna Arendt, translated by Harry Zohn. 217–251. New York: Schocken Books, 1968. First published 1936 by *Zeitschrift für Sozialforschung*.

Bernstein, Stephen. "Modernist Spatial Nostalgia: Forster, Conrad, Woolf." In *Virginia Woolf: Texts and Contexts*, edited by Beth Rigel Daugherty and Eileen Barrett, 10–44. New York: Pace University Press, 1996.

Bial, Henry. *The Performance Studies Reader*. London: Routledge, 2004.

Bloom, Harold, ed. *George Bernard Shaw's Major Barbara*. New York: Chelsea House, 1988.

Born, Daniel. "Private Gardens, Public Swamps: *Howards End* and the Revaluation of Liberal Guilt." *Novel: A Forum on Fiction* 25 (1992): 141–159.

Bornstein, George. *Material Modernism: The Politics of the Page*. Cambridge: Cambridge University Press, 2001.

Bourdieu, Pierre. *Distinction: A Social Critique of the Judgment of Taste*. Translated by Richard Nice. Cambridge, MA: Harvard University Press, 1984.

Bowlby, Rachel. *Carried Away: The Invention of Modern Shopping*. New York: Columbia University Press, 2001.

———. *Just Looking: Consumer Culture in Dreiser, Gissing, and Zola*. New York: Methuen, 1985.

———. "Walking, Women, and Writing: Virginia Woolf as *Flâneuse*." In *New Feminist Discourses: Critical Essays on Theories and Texts*, edited by Isobel Armstrong, 26–47. London: Routledge, 1992.

Boym, Svetlana. *The Future of Nostalgia*. New York: Basic Books, 2002.

Bradbury, Malcolm. *The Modern British Novel*. London: Penguin, 1993.

Bradley, John R., ed. *Henry James and Homo-erotic Desire*. New York: St. Martin's Press, 1999.

Burnett, John. *A Social History of Housing: 1815–1970*. Newton Abbot, UK: David and Charles, 1978.

Butler, Judith. *Gender Trouble: Feminism and the Subversion of Identity*. New York: Routledge, 1990.

Cadbury, Edward. *Experiments in Industrial Organization*. London: Longmans, Green, 1912.

Cadbury, Jr., George. *Town Planning, with Special Reference to the Birmingham Schemes*. London: Longmans, Green, 1915.

Claeys, Gregory. *Citizens and Saints: Politics and Anti-politics in Early British Socialism*. Cambridge: Cambridge University Press, 1989.

Cohen, Deborah. *Household Gods: The British and Their Possessions*. New Haven, CT: Yale University Press, 2006.

Comentale, Edward P. *Modernism, Cultural Production, and the British Avant-garde*. Cambridge: Cambridge University Press, 2004.

Conor, Liz. *The Spectacular Modern Woman: Feminine Visibility in the 1920s*. Bloomington: Indiana University Press, 2004.

Cooper, John Xiros. *Modernism and the Culture of Market Society*. Cambridge: Cambridge University Press, 2004.

Creese, Walter L., ed. *The Legacy of Raymond Unwin: A Human Pattern for Planning*. Cambridge, MA: MIT Press, 1967.

———. *The Search for Environment: The Garden City, Before and After*. New Haven, CT: Yale University Press, 1966.

Cucullu, Lois. "Shepherds in the Parlor: Forster's Apostles, Pagans, and Native Sons." *Novel: A Forum on Fiction* 32 (1988): 19–50.

Dale, Tim. *Harrods: The Store and the Legend*. London: Pan Books, 1981.

Davidoff, Leonore, and Catherine Hall. *Family Fortunes: Men and Women of the English Middle Class, 1780–1850*. Chicago: University of Chicago Press, 1987.

Davison, T. Raffles. *Port Sunlight: A Record of Its Artistic and Pictorial Aspect*. London: B. T. Batsford, 1916.

Delany, Paul. "'Islands of Money': Rentier Culture in *Howards End*." *English Literature in Translation* 31 (1988): 285–296. Reprinted in *E. M. Forster*, edited by Jeremy Tambling, 67–80. New York: St. Martin's Press, 1995.

Dettmar, Kevin J. H. "Bookcases, Slipcases, Uncut Leaves: The Anxiety of the Gentleman's Library." *Novel: A Forum on Fiction* 39 (2005): 5–24.

Dettmar, Kevin J. H., and Stephen Watt, eds. *Marketing Modernisms: Self-Promotion, Canonization, and Rereading*. Ann Arbor: Michigan University Press, 1996.

DiBattista, Maria, and Lucy McDiarmid, eds. *High and Low Moderns: Literature and Culture, 1889–1939*. New York: Oxford University Press, 1996.

Doughty, Martin, ed. *Building the Industrial City*. Leicester, UK: Leicester University Press, 1986.

Dukore, Bernard F. "Shaw's Big Three." *Shaw: The Annual of Bernard Shaw Studies* 4 (1984): 33–67.

Edel, Leon. *Henry James: A Biography*. Vol. 4, *The Treacherous Years: 1895–1901*. Philadelphia: Lippincott, 1969.

Evans, T. F., ed. *Shaw: The Critical Heritage*. London: Routledge and Kegan Paul, 1976.

Ewen, Stuart. *Captains of Consciousness: Advertising and the Social Roots of the Consumer Culture*. New York: McGraw-Hill, 1977.

Felski, Rita. *The Gender of Modernity*. Cambridge, MA: Harvard University Press, 1995.

Fishman, Robert. *Urban Utopias in the Twentieth Century: Ebenezer Howard, Frank Lloyd Wright, and Le Courbusier*. Cambridge, MA: MIT Press, 1982.

Forster, E. M. "Boyhood Recollection of Rooksnest." In *Howards End*, edited by Oliver Stallybrass, 286–290. London: Arnold, 1973. Reprinted by Paul B. Armstrong. New York: Norton, 1998.

———. *Howards End*. Edited by Paul B. Armstrong. New York: Norton, 1998. First published 1910 by E. Arnold.

Freedman, Jonathan. *Professions of Taste: Henry James, British Aestheticism, and Commodity Culture*. Stanford, CA: Stanford University Press, 1990.

Friedberg, Anne. "Les Flâneurs du Mal(l): Cinema and the Postmodern Condition." *PMLA* 3, no. 106 (1991): 419–431.

———. *Window Shopping: Cinema and the Postmodern*. Berkeley: University of California Press, 1993.

Furbank, P. N. *E. M. Forster: A Life*. San Diego: Harvest-Harcourt Brace, 1981.

George, W. L. *Labour and Housing at Port Sunlight*. London: Alson Rivers, 1909.

Gifford, Don. *Ulysses Annotated: Notes for James Joyce's Ulysses*. 2nd ed. Berkeley: University of California Press, 1988.

Gregory, Lady Isabella Augusta. *Our Irish Theatre*. New York: Putnam, 1914.

Grene, Nicholas. "The Edwardian Shaw, or the Modernist that Never Was." In *High and Low Moderns*, edited by Maria DiBattista and Lucy McDiarmid, 135–147. New York: Oxford University Press, 1996.

Griffin, Philip. "'X2': The Final Chapter of *Tono-Bungay*." *Critical Survey* 13 (2001): 78–88.

Gunn, Daniel P. "Beware of Imitations: Advertisement as Reflexive Commentary in *Ulysses*." *Twentieth Century Literature* 42, no. 4 (Winter 1996): 481–493.

Hapgood, Lynne, and Nancy L. Paxton, eds. *Outside Modernism: In Pursuit of the English Novel, 1900–1930*. New York: St. Martin's Press, 2000.

Harrison, Michael. *Bournville: Model Village to Garden Suburb*. Chichester, UK: Phillimore and Company, 1999.

Harvey, W. Alexander. *The Model Village and Its Cottages: Bournville*. London: B. T. Batsford, 1906.

Hawkes, Dean, ed. *Modern Country Homes in England: The Arts and Crafts Architecture of Barry Parker.* Cambridge: Cambridge University Press, 1986.

Hegglund, Jon. "Defending the Realm: Domestic Space and Mass Cultural Contamination in *Howards End* and *An Englishman's Home.*" *English Literature in Transition, 1880–1920* 40, no. 4 (September 1997): 398–423.

Hewison, Robert. *The Heritage Industry: Britain in the Climate of Decline.* London: Methuen, 1987.

Higson, Andrew. *English Heritage, English Cinema: Costume Drama since 1980.* Oxford, Oxford University Press, 2003.

Hobsbawm, Eric, and Terence Ranger, eds. *The Invention of Tradition.* Cambridge: Cambridge University Press, 1992.

Holroyd, Michael. *Bernard Shaw: 1918–1950.* Vol. 3, *The Lure of Fantasy.* New York: Random House, 1991.

Honeycombe, Gordon. *Selfridges: Seventy-five Years, The Story of the Store, 1909–1984.* London: Park Lane Press, 1984.

Horkheimer, Max, and Theodor Adorno. *The Dialectic of Enlightenment.* Translated by John Cumming. New York: Continuum, 1994.

Howard, Ebenezer. *To-morrow: A Peaceful Path to Real Reform.* Edited by Peter Hall, Dennis Hardy, and Colin Ward. London: Routledge, 2003. Reprint of the first London edition of 1898, by Swan Sonnerschein.

Howkins, Alun. "The Discovery of Rural England." In *Englishness: Politics and Culture 1880–1920,* edited by Robert Colls and Philip Dodd, 62–88. London: Croom Helm, 1986.

Huyssen, Andreas. *After the Great Divide: Modernism, Mass Culture, Postmodernism.* Bloomington: Indiana University Press, 1986.

Hynes, Samuel. *A War Imagined: The First World War and English Culture.* New York: Atheneum, 1991.

Innes, Christopher, ed. *The Cambridge Companion to George Bernard Shaw.* Cambridge: Cambridge University Press, 1998.

Inskip, Peter. *Edwin Lutyens.* London: Academic Editions, 1986.

Ishii, Michiyo. "Two Political Implications of Shaw's *Major Barbara.*" *Studies in English Literature* (1984): 21–32.

James, Henry. "The Great Good Place." In *The Complete Tales of Henry James,* edited by Leon Edel, vol. 11, 13–42. Philadelphia: Lippincott, 1962. First published 1900 by *Scribner's Magazine.*

Jameson, Fredric. "Modernism and Imperialism." In *Nationalism, Colonialism, and Literature,* by Terry Eagleton, Fredric Jameson, and Edward W. Said, 43–66. Minneapolis: University of Minnesota Press, 1990.

———. "The Politics of Theory: Ideological Positions in the Postmodern Debate." *New German Critique* 33 (Autumn 1984): 53–65.

Jenckes, Norma. "The Rejection of Shaw's Irish Play: *John Bull's Other Island.*" *Eire-Ireland: A Journal of Irish Studies* 10 (1975): 38–53.

Joyce, James. *Ulysses.* Edited by Hans Walter Gabler. New York: Random House, 1984. First published 1922 by Shakespeare and Company.

Kalliney, Peter J. *Cities of Affluence and Anger: A Literary Geography of Modern Englishness.* Charlottesville: University Press of Virginia, 2006.

Kelly, Katherine E. "Imprinting the Stage: Shaw and the Publishing Trade, 1883–1903." In *The Cambridge Companion to George Bernard Shaw*, edited by Christopher Innes, 25–54. Cambridge: Cambridge University Press, 1998.

Kelsall, Malcolm. *The Great Good Place: The Country House and English Literature*. New York: Columbia University Press, 1993.

Kern, Stephen. *The Culture of Time and Space: 1880–1918*. Cambridge, MA: Harvard University Press, 1983.

Kirshenblatt-Gimblett, Barbara. *Destination Culture: Tourism, Museums, and Heritage*. Berkeley: University of California Press, 1998.

Knox, Andrew. *Coming Clean: A Postscript after Retirement from Unilever*. London: Heinemann, 1976.

Kumar, Kishan. *Utopia and Anti-utopia in Modern Times*. Oxford: Basil Blackwell, 1987.

Kupinse, William. "Wasted Value: The Serial Logic of H. G. Wells's *Tono-Bungay*." *Novel: A Forum on Fiction* 33 (1999): 51–72.

Lang, M. H. *Designing Utopia: John Ruskin's Urban Vision for Britain and America*. Montréal, Canada: Black Rose Books, 1998.

Lawrence, D. H. *Women in Love*. New York: Penguin Books, 2006. First published 1922 by T. Seltzer.

Leach, William. *Land of Desire: Merchants, Power, and the Rise of a New American Culture*. New York: Vintage Books, 1994.

Lee, Hermione. *Virginia Woolf*. New York: Knopf, 1997.

Leonard, Garry. *Advertising and Commodity Culture in Joyce*. Gainesville: University Press of Florida, 1998.

Levenson, Michael. "Liberalism and Symbolism in *Howards End*." In *Modernism and the Fate of Individuality*, 78–101. Cambridge: Cambridge University Press, 1991.

Leverhulme, William Hesketh Lever, Viscount. *The Six-Hour Day and Other Industrial Questions*. Edited by Stanley Unwin. New York: Henry Holt, 1919.

Lodge, David. *Language of Fiction: Essays in Criticism and Verbal Analysis of the English Novel*. New York: Columbia University Press, 1966.

Loeb, Lori Anne. *Consuming Angels: Advertising and Victorian Women*. Oxford: Oxford University Press, 1994.

Lowenthal, David. *The Heritage Crusade and the Spoils of History*. London: Viking, 1997.

———. *The Past Is a Foreign Country*. Cambridge: Cambridge University Press, 1985.

Lyall, Sutherland. *Dream Cottages: From Cottage Orneé to Stockbroker Tudor, Two Hundred Years of the Cult of the Vernacular*. London: Robert Hale, 1988.

Mansfield, Katherine. *The Collected Letters of Katherine Mansfield*. Vol. 3, *1919–1920*. Edited by Vincent O'Sullivan with Margaret Scott. Oxford: Clarendon Press, 1993.

Marcus, Leonard S. *The American Store Window*. New York: Whitney Library of Design, 1978.

Marx, Karl. *Capital*. Vol. 1. Translated by Ben Fowkes. New York: Penguin, 1990. First published 1867.

Masterman, C. F. G. *The Condition of England*. London: Methuen, 1910. First published 1909 by Methuen.

McDonald, Jan. "Shaw and the Court Theatre." In *The Cambridge Companion to George Bernard Shaw*, edited by Christopher Innes, 261–282. Cambridge: Cambridge University Press, 1998.

McKenzie, Jon. *Perform or Else: From Discipline to Performance.* New York: Routledge, 2001.

Meacham, Standish. *Regaining Paradise: Englishness and the Early Garden City Movement.* New Haven, CT: Yale University Press, 1999.

Meisel, Martin. "Shaw and Revolution: The Politics of the Plays." In *Shaw: Seven Critical Essays*, edited by Norman Rosenblood, 106–134. Toronto: University of Toronto Press, 1971.

Miller, Andrew. *Novels behind Glass.* Cambridge: Cambridge University Press, 1995.

Miller, Mervyn. *Barry Parker and Raymond Unwin.* Letchworth: Letchworth Garden City Heritage Foundation, 1999.

———. *Letchworth: The First Garden City.* 2nd ed. Chichester, UK: Phillimore, 2002.

Milling, Jane, and Graham Ley, eds. *Modern Theories of Performance: From Stanislavski to Boal.* New York: Palgrave, 2001.

Morris, William. *News from Nowhere and Other Writings.* London: Penguin, 1998. First published 1890 as a serial story in *Commonweal.*

Muthesius, Hermann. *The English House.* Edited by Dennis Sharp. Translated by Jan Seligman. New York: Rizzoli, 1987. First published 1904 by E. Wasmuth.

Nevett, T. R. *Advertising in Britain: A History.* London: Heinemann, 1982.

Nicolson, Nigel. *Lord of the Isles: Lord Leverhulme in the Hebrides.* London: Weidenfeld and Nicolson, 1960.

Oliver, Basil. *Old Houses and Village Buildings in East Anglia, Norfolk, Suffolk and Essex.* London: B. T. Batsford, 1912.

Opie, Robert. *Rule Britannia: Trading on the British Image.* New York: Viking Penguin, 1985.

Parry, Benita. "*Tono-Bungay*: Modernisation, Modernity, Modernism, and Imperialism, or The Failed Electrification of the Empire of Light." *New Formations* 34 (Summer 1998): 91–108.

Parsons, Kermit C., and David Schuyler, eds. *From Garden City to Green City: The Legacy of Ebenezer Howard.* Baltimore: Johns Hopkins University Press, 2002.

Poovey, Mary. *Uneven Developments: The Ideological Work of Gender in Mid-Victorian England.* Chicago: University of Chicago Press, 1988.

Pound, Reginald. *Selfridge: A Biography.* London: Heinemann, 1960.

Rainey, Lawrence. *Institutions of Modernism: Literary Elites and Public Culture.* New Haven, CT: Yale University Press, 1998.

Rappaport, Diane Erika. *Shopping for Pleasure: Women in the Making of London's West End.* Princeton, NJ: Princeton University Press, 2000.

Richards, Thomas. *The Commodity Culture of Victorian England: Advertising and Spectacle, 1851–1914.* Stanford, CA: Stanford University Press, 1990.

Rojek, Chris, and John Urry, eds. *Touring Cultures: Transformations of Travel and Theory.* London: Routledge, 1997.

Ryan, Deborah S. *The Ideal Home through the 20th Century.* London: Hazar, 1997.

Saddlemyer, Ann. *Becoming George: The Life of Mrs. W. B. Yeats.* New York: Oxford University Press, 2004.

Samuel, Raphael. *Theatres of Memory: Past and Present in Contemporary Culture.* 2 vols. London: Verso, 1994.

Schechner, Richard. *Performance Studies: An Introduction*. London: Routledge, 2002.

———. *Performance Theory*. 2nd ed. London: Routledge, 1988.

Selfridge, H. Gordon. *The Romance of Commerce*. London: John Lane, 1918.

Sennett, A. R. *Garden Cities in Theory and Practice*. 2 vols. London: Bemrose and Sons, 1905.

Shaw, George Bernard. *Collected Letters*. 4 vols. Edited by Dan H. Laurence. New York: Viking Penguin, 1965–1988.

———. *John Bull's Other Island*. 1904. In *The Bodley Head Bernard Shaw: Collected Plays with Their Prefaces*, edited by Dan Laurence, vol. 2, 503–611. London: The Bodley Head, 1970–1974.

———. *Major Barbara*. 1905. In *The Bodley Head Bernard Shaw: Collected Plays with their Prefaces*, edited by Dan Laurence, vol. 3, 11–200. London: The Bodley Head, 1970–1974.

———. *Our Theatres in the Nineties*. Vol. 2. London: Constable, 1932.

———. "Preface for Politicians." 1906. In *Complete Plays with Prefaces*, vol. 2, 443–502. New York: Dodd, Mead, 1963.

Simpson, Michael. *Thomas Adams and the Modern Planning Movement: Britain, Canada, and the United States, 1900–1940*. London: Alexandrine Press Book, 1985.

Smith, Wareham. *Spilt Ink*. London: E. Benn, 1932.

Sparrow, W. Shaw. *The English House: How to Judge Its Periods and Styles*. London: Eveleigh Nash, 1908.

Squier, Susan Merrill. "Tradition and Revision: The Classic City Novel and Virginia Woolf's *Night and Day*." In *Women Writers in the City: Essays in Feminist Literary Criticism*, edited by Susan Merrill Squier, 114–133. Knoxville: University of Tennessee Press, 1984.

Stamp, Gavin, and André Goulancourt. *The English House 1860–1914: The Flowering of English Domestic Architecture*. Chicago: University of Chicago Press, 1986.

Stape, J. H., ed. *E. M. Forster: Interviews and Recollections*. London: St. Martin's Press, 1993.

Stone, Wilfred. *The Cave and the Mountain: A Study of E. M. Forster*. Stanford, CA: Stanford University Press, 1966.

Strychacz, Thomas. *Modernism, Mass Culture, and Professionalism*. Cambridge: Cambridge University Press, 1993.

Tambling, Jeremy, ed. *E. M. Forster*. New York: St. Martin's Press, 1995.

Taylor, Charles. *The Ethics of Authenticity*. Cambridge, MA: Harvard University Press, 1991.

Terdiman, Richard. *Present Past: Modernity and the Memory Crisis*. Ithaca, NY: Cornell University Press, 1993.

Thormählen, Marianne, ed. *Rethinking Modernism*. New York: Palgrave Macmillan, 2003.

Tintner, Adeline R. "Henry James and the Symbolist Movement in Art." *Journal of Modern Literature* 7, no. 3 (1979): 397–415.

Trilling, Lionel. *E. M. Forster*. Norfolk, CT: New Directions, 1943.

———. *Sincerity and Authenticity*. New York: Harcourt Brace Jovanovich, 1972.

Turner, Catherine. *Marketing Modernism between the Two World Wars*. Amherst: University of Massachusetts Press, 2003.

Unwin, Raymond. *Town Planning in Practice: An Introduction to the Art of Designing Cities and Suburbs*. London: Longmans, Green, 1909.

Vaid, Krishna Baldev. *Technique in the Tales of Henry James*. Cambridge, MA: Harvard University Press, 1964.

Veblen, Thorstein. *The Theory of the Leisure Class.* New York: Penguin, 1979. First published 1899 by Macmillan.

Weaver, Lawrence. *Houses and Gardens by E. L. Lutyens.* Suffolk: Antique Collectors' Club, 1987.

Wegner, Phillip E. *Imagined Communities: Utopia, the Nation, and the Spatial History of Modernity.* Berkeley: University of California Press, 2002.

Weissman, Judith. "*Howards End:* Gasoline and Goddesses." In *Howards End*, edited by Alistair M. Duckworth, 432–446. Boston: Bedford Books, 1997.

Wells, H. G. *A Modern Utopia.* Lincoln: University of Nebraska Press, 1967. First published 1905 by C. Scribner and Sons.

———. *Tono-Bungay.* Boston: Houghton Mifflin, 1966. First published in book form in 1909 by Duffield and Company.

Wexler, Joyce. "Selling Sex as Art." In *Marketing Modernisms*, edited by Kevin J. H. Dettmar and Stephen Watt, 91–108. Ann Arbor: University of Michigan Press, 1996.

Whelan, Robert, ed. *Octavia Hill and the Social Housing Debate.* London: IEA Health and Welfare Unit, 1998.

Wicke, Jennifer. *Advertising Fictions: Literature, Advertisement, and Social Reading.* New York: Columbia University Press, 1988.

———. "Coterie Consumption: Bloomsbury, Keynes, and Modernism as Marketing." In *Marketing Modernisms*, edited by Kevin J. H. Dettmar and Stephen Watt, 109–132. Ann Arbor: University of Michigan Press, 1996.

———. "Enchantment, Disenchantment, Re-enchantment: Joyce and the Cult of the Absolutely Fabulous." *Novel: A Forum on Fiction* 29 (1995): 128–137.

———. "Joyce and Consumer Culture." In *James Joyce*, edited by Derek Attridge, 234–253. Cambridge: Cambridge University Press, 2004.

———."Modernity Must Advertise: Aura, Desire, and Decolonization in Joyce." *James Joyce Quarterly* 30, no. 4 (1993); 31, no. 1 (1993): 593–613.

———. "*Mrs. Dalloway* goes to Market: Woolf, Keynes, and Modern Markets." *Novel: A Forum on Fiction* 28 (1994): 5–23.

———. " 'Who's She When She's at Home?' Molly Bloom and the Work of Consumption." *James Joyce Quarterly* 28, no. 4 (1991): 749–764.

Widdowson, Peter. *E. M. Forster's Howards End: Fiction as History.* London: Sussex University Press, 1977.

Wiener, Martin. *English Culture and the Decline of the Industrial Spirit, 1850–1980.* Cambridge: Cambridge University Press, 1981.

Williams, A. H. *No Name on the Door: A Memoir of Gordon Selfridge.* London: W. H. Allen, 1956.

Williams, Iolo A. *The Firm of Cadbury: 1888–1931.* London: Constable, 1931.

Williams, Raymond. *The Country and the City.* New York: Oxford University Press, 1973.

Willison, Ian, Warwick Gould, and Warren Chernaik, eds. *Modernist Writers and the Marketplace.* London: Macmillan, 1996.

Wood, Barry James. *Show Windows: 75 Years of the Art of Display.* New York: Congdon and Weed, 1982.

Woolf, Virginia. *The Diary of Virginia Woolf.* 5 vols. Edited by Anne Olivier Bell and assisted by Andrew McNeillie. New York: Harvest-Harcourt Brace, 1977–1984.

———. *The Essays of Virginia Woolf.* Edited by Andrew McNeillie. 3 vols. New York: Harvest-Harcourt Brace, 1986–1988.

———. *The Letters of Virginia Woolf.* Edited by Nigel Nicolson and Joanne Trautmann. 6 vols. New York: Harcourt Brace Jovanovich, 1975–1980.

———. *Moments of Being.* 2nd edition. San Diego: Harcourt Brace Jovanovich, 1985.

———. *Night and Day.* San Diego, Harvest-Harcourt Brace, 1948. First published 1919 by Duckworth.

———. "Oxford Street Tide." In *The London Scene: Five Essays by Virginia Woolf,* 16–22. New York: Random House, 1975.

———. *To the Lighthouse.* New York: Harcourt Brace Jovanovich, 1989. First published 1927 by Harcourt, Brace.

Worthen, John. "D. H. Lawrence and the 'Expensive Edition Business.'" In *Modernist Writers and the Marketplace,* edited by Ian Willison, Warwick Gould, and Warren Chernaik, 105–123. London: Macmillan, 1996.

Wright, Patrick. *On Living in an Old Country: The National Past in Contemporary Britain.* London: Verso, 1985.

Wussow, Helen. "Conflict of Language in Virginia Woolf's *Night and Day.*" *Journal of Modern Literature* 15 (1989): 61–73.

Zwerdling, Alex. *Virginia Woolf and the Real World.* Berkeley: University of California Press, 1986.

Index

Literary works are listed under the names of individual authors. Page numbers in italics refer to figures.